Office 2013

FOR

DUMMIES®

A Wiley Brand

*e*LEARNING KIT

by Faithe Wempen

FOR

DUMMIES®

A Wiley Brand

Office 2013 For Dummies® eLearning Kit

Published by: **John Wiley & Sons, Inc.,** 111 River Street, Hoboken, NJ 07030-5774, www.wiley.com

Copyright © 2014 by John Wiley & Sons, Inc., Hoboken, New Jersey

Published simultaneously in Canada

For general information on our other products and services, please contact our Customer Care Department within the U.S. at 877-762-2974, outside the U.S. at 317-572-3993, or fax 317-572-4002. For technical support, please visit www.wiley.com/techsupport.

Wiley publishes in a variety of print and electronic formats and by print-on-demand. Some material included with standard print versions of this book may not be included in e-books or in print-on-demand. If this book refers to media such as a CD or DVD that is not included in the version you purchased, you may download this material at http://booksupport.wiley.com. For more information about Wiley products, visit www.wiley.com.

Library of Congress Control Number: 2013952431

ISBN 978-1-118-49032-7 (pbk); ISBN 978-1-118-49033-4 (ebk); ISBN 978-1-118-49050-1 (ebk)

Manufactured in the United States of America

10 9 8 7 6 5 4 3 2 1

Contents at a Glance

Introduction *1*

Chapter 1: Getting to Know Office.. 7

Chapter 2: Creating a Word Document..57

Chapter 3: Paragraph and Page Formatting in Word...................................97

Chapter 4: Working with Tables and Graphics in Word.............................143

Chapter 5: Creating Basic Worksheets in Excel..175

Chapter 6: Creating Formulas and Functions in Excel..............................203

Chapter 7: Formatting and Printing Excel Worksheets 235

Chapter 8: Managing E-Mail with Outlook 267

Chapter 9: Using Outlook Contacts and Tasks..311

Chapter 10: Getting Started with PowerPoint 337

Chapter 11: Formatting a Presentation...369

Chapter 12: Adding Movement and Sound to a Presentation...................409

Chapter 13: Presenting a Slide Show..431

Index *447*

Table of Contents

Introduction *1*

About This Kit 1
Foolish Assumptions 3
Icons Used in This Kit 3
Accessing the Office 2013 eCourse 4
Beyond the Book 5
Where to Go from Here 5

Chapter 1: Getting to Know Office **7**

Starting an Office Application 9
   Starting an Office application in Windows 8 10
   Starting an Office application in Windows 7 12
Exploring the Office Interface 13
   Exploring the Ribbon and tabs 13
   Understanding the File menu 19
Creating Your First Document 22
   Starting a new document 22
   Typing text 23
   Inserting a picture 26
Moving Around 29
   Moving using the mouse 29
   Moving using the keyboard 32
Changing the Onscreen View 33
   Zooming in and out 33
   Changing views 35
Saving and Opening Documents 40
   Saving your work for the first time 40
   Navigating in the Save As dialog box 44
   Opening a document 50
   Recovering lost work 51
Summing Up 53
   Try-it-yourself lab 54
   Know this tech talk 54

Chapter 2: Creating a Word Document **57**

Creating a New Document Using a Template 59
Adjusting Page Settings 62
   Setting page margins 63
   Setting paper size and orientation 65

Editing Text 67
    Filling text placeholders... 67
    Typing and editing text 69
Selecting Text.. 71
Formatting Text 73
    Choosing text font, size, and color 73
    Applying text attributes and effects 76
    Working with themes 80
    Applying style sets.. 83
Checking Spelling and Grammar... 85
Sharing Your Document with Others.. 88
    E-mailing your document to others.. 88
    Sharing your document in other formats 90
Printing Your Work 92
Summing Up 93
    Try-it-yourself lab 94
    Know this tech talk.. 94

Chapter 3: Paragraph and Page Formatting in Word .... .97
Formatting Paragraphs... 99
    Applying horizontal alignment.. 100
    Indenting a paragraph 102
    Changing vertical spacing.. 105
Adding Borders and Shading 109
    Placing a border around a paragraph 110
    Shading a paragraph's background....................................... 112
Creating Bulleted and Numbered Lists.. 114
    Creating a basic numbered or bulleted list 115
    Changing the bullet character... 115
    Changing the numbering style 118
Working with Styles.. 121
    Applying a style.. 122
    Modifying a style.. 125
    Creating a new style 128
Copying Formats with Format Painter.. 130
Using Headers and Footers 132
    Numbering the pages 133
    Using a header or footer preset.. 135
    Creating a custom header or footer 137
Summing Up 139
    Try-it-yourself lab 140
    Know this tech talk.. 141

Chapter 4: Working with Tables and Graphics in Word **143**

Creating a Table 145
  Converting text to a table 147
  Selecting rows and columns 149
  Resizing rows and columns 150
  Formatting table borders 153
Inserting Pictures from the Web 156
  Understanding vector and raster graphics 157
  Finding and inserting pictures from the web 158
Inserting Photos from Files 161
Managing Picture Size and Placement 162
  Changing the text wrap setting for a picture 162
  Moving a picture 165
  Resizing a picture 169
Summing Up 171
  Try-it-yourself lab 171
  Know this tech talk 172

Chapter 5: Creating Basic Worksheets in Excel **175**

Understanding the Excel Interface 177
  Touring the Excel interface 178
  Moving the cell cursor 182
  Selecting ranges 183
Typing and Editing Cell Content 186
  Typing text or numbers into a cell 186
  Editing cell content 188
  Copying and moving data between cells 190
  Using AutoFill to fill cell content 192
  Using Flash Fill to extract content 193
Changing the Worksheet Structure 195
  Inserting and deleting rows and columns 195
  Inserting and deleting cells and ranges 196
Working with Worksheets 197
Summing Up 199
  Try-it-yourself lab 200
  Know this tech talk 201

Chapter 6: Creating Formulas and Functions in Excel **203**

Finding Out About Formulas 205
  Writing formulas that calculate 205
  Writing formulas that reference cells 207
  Referencing a cell on another sheet 209
Moving and Copying Formulas 210
  Copying formulas with relative referencing 210
  Copying formulas with absolute referencing 213

Introducing Functions 215
    Using the SUM function 215
    Inserting a function 218
    Touring some basic functions 221
Working with Named Ranges 222
    Naming a range 223
    Using a named range in a formula 225
Using Quick Analysis 226
Summing Up 231
    Try-it-yourself lab 232
    Know this tech talk 233

Chapter 7: Formatting and Printing Excel Worksheets 235

Adjusting Rows and Columns 237
    Changing a row's height 238
    Changing a column's width 240
Formatting an Entire Worksheet 242
    Applying a worksheet background 242
    Creating a header or footer 245
Using Theme Formatting 247
    Applying a workbook theme 248
    Customizing a theme 250
    Formatting a range as a table 252
    Creating a custom table style 254
Printing Worksheets 257
    Previewing and print the active worksheet 257
    Setting and using a print range 258
    Adjusting the page size, orientation, and
        margins while printing 260
Summing Up 264
    Try-it-yourself lab 264
    Know this tech talk 265

Chapter 8: Managing E-Mail with Outlook 267

Touring the Microsoft Outlook Interface 269
Setting Up Outlook for E-Mail 275
    Changing account settings during setup 277
    Setting up additional mail accounts 279
    Troubleshooting mail setup problems 280
Composing a New Message 284
The Three Rs of Mail: Receiving, Reading, and Replying 286
    Sending and receiving e-mail manually 286
    Setting the send/receive interval 287
    Reading an e-mail message 288
    Replying to a message 290

Working with Attachments 292
    Attaching a file to a message..292
    Viewing and saving an e-mail attachment 294
Managing Incoming Mail..296
    Creating folders for managing mail 296
    Moving a message to a folder...297
    Creating a rule that moves messages............................299
    Customizing the Favorites list..302
    Deleting e-mail...303
    Flagging an e-mail..305
    Configuring the Junk Mail filter 306
Summing Up 307
    Try-it-yourself lab 308
    Know this tech talk..308

Chapter 9: Using Outlook Contacts and Tasks 311

Storing Contact Information...313
    Adding and editing a contact 313
    Navigating the Contacts list..316
    Changing how a contact is filed 319
    Deleting and restoring a contact....................................320
Using Contact Information 322
    Sending an e-mail message to a contact 322
    Attaching contact info to an e-mail................................324
Using Tasks and the To-Do List 325
    Displaying the Tasks list 325
    Creating a task...327
    Updating a task...329
    Setting a task reminder 331
    Deleting a task 333
Summing Up 334
    Try-it-yourself lab 334
    Know this tech talk..335

Chapter 10: Getting Started with PowerPoint. 337

Exploring the PowerPoint Interface..339
    Moving around in a presentation....................................340
    Understanding PowerPoint views....................................342
Creating a New Presentation..346
    Creating a blank presentation 346
    Creating a presentation with a template 347
Creating New Slides..349
    Creating a new slide with the Ribbon 349
    Creating a new slide in the Slides pane or Outline pane 350
    Duplicating a slide 353
    Deleting a slide...354

Adding Text to a Slide...356
    Typing in a slide placeholder...............................356
    Manually placing text on a slide 358
Manipulating Slide Content......................................360
    Moving a slide object...360
    Resizing a slide object..363
    Deleting a slide object...365
Summing Up...366
    Try-it-yourself lab..367
    Know this tech talk..367

Chapter 11: Formatting a Presentation......................369

Understanding and Applying Themes 371
    Changing the presentation theme 371
    Changing the presentation variant and colors 373
    Changing the presentation fonts..........................376
Formatting Text Boxes and Placeholders 378
    Applying shape styles 378
    Applying a background fill....................................380
    Applying and removing borders 383
    Applying shape effects 385
    Turning text Autofit on or off 388
Inserting Graphics 389
    Inserting an online image from Office.com.................390
    Inserting your own pictures 393
Creating SmartArt...395
    Converting text to SmartArt 395
    Inserting a SmartArt graphic 395
    Modifying a SmartArt graphic 399
    Formatting a SmartArt graphic 402
Summing Up 405
    Try-it-yourself labs...406
    Know this tech talk..407

Chapter 12: Adding Movement and Sound to a Presentation.......409

Adding Slide Transition Effects 411
    Applying a transition to a slide...........................412
    Changing a transition's options 414
    Setting slides to advance manually or automatically............415
Animating Objects 417
    Creating an entrance animation...........................417
    Creating an emphasis animation 419
    Creating an exit animation....................................421
    Changing an animation's options 423

Inserting Sounds and Videos...425
    Inserting a sound clip on a slide 425
    Inserting a video clip on a slide 427
Summing Up 429
    Try-it-yourself lab 430
    Know this tech talk...430

Chapter 13: Presenting a Slide Show 431

Displaying a Slide Show Onscreen 433
    Moving between slides...433
    Annotating slides with the pen tools................................437
Creating Handouts...439
    Printing handouts 439
    Exporting handouts to Word...441
Summing Up 445
    Try-it-yourself lab 445
    Know this tech talk...446

Index *447*

Introduction

*I*f you've been thinking about taking a class on the Internet (it is all the rage these days), but you're concerned about getting lost in the electronic fray, worry no longer. *Office 2013 eLearning Kit For Dummies* is here to help you, providing you with a hands-on learning experience that includes not only the book and CD you hold in your hands, but also an online course at `http://learn.dummies.com`. Consider this introduction your primer.

About This Kit

Whether you follow along with the book, go online for the courses, or some combination of the two, the 13 chapters in *Office 2013 eLearning Kit For Dummies* walk you through examples and exercises so that you learn how to do the following:

- ✔ Master the basic features that all Office products have in common, like ribbons, scroll bars, and keyboard shortcuts.
- ✔ Create and format Word documents that include text, headers and footers, tables, and various types of graphics.
- ✔ Use Excel to store, format, and calculate numeric data and present it in easy-to-read formats.
- ✔ Send and receive e-mail in Outlook and manage a calendar and To-Do list items.
- ✔ Create a PowerPoint presentation that contains text, graphics, animation effects, and even sound and video.

Each piece of this kit works in conjunction with the others, although you don't need them all to gain valuable understanding of the key concepts.

This book uses a tutorial approach to explain how to use Office features. In each lesson, you'll find the following elements:

- ✔ **Lesson opener questions:** To get you warmed up and ready for the lesson material, the questions quiz you on particular points of interest. If you don't know the answer, a page number heads you in the right direction to find it.

- ✔ **Tutorial step-by-step instruction with sample data files:** Each lesson introduces an important task you can do in an Office application. You then find step-by-step tutorials that walk you through using the feature or combining skills you've learned so far to accomplish a specific goal. Often, you need to download a sample file that goes with the steps. See the "Beyond the Book" section later in this introduction for details on downloading the sample files.

- ✔ **Summing Up:** This section appears at the end of each chapter; it briefly reiterates the content you just learned.

- ✔ **Try-it-yourself lab:** Test your knowledge of the content just covered by performing an activity *from scratch* — that is, using general steps only and no sample files.

- ✔ **Know this tech talk:** Each lesson contains a brief glossary of related terms.

A few style conventions help you navigate the book piece of this kit efficiently:

- ✔ Instructions and names of the files needed to follow along with the step lists are *italicized*.

- ✔ Website addresses, or URLs, and filenames are shown in a special typeface `like this`.

- ✔ Numbered steps that you need to follow and characters you need to type are set in **bold.**

Used in conjunction with the tutorial text, the online course that goes with this kit gives you the tools you need for a productive and self-guided eLearning experience. Here's how the course helps you get up-to-speed in Microsoft Office:

- ✔ **Multimedia-based instruction:** After each feature is introduced, you'll find plentiful video clips, illustrations, and interactive widgets that show you how a feature or task works. The course is like having a tutor ready and willing to show you how a process works as many times as you need until you're confident in what you've learned. Or if you're pretty comfortable with certain parts of Microsoft Office, you can breeze past those parts of the course instead.

✔ **Interactive quizzes and activities:** Ample interactive elements enable you to understand how Microsoft Office works and check what you've learned. Hands-on activities enable you to try working in Office yourself and receive feedback on what skills you still need to practice.

✔ **Resources:** Throughout the online course, you'll find extra resources relevant to what you're learning.

Foolish Assumptions

For starters, I assume you need to find out how to use Office (and fast!) and want to get a piece of this academic action the fun and easy way with *Office 2013 eLearning Kit For Dummies.*

I assume you have basic Windows and computer skills, such as starting the computer and using the mouse.

To get the most out of this kit, you need a Windows computer running Office 2013. That way, you can experience the benefit of the tutorial steps in the book and the hands-on instruction in the online course.

Icons Used in This Kit

The familiar and helpful *For Dummies* icons point you in the direction of really great information that's sure to help you as you work your way through this kit. Look for these icons throughout the book and online course:

The Tip icon points out helpful information that's likely to make your job easier.

This icon marks an interesting and useful fact — something that you might want to remember for later.

The Warning icon highlights lurking danger. When you see this icon, you know to pay attention and proceed with caution.

Sometimes I might change things up by directing you to repeat a set of steps but with different parameters. If you're up for the challenge, look for the Practice icon.

In addition to the icons, you also find two friendly study aids that bring your attention to certain pieces of information:

- **Lingo:** When you see the Lingo box, look for a definition of a key term or concept.
- **Extra Info:** This box highlights something to pay close attention to in a figure or points out other useful information that's related to the discussion.

Accessing the Office 2013 eCourse

Your purchase of this For Dummies eLearning Kit includes access to the course online at the For Dummies eLearning Center. If you have purchased an electronic version of this book, please visit www.dummies.com/go/getelearningcode to gain your access code to the online course. If you purchased the paperback book, you find your access code inside the front cover of this book.

Dummies eCourses require an HTML5-capable browser. If you use the Firefox or Chrome browser, make sure you have the latest version. Internet Explorer 10 is also HTML5-capable.

Beyond the Book

This section is your handy guide to finding all the content that goes with the book and eCourse, which includes the following:

- ✔ **Companion files:** You can download the companion files that go with the tutorial steps in this book online at `www.dummies.com/go/office2013elearning`.

- ✔ **Bonus appendix:** If you're interested in finding out more about using SkyDrive, Microsoft's cloud-based storage space, check out the online bonus appendix, "Essential SkyDrive Skills." You can download it for free at `www.dummies.com/go/office2013elearning`.

- ✔ **Online articles and extras:** If you have questions about Office that you don't find answered in this kit, check out the free online articles at Dummies.com. You can also find help with evolving features that are related to Office, but that Microsoft is likely to change independently of Office, such as Microsoft's cloud storage space (that is, a free service for storing your files online so you can access them from anywhere).

Where to Go from Here

Now that you're primed and ready, time to begin.

Chapter 1
Getting to Know Office

✔ The Office interface *is consistent across all Office programs* and includes the Ribbon, the File menu, Zoom controls, and standard dialog boxes for saving and opening files.

✔ Moving around in a document *enables you to view different parts of the document* that may not be onscreen at the moment. You can use scroll bars, arrow keys, and keyboard shortcuts in any combination.

✔ Changing the onscreen view *helps you focus on the important parts of the document* for the task you want to perform. Each application has its own unique set of views, as well as a Zoom control.

✔ Saving and opening documents *lets you store your work for later use* and then recall it to the screen when you're ready to continue. The Save As and Open dialog boxes share a common look and feel in all applications.

1. How do you start an Office application?

Find out on page 9

2. How can you find out what a certain button on the Ribbon is for?

Find out on page 14

3. What is Backstage view?

Find out on page 19

4. How can you make the text you're typing appear larger so that it's easier to see onscreen?

Find out on page 34

5. After you've saved a file once, how can you reopen the Save As dialog box so you can save it with a different name?

Find out on page 40

6. How can you quickly reopen a recently opened document?

Find out on page 50

icrosoft Office is a suite of applications. A *suite* is a group of applications that are designed to work together and to have similar user interfaces that cut down on the learning curve for each one. Office 2013 includes a word processor (Word), a spreadsheet program (Excel), a presentation graphics program (PowerPoint), and an e-mail program (Outlook). Depending on the version of Office, it may also include other programs. Sweet, eh? Er . . . suite.

Because all the Office apps have similar interfaces, many of the skills you pick up while working with one program also translate to the others. In this chapter, I introduce you to the Office interface and show you some things the programs have in common. For the examples in this chapter, I mostly use Word, the word processor, because it's the most popular of the applications. Keep in mind, though, that the skills you're learning here apply to the other applications too.

Starting an Office Application

The most straightforward way to start an Office application is to select it from the Windows 8 Start screen (or Windows 7 Start menu). You can browse through the list of programs, or you can start typing the application's name and then click its name when it appears.

Depending on how your PC is set up, you may also have shortcuts to one or more of the Office apps on your desktop and/or on the taskbar.

You can double-click a data file that's associated with one of the apps, but because you haven't created any documents yet, you can't do that now.

LINGO

Technically, a **program** can be any type of software, including Windows itself, whereas an **application** is a specific type of program that performs a useful user task, such as word processing.

Most nongeeky computer users don't recognize that distinction, though, and they use the terms interchangeably. So does this book.

When you're finished with an application, you can click its Close (X) button in its upper-right corner to exit. If you have any unsaved work, you're prompted to save it.

Starting an Office application in Windows 8

In this exercise, you practice opening and closing Office applications. This exercise is for Windows 8 users; if you have Windows 7, use the exercise in the next section instead.

Files needed: None

1. **In Windows 8, press the Windows key to display the Start screen.**

2. **Click Excel 2013. (Scroll to the right to locate that tile if needed, as shown in Figure 1-1.)**

   The Excel application opens.

EXTRA INFO

Note: If you're working with a touchscreen, another way to display the Start screen is to swipe in from the right and then tap the Start charm.

Excel tile

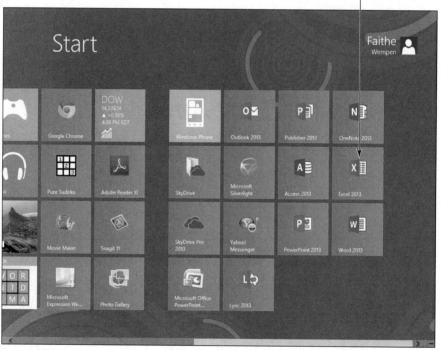

Figure 1-1

3. **Click the Close (X) button in the upper-right corner of the Excel window.**

   The Excel application window closes.

4. **Press the Windows key to reopen the Start screen.**

5. **Click PowerPoint 2013.**

   The PowerPoint application opens.

6. **Click the Close (X) button in the upper-right corner of the PowerPoint window.**

   The PowerPoint application window closes.

7. **Press the Windows key to reopen the Start screen.**

8. **Type Word.**

   The Search panel appears, and the Apps list is filtered to show only applications with "Word" in their names, as shown on the left in Figure 1-2.

Click Word 2013.

Apps list is filtered to show only names containing "word."

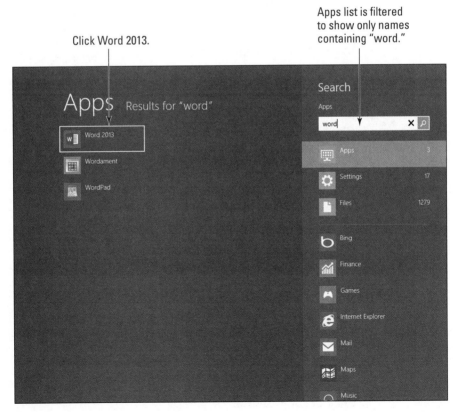

Figure 1-2

9. From the list of applications that appears, click Word 2013.

The Word application opens.

Leave Word open for the "Exploring the Office Interface" exercise later in the chapter.

Starting an Office application in Windows 7

In this exercise, you practice opening and closing Office applications. This exercise is for Windows 7 users; if you have Windows 8, use the preceding exercise instead.

Files needed: None

1. Click the Start button.

The Start menu opens.

2. Click All Programs.

A list of all installed applications appears. Some of the applications are organized into folders.

3. Click the Microsoft Office folder.

A list of the Microsoft Office 2013 applications appears.

4. Click Microsoft Excel 2013.

The Excel application opens.

5. Click the Close (X) button in the upper-right corner of the Excel window.

The Excel application window closes.

6. Repeat Steps 1–3 (choose Start ➪ All Programs ➪ Microsoft Office) to reopen the Microsoft Office folder on the Start menu.

7. Click Microsoft PowerPoint 2013.

The PowerPoint application opens.

8. Click the Close (X) button in the upper-right corner of the PowerPoint window.

The PowerPoint application window closes.

9. Click the Start button.

EXTRA INFO

On the left side of the Start menu, shortcuts to recently or frequently used applications appear. If the application you want happens to appear there after Step 1, you can click it to open the application. If not, continue to Step 2.

EXTRA INFO

In Excel, you can find two Close (X) buttons. The upper one closes the entire application; the lower one closes only the current workbook.

10. **Type** Word.

The Start menu is filtered to show applications that contain those letters in their names.

11. **From the list of applications that appears, click Microsoft Word 2013.**

The Word application opens.

Leave Word open for the next exercise.

Exploring the Office Interface

The Office 2013 interface in each program consists of a tabbed Ribbon, a File menu, a status bar at the bottom, window controls, and other common features. In the following sections, you become familiar with these common elements.

Exploring the Ribbon and tabs

All Office 2013 applications have a common system of navigation called the *Ribbon,* which is a tabbed bar across the top of the application window. Each tab is like a page of buttons. You click different tabs to access different sets of buttons and features.

In this exercise, you practice using the commands on the Ribbon in Microsoft Word.

Files needed: None

1. **If Word isn't already open from the previous exercise, open it.**

Word's Start screen appears.

2. **Press Esc or click Blank Document to start a new document.**

3. **On the Ribbon, click the Insert tab.**

The buttons on the Ribbon change to show the ones for inserting various types of content.

TIP

Notice that the buttons are organized into *groups;* the group names appear at the bottom of the Ribbon. For example, the Symbols group is the rightmost group on the Insert tab.

4. In the Symbols group, hover the mouse pointer over the Equation button, as shown in Figure 1-3.

A ScreenTip appears, telling you the button's name and purpose and showing a keyboard shortcut (Alt+=) that you can optionally use to select that command.

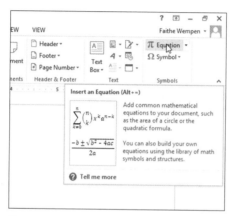

Figure 1-3

5. Click the Equation button.

A new equation box appears in the document, and the Equation Tools Design tab appears on the Ribbon, as shown in Figure 1-4.

Equation Tools Design tab

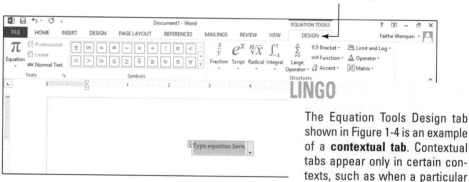

Figure 1-4

LINGO

The Equation Tools Design tab shown in Figure 1-4 is an example of a **contextual tab**. Contextual tabs appear only in certain contexts, such as when a particular type of object is active — in this case, an equation box.

6. **Press Delete to remove the equation box.**

   The Home tab reappears.

7. **Click the Insert tab again, and in the Header & Footer group, click the Header button.**

   A menu opens, as shown in Figure 1-5.

Header button (opens menu)

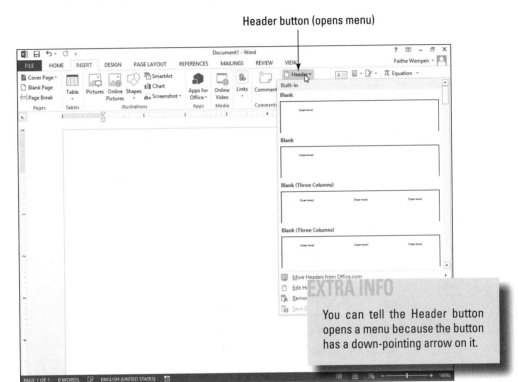

Figure 1-5

You can tell the Header button opens a menu because the button has a down-pointing arrow on it.

8. **Click away from the menu to close it without making a selection.**

9. **In the Illustrations group, click SmartArt.**

   The Choose a SmartArt Graphic dialog box opens, as shown in Figure 1-6.

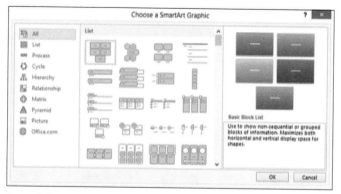

Figure 1-6

10. **Click Cancel to close the dialog box without creating a graphic.**

11. **Click the Home tab, and in the Font group, click the Bold button (the B icon shown in Figure 1-7).**

    The Bold attribute is toggled on.

12. **Type your first name.**

    Your first name appears in bold, as shown in Figure 1-7.

13. **Click the Bold button again.**

    The Bold attribute is toggled off.

14. **Press the space bar and then type your last name.**

    Your last name does not appear in bold.

    In the Paragraph group, notice that the Align Left button (shown in Figure 1-7) is selected; this is the default setting when you create a new blank document.

15. **Click the Center button in the Paragraph group.**

    Your name is centered horizontally on the page, as shown in Figure 1-8.

Bold button   Align Left button

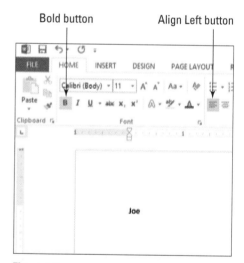

Figure 1-7

EXTRA INFO

The Align Left, Center, Align Right, and Justify buttons operate as a set to select horizontal alignment. Because these buttons are a set, when you select one, the previously selected button is deselected.

Center

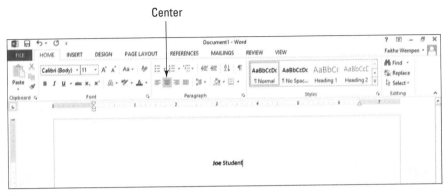

Figure 1-8

16. **Click the Undo button on the Quick Access Toolbar, as shown in Figure 1-9.**

   The last action is undone, and the paragraph alignment goes back to left alignment.

Undo

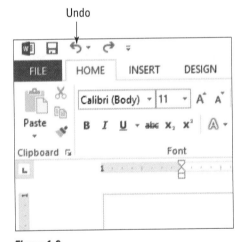

Figure 1-9

LINGO

The **Quick Access Toolbar** is the row of buttons above the Ribbon. It contains shortcuts to a few commonly used commands, and you can add your own shortcuts to it as well. You can right-click any command on the Ribbon and choose Add to Quick Access Toolbar, or you can customize it from the Options dialog box (File ⇨ Options).

17. **Click the dialog box launcher in the bottom-right corner of the Paragraph group.**

   The dialog box launcher is tiny and has an arrow pointing to its bottom-right corner.

   The Paragraph dialog box opens, as shown in Figure 1-10.

18. **Click Cancel to close the Paragraph dialog box.**

19. **If the Word window is maximized (meaning it fills the screen), click the Restore Down button in the upper-right corner, as shown in Figure 1-11, so that the window is resizable.**

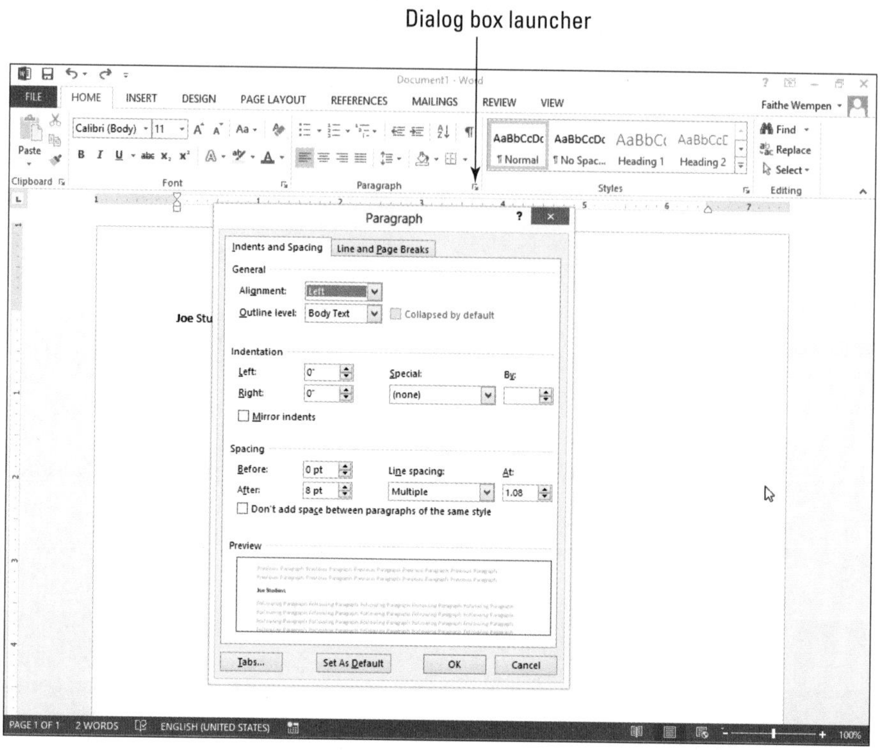

Dialog box launcher

Figure 1-10

Restore/Restore Down

Figure 1-11

20. **Note the three buttons available in the Editing group on the Home tab, as shown in Figure 1-11.**

21. **Drag the right border of the Word window toward the left, decreasing the size of the Word window, until the Editing group collapses into a single large button, as shown in Figure 1-12.**

    The mouse pointer appears as a double-headed arrow as you drag.

22. **Click the Editing button.**

    The menu that opens contains the buttons that were previously available from the Editing group, as shown in Figure 1-13.

23. **Drag the right border of the Word window toward the right until the Editing group is expanded again. Click the Maximize button if you want to maximize the window to fill the screen.**

24. **Click the Close (X) button in the Word window's upper-right corner to exit the Word application. When you're prompted to save changes, click Don't Save.**

The next exercise uses a different application.

Understanding the File menu

In each Office application, clicking the File tab opens the File menu, also known as *Backstage view.* Backstage view provides access to commands that have to do with the data file you're working with — commands such as saving, opening, printing, mailing, and checking its properties. The File tab is a different color in each application. In Excel, for example, it's green. To leave Backstage view, press the Esc key or click the left-pointing arrow button in the upper-left corner.

In the following exercise, you practice using the File menu in Excel.

The Editing group has been collapsed into a single large button.

Figure 1-12

Clicking the collapsed group's button opens a menu containing the group's commands.

Figure 1-13

Files needed: None

1. **Start Excel, and when Excel's Start screen appears, press Esc to display a new blank worksheet.**

2. **Click the File tab on the Ribbon.**

   The File menu opens. Categories of commands are listed at the left.

   The category that appears by default depends on the application and whether any changes have been made to the blank document that opens by default when the application starts.

3. **Click Open if that category doesn't already appear by default.**

4. **Click Recent Workbooks if that subcategory doesn't already appear by default.**

   This subcategory provides shortcuts for reopening recently used files, as shown in Figure 1-14.

5. **Click the Info category and examine the commands available.**

   This category provides commands for inspection, protection, and versions, as well as basic information about the file itself.

Click a category.   Click a subcategory (if available).

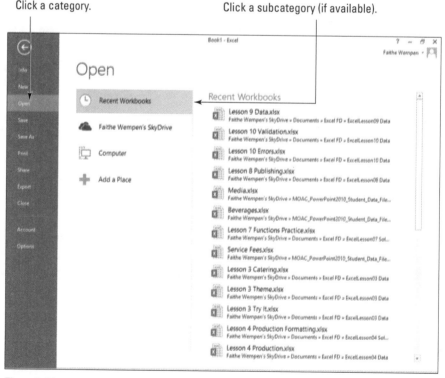

Figure 1-14

6. Click the Manage Versions button.

This button opens a menu of additional commands, as shown in Figure 1-15.

7. Click away from the menu without selecting a command from it.

The menu closes.

8. Click the New category.

Buttons appear for creating a new workbook based on a variety of templates.

9. Click the Print category.

Buttons appear for printing the active workbook.

10. Click the Share category.

Buttons appear for sharing your workbook online or e-mailing it to others.

11. Click the Export category.

Buttons appear for creating a PDF or XPS document and for changing the file type.

Some categories contain buttons that open menus.

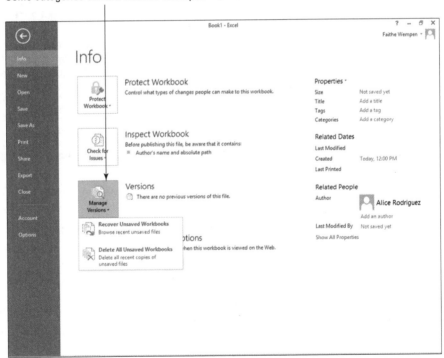

Figure 1-15

12. Click Close.

The active workbook closes, and so does Backstage view. Excel itself remains open.

13. Click the Close (X) button in the upper-right corner of the window.

The Excel application window closes.

Creating Your First Document

In all the Office applications discussed in this book (except Outlook, which works somewhat differently), when you start the application, a Start screen appears, and if you press Esc from there, a new blank document appears. You can begin creating new content in this document and then save your work when you're finished editing. Alternatively, you can open an existing document or start a different type of document.

After starting a new document, you type or insert content into it. Documents can contain text, graphic objects, or a combination of the two. You can use many types of graphic objects, such as photos, clip art, drawings, diagrams, and charts. You learn about these object types in a later chapter.

LINGO

Because this chapter is about Office in general, I use the term **document** generically to refer to a data file from Word, Excel, or PowerPoint. *Document* is actually the preferred term for a Word document. An Excel document is more commonly called a **workbook**, and a PowerPoint document is more commonly called a **presentation**.

Starting a new document

In this exercise, you start several new PowerPoint presentations by using various methods.

Files needed: None

1. Start PowerPoint.

The PowerPoint start screen appears. Icons for various template types appear, as shown in Figure 1-16.

2. Click the Welcome to PowerPoint template.

Information about that template appears.

3. Click the Create button.

A new presentation appears with several slides containing sample content.

4. Choose File ⇨ Close to close the new presentation.

Now no presentations are open.

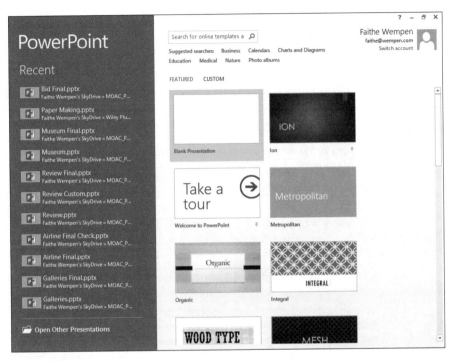

Figure 1-16

5. **Press Ctrl+N to start a new blank presentation.**

6. **Choose File ⇨ New and click the Blank Presentation template.**

   A second blank presentation opens.

7. **Click the Close (X) button in the upper-right corner of the window to close one of the blank presentations, and then repeat to close the second one and exit PowerPoint.**

Neither file is saved. You aren't prompted to save changes because you didn't enter any content into the presentations.

Typing text

Because of the layout differences among Excel, Word, and PowerPoint, the process of entering text in each program differs. Excel stores text in *cells*, which are boxes at the intersections of rows and columns. Word stores text directly on the document page. PowerPoint places text in movable, resizable text boxes on slides.

In this exercise, you place text into documents in Word, Excel, and PowerPoint.

Files needed: None

1. **Start Word and press Esc to start with a new blank document.**

2. **Type this text:** ACME Engineering.

3. **Press Enter to start a new paragraph and then type this text:** Making smart engineering decisions since 1962.

   Figure 1-17 shows the text entered in Steps 2 and 3.

4. **Leave Word open and start Excel. Press Esc to start a new blank workbook.**

5. **Type** ACME Engineering **and press Enter.**

   The text you just typed appears in cell A1 (that is, the cell at the intersection of column A and row 1). The text overlaps into column B, too, because column A isn't wide enough to hold it. An outline appears around cell A2, indicating that it's active. The next text you type will appear there.

6. **Type this text:** Making smart engineering decisions since 1962.

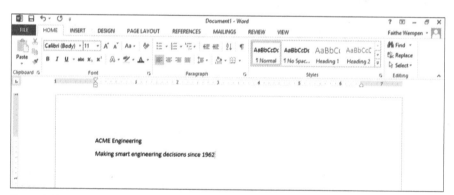

Figure 1-17

7. **Press Enter.**

   The text you typed appears in A2, as shown in Figure 1-18.

8. **Leave Excel open and open PowerPoint. Press Esc to start a new blank presentation.**

9. **Click in the Click to Add Title box and type** ACME Engineering.

10. **Click in the Click to Add Subtitle box and type the following:** Making smart engineering decisions since 1962.

    See Figure 1-19.

Leave Word, Excel, and PowerPoint open for the next exercise.

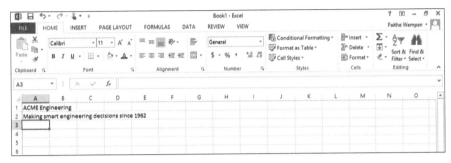

Figure 1-18

LINGO

The outline that appears around a cell is called the **cell cursor**. It indicates which cell is active. Do not confuse the cell cursor, which can be on only one cell at a time, with a selection area, which can contain multiple cells. See "Selecting Ranges" in Chapter 5 for more information about multi-cell selections.

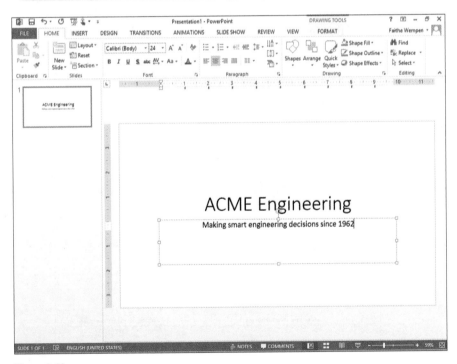

Figure 1-19

Inserting a picture

One of the most common types of graphic is what Office calls a *picture from file* (a picture that's saved as a separate file outside of Office). You can get pictures from the Internet, from friends, or from your own scanner or digital camera.

In this exercise, you place the same graphic into documents in Word, Excel, and PowerPoint.

Files needed: 01Graphic01.jpg

1. **On the Windows taskbar, click the Word button to switch to the already-open Word document from the previous exercise.**

   If you didn't do the previous exercise, go back and perform Steps 1–3 there.

2. **Click at the end of the second paragraph to move the insertion point there; then press Enter to start a new paragraph.**

3. **Click the Insert tab on the Ribbon and then click the Pictures button.**

   The Insert Picture dialog box opens.

4. **Navigate to the folder containing the data files for this chapter and select** 01Graphic01.jpg, **as shown in Figure 1-20.**

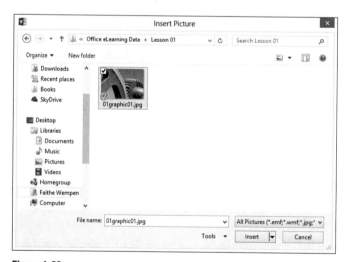

Figure 1-20

5. **Click the Insert button.**

   The picture is inserted in the document at the insertion point position.

6. **On the Windows taskbar, click the Excel button to switch to the already-open Excel workbook from the previous exercise.**

   If you didn't do the previous exercise, go back and perform Steps 4–7 there.

7. **Click the Insert tab on the Ribbon and then click the Pictures button. (If you don't see a Pictures button, click the Illustrations button and then click Pictures on the submenu that appears.)**

   The Insert Picture dialog box opens. (Refer to Figure 1-20.)

8. **Navigate to the folder containing the data files for this chapter and select 01Graphic01.jpg.**

9. **Click the Insert button.**

   The picture is inserted in the workbook as a free-floating object. You can drag it around to change its position.

LINGO

The **insertion point** is the flashing vertical bar that shows where the next text or graphic will appear. You can move it by clicking where you want it or by using the arrow keys. Moving the insertion point is covered later in this chapter in more detail.

The picture appears very large — larger than you might want it to be. You can resize the picture to make it more manageable. Chapter 4 covers resizing a picture.

10. **On the Windows taskbar, click the PowerPoint button to switch to the already-open PowerPoint presentation from the previous exercise.**

    If you didn't do the previous exercise, go back and perform Steps 8–10 there.

11. **Click below the thumbnail image of the slide on the left side of the PowerPoint window.**

    A flashing horizontal line appears there, as shown in Figure 1-21.

12. **Press Enter to create a new slide.**

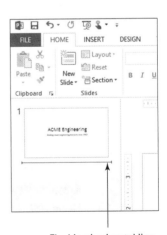

Flashing horizontal line

Figure 1-21

13. **In the placeholder box in the center of the slide, click the Pictures icon, shown in Figure 1-22.**

    The Insert Picture dialog box opens (refer to Figure 1-20).

14. **Navigate to the folder containing the data files for this chapter and select 01Graphic01.jpg.**

15. **Click the Insert button.**

    The picture is inserted in the slide placeholder and sized to fit the placeholder box, as shown in Figure 1-23.

16. **Close all open Office applications.**

    Don't save your work.

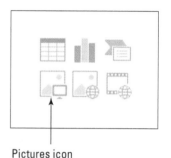

Pictures icon

Figure 1-22

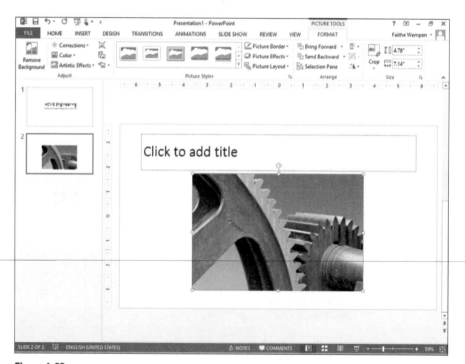

Figure 1-23

Moving Around

As you work in one of the Office applications, you may add so much content that you can't see it all onscreen at once. You might need to scroll through the document to view different parts of it. The simplest way to scroll through a document is by using the *scroll bars* with your mouse.

> Scrolling through a document with the scroll bars doesn't move the insertion point, so what you type or insert doesn't necessarily appear in the location that shows onscreen.

You can also get around by moving the insertion point. When you do so, the document view scrolls automatically so you can see the newly selected location. You can move the insertion point either by clicking where you want it or by using keyboard shortcuts.

Moving using the mouse

Here's a summary of how to move in your document using the scroll bar:

- ✔ Click a scroll arrow to scroll a small amount in that direction. In Excel, that's one row or column; in other applications, the exact amount varies per click.
- ✔ Hold down the left mouse button as you point to the scroll arrow to scroll continuously in that direction until you release the mouse button.
- ✔ Click above or below the scroll box to scroll one full screen in that direction if the document is tall/wide enough that there's undisplayed content in that direction.
- ✔ Drag the scroll box to scroll quickly in the direction you're dragging.

In this exercise, you practice moving around in an Excel worksheet by using the mouse.

Files needed: None

1. **Start Excel 2013 and press Esc to display a new blank workbook.**

2. **Click cell E10 (that is, the cell at the intersection of column E and row 10).**

   The cell cursor moves there, as shown in Figure 1-24.

Cell address appears in Name box.   Cell E10 is active.

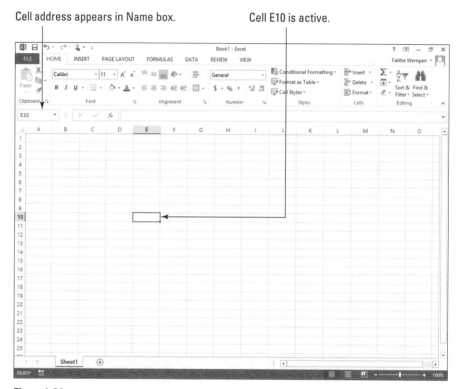

Figure 1-24

3. **Click the down-pointing arrow at the bottom of the vertical scroll bar.**

The display scrolls down one row. Notice that row 1 is no longer visible.

4. **Click the up arrow at the top of the vertical scroll bar.**

Row 1 comes back into view.

5. **Click the space below the scroll box on the scroll bar.**

The display scrolls down one full screen. Notice that the selected cell, E10, is no longer visible.

6. **Click the space above the scroll box.**

The display scrolls back up one full screen.

7. **Drag the scroll box downward.**

The display scrolls down quickly, according to the distance you dragged.

EXTRA INFO

The size of the scroll box is an indicator of how much of the document is undisplayed at the moment. In Figure 1-24, the scroll boxes takes up most of the scroll bar, indicating that almost all of the document fits onscreen at once.

8. **Click the right-pointing arrow on the horizontal scroll bar three times.**

The display scrolls to the right one column for each click. See Figure 1-25.

9. **Click the space to the left of the scroll box on the horizontal scroll bar.**

The display scrolls to the left one full screen.

Leave Excel open for the next exercise.

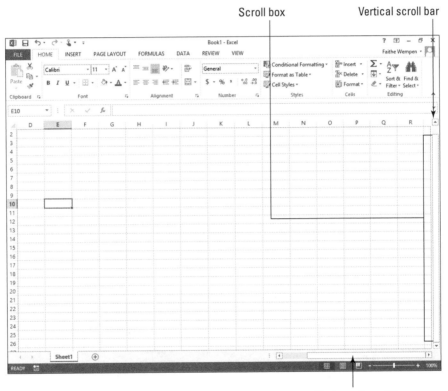

Scroll box   Vertical scroll bar

Horizontal scroll bar

Figure 1-25

Moving using the keyboard

Here's a summary of the ways you can move around in a document by using the keyboard:

- ✔ Press an arrow key to move the insertion point or cell cursor in the direction of the arrow. The exact amount of movement depends on the application; for example, in Excel, one arrow click moves the cursor by one cell. In Word, the up and down arrows move the cursor by one line, and the right and left arrows move it by one character.

- ✔ Press Page Up or Page Down to scroll one full screen in that direction.

- ✔ Press Home to move to the left side of the current row or line.

- ✔ Press End to move to the right side of the current row or line.

- ✔ Press Ctrl+Home to move to the upper-left corner of the document.

- ✔ Press Ctrl+End to move to the lower-right corner of the document.

In this exercise, you practice moving around in an Excel worksheet by using the keyboard.

Files needed: None

1. **If Excel isn't already open from the previous exercise, start Excel and press Esc to display a new blank worksheet.**

2. **If A1 is not the active cell, click it to make it so.**

3. **Press the right-arrow key on the keyboard twice.**

   The cell cursor moves to cell C1.

4. **Press the down-arrow key twice.**

   The cell cursor moves to cell C3, as shown in Figure 1-26.

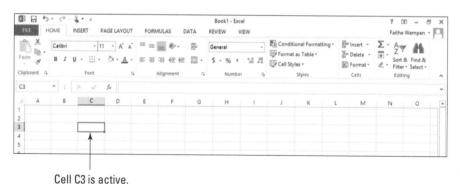

Cell C3 is active.

Figure 1-26

5. **Hold down the Ctrl key and press the down-arrow key.**

   The cell cursor moves to the bottom row of the worksheet (row 1,048,576).

6. **Hold down the Ctrl key and press the right-arrow key.**

   The cell cursor moves to the rightmost column of the worksheet (column XFD).

7. **Press the Home key.**

   The cell cursor moves back to column A.

8. **Press the Page Up key.**

   The cell cursor moves up one full screen.

9. **Press Ctrl+Home.**

   The cell cursor moves to cell A1.

Close Excel without saving your changes.

Changing the Onscreen View

All Office applications have Zoom commands that can make the data appear larger or smaller onscreen. In addition, depending on what you're doing to the data in a particular application, you may find that changing the view is useful. Some applications have multiple viewing modes you can switch among; for example, PowerPoint's Normal view is suitable for slide editing, and its Slide Sorter view is suitable for rearranging the slides.

Zooming in and out

Zooming changes the magnification of the data shown on the screen. It doesn't change the magnification of the application window itself (for example, the Ribbon), and it doesn't change the size of the data on printouts.

Zooming in increases the magnification, and zooming out decreases it.

In this exercise, you explore the Zoom feature in Word.

Files needed: None

1. **Open Word. Press Esc to start a new blank document.**

2. **Type** On Sale Now.

3. **Drag the Zoom slider to the right until the percentage shown is approximately 180.**

   The Zoom slider is located in the bottom-right corner of the Word window, as shown in Figure 1-27.

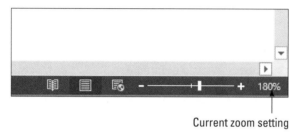

Current zoom setting

Figure 1-27

4. **If the text you typed in Step 2 has scrolled to the left, use the horizontal scroll bar to bring it back into view.**

5. **Drag the Zoom slider to the left until the percentage shown is approximately 75%.**

   The Zoom magnification decreases.

6. **Click the plus sign at the right end of the Zoom slider.**

   The zoom increases to 80%, to the next higher multiple of 10%.

7. **Click the minus sign at the left end of the Zoom slider.**

   The zoom decreases to 70%, to the next lower multiple of 10%.

8. **Click the current zoom percentage (the number to the left of the Zoom slider).**

   The Zoom dialog box opens, as shown in Figure 1-28.

You can also open the Zoom dialog box by clicking the View tab on the Ribbon and clicking the Zoom button.

9. **In the Zoom dialog box, click 100%.**

10. **Click OK.**

    The zoom changes back to 100% (the default).

Leave the Word document open for the next exercise.

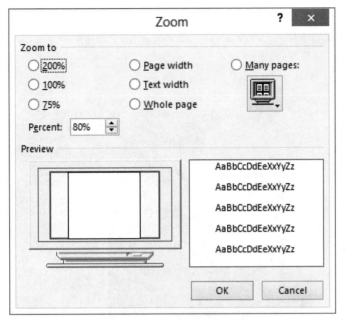

Figure 1-28

Changing views

Each application has its own views suited to working with the unique type of content it generates.

In this exercise, you explore the available views in Word and PowerPoint.

Files needed: None

1. **In Word, choose File ⇨ New and click the Seasonal Event Flyer template.**

   If you don't see the Seasonal Event Flyer template, click in the Search for Online Templates text box at the top of the window, type **Seasonal Event**, and press Enter.

2. **Click Create to start a new document based on that template.**

   Steps 1 and 2 give you a sample document to practice with. Word is now in Print Layout view, as shown in Figure 1-29.

Print Layout view is useful for editing documents in a format that approximates how they'll look when printed.

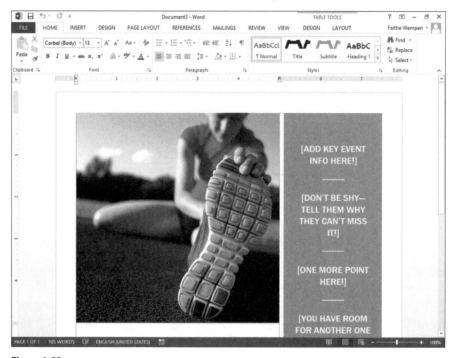

Figure 1-29

3. **Click the View tab on the Ribbon and then click the Draft button.**

   The document appears in Draft view, as shown in Figure 1-30.

4. **On the View tab, click the Read Mode button.**

   The document appears in Full Screen Reading view, which is suitable for reading the content onscreen.

5. **Click View in the upper-left corner, and from the menu that appears, choose Edit Document, as shown in Figure 1-31.**

   The document returns to Print Layout view.

6. **Exit Word. Do not save changes.**

EXTRA INFO

Draft view shows the text in a very basic format, without multiple columns, headers, footers, or other layout elements.

Document views.   Pictures do not appear in Draft view.

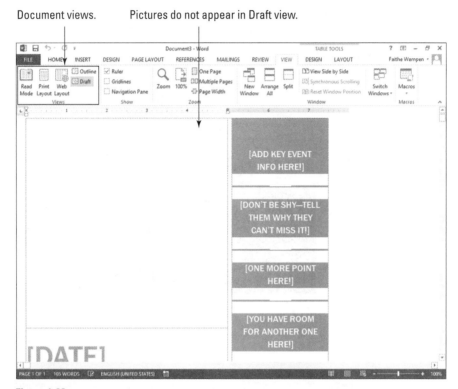

Figure 1-30

7. **Open PowerPoint.**

   PowerPoint's Start screen appears, showing several template thumbnails.

8. **Click the Welcome to PowerPoint template and then click the Create button.**

   This step gives you a sample presentation to practice with, as shown in Figure 1-32.

   When you complete Step 8, PowerPoint is in Normal view. Normal view has three panes: thumbnails of the slides appear in the Slides pane at the left, the active slide appears in a large pane on the right, and any notes for the slide appear in the Notes pane at the bottom. This view is useful for editing slide content.

Read Mode has a menu bar for selecting
commands rather than a Ribbon.

Figure 1-31

9. **Click the View tab and then click the Slide Sorter button.**

   The presentation appears in Slide Sorter view, as shown in Figure 1-33.

10. **On the View tab, click the Outline View button.**

    Outline view appears. It's like Normal view (refer to Figure 1-32) except the slide text appears in outline format on the left instead of slide thumbnails appearing there.

11. **Close PowerPoint without saving your changes.**

Leave Word open for the next exercise.

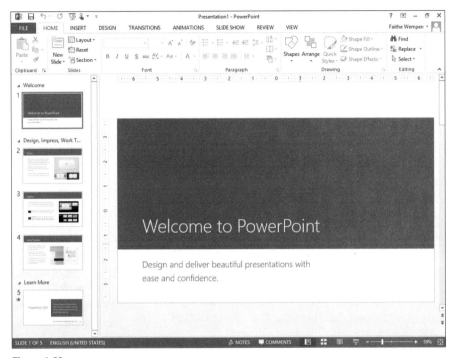

Figure 1-32

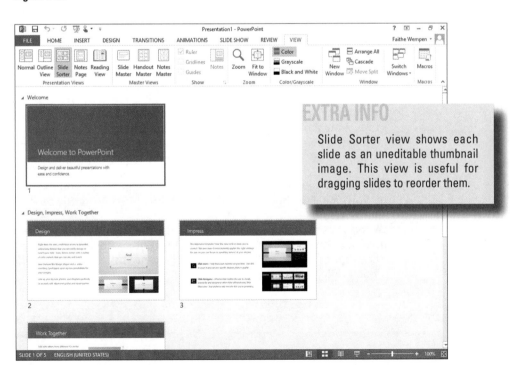

EXTRA INFO

Slide Sorter view shows each slide as an uneditable thumbnail image. This view is useful for dragging slides to reorder them.

Figure 1-33

Saving and Opening Documents

In each Office app, you can create, open, and save data files. A data file stores your work in a particular application. If you don't save your work, whatever you've entered disappears when you close the application or turn off your computer.

Each Office 2013 application has its own data file format. For example:

- ✔ **Word:** Document files, `.docx`
- ✔ **Excel:** Workbook files, `.xlsx`
- ✔ **PowerPoint:** Presentation files, `.pptx`
- ✔ **Outlook:** Personal folders files, `.pst`

Word, Excel, and PowerPoint use a separate data file for each project you work on. Every time you use one of these programs, you open and save data files. Outlook uses just one data file for all your activities. This file is automatically saved and opened for you, so you usually don't have to think about data file management in Outlook.

The steps for saving and opening data files are almost exactly the same in each application, so mastering them in one program gives you a big head start in the other programs. Throughout the rest of this book, many of the exercises begin with an instruction to open a particular data file and end with an instruction to save it.

Saving your work for the first time

As you work in an application, the content you create is stored in the computer's memory. This memory is only temporary storage. When you exit the application or shut down the computer, whatever is stored in memory is flushed away forever — unless you save it.

The first time you save a file, the application prompts you to enter a name for it. You can also choose a different save location and/or file type.

When you resave a previously saved file, the Save As dialog box doesn't reappear; the file saves with the most recent settings. If you want to change the settings (such as the location or file type) or save under a different name, choose File➪Save As.

Each application has three important file types:

- ✔ **Default:** The default format in each application supports most Office 2007 and higher features except macros. The file extension ends in the letter *X* for each one: Word is `.docx`; Excel is `.xlsx`; PowerPoint is `.pptx`.

- ✔ **Macro-enabled:** This format supports most Office 2007 and higher features, including macros. The file extension ends in the letter *M* for each one: `.docm`, `.xlsm`, and `.pptm`.

> *Macros* are recorded bits of code that can automate certain activities in a program, but they can also carry viruses. The default formats don't support macros for that reason. If you need to create a file that includes macros, you can save in a macro-enabled format.

- ✔ **97–2003:** Each application includes a file format for backward compatibility with earlier versions of the application (Office versions 97 through 2003). Some minor functionality may be lost when you save in this format. The file extensions are `.doc`, `.xls`, and `.ppt`.

In this exercise, you save a document in Word several times with different names and file types.

Files needed: None

1. **Open Word. Click the Welcome to Word template to start a new document based on it.**

2. **Choose File ⇨ Save.**

   The Save As screen of Backstage view appears. Note that your SkyDrive is the default location selected under the Save As heading. In this exercise, however, you save to your local computer. (See the next section for the lowdown on SkyDrive.)

3. **Click Computer.**

   A list of recently used folders on your local computer appears, as shown in Figure 1-34.

4. **Click Browse.**

   The Save As dialog box opens, showing the default local location (probably your Documents library).

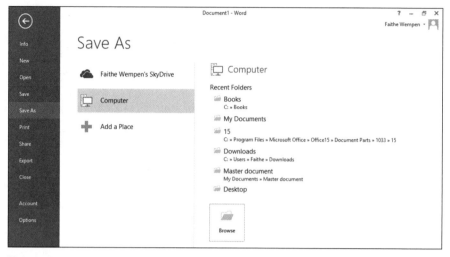

Figure 1-34

5. **In the File Name text box, type** Tour of Word, **as shown in Figure 1-35.**

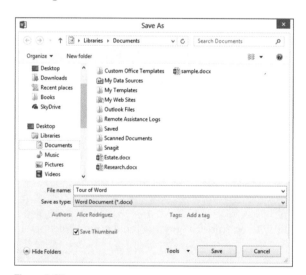

Figure 1-35

6. **Click Save.**

   The file is saved. The file's name appears in Word's title bar at the top of the window.

7. **In the document, scroll down to the picture of the blue flowers. Click the picture to select it and then press the Delete key to remove it.**

8. **On the Quick Access Toolbar, click the Save button, shown in Figure 1-36.**

   The changes to the document are saved.

9. **In the document, press the Delete key four more times to remove the extra blank lines where the picture used to be.**

10. **Press Ctrl+S.**

    The changes are saved.

11. **Drag across the words** *live layout* **in item 1 to select those words and then press Ctrl+I to italicize them.**

12. **Choose File ⇨ Save As and click the Browse button.**

    The Save As dialog box opens.

Save

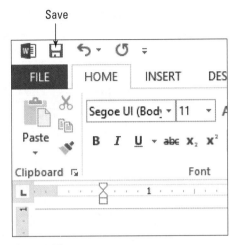

Figure 1-36

13. **In the File Name text box, change the filename to** Tour of Word Revised.

14. **Click the drop-down list to the right of Save as Type.**

    A list of document types opens.

15. **Select the Word 97–2003 Document option, as shown in Figure 1-37.**

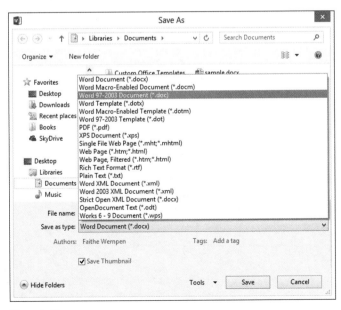

Figure 1-37

16. Click Save.

A Compatibility Checker dialog box opens, as shown in Figure 1-38.

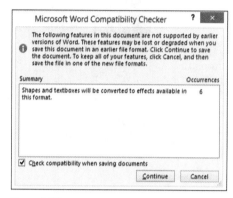

The Compatibility Checker points out any features that might appear differently in an earlier-format version of the file. In most cases, the losses are minimal.

Figure 1-38

17. Click the Continue button.

The document is resaved with a different name and a different file type.

Leave the document open in Word for the next exercise.

Navigating in the Save As dialog box

Office 2013 uses the current Windows user's SkyDrive as the default storage location. SkyDrive is a cloud-based online storage area hosted by Microsoft. Anyone who registers for the service, or who logs into Windows 8 with a Microsoft ID, is given a certain amount of free storage space, and can purchase more. For more information about SkyDrive, see Appendix A.

You can also save your files locally, where the default location is your Documents library, as it was with Office 2010. In Windows, each user has his own Documents folder (based on who is logged in to Windows at the moment).

LINGO

The **cloud** is a generic way of referring to secure, Internet-based storage and applications. For example, SkyDrive is Microsoft's cloud-based storage area, and Office 365 is Microsoft's cloud-based version of Office.

New in Office 2013 applications, when you choose File ⇨ Save As, a dialog box doesn't open immediately. Instead, a Save As screen in Backstage view opens, prompting you to choose an overall save location, whether it's your SkyDrive, your computer, or some custom location you might have set up. (See Figure 1-39.) Only after you make that choice and click Browse does the Save As dialog box appear.

To understand how to change save locations, you should first understand the concept of a file path. Files are organized into folders, and you can have folders *inside* folders. For example, you might have

✔ A folder called *Work*

✔ Within that folder, another folder called *Job Search*

✔ Within that folder, a Word file called `Resume.docx`

The path for such a file would be

`C:\Work\Job Search\Resume.docx`

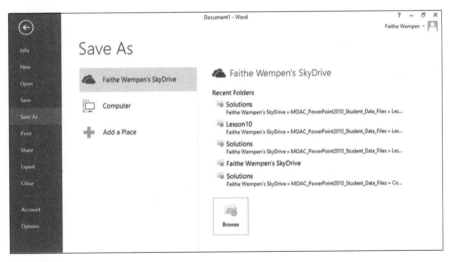

Figure 1-39

When you change the save location, you're changing to a different path for the file. You do that by navigating through the file system via the Save As dialog box. The Save As dialog box provides several ways of navigating, so you can pick the one you like best.

In this exercise, you experiment with several ways of changing the save location in the Save As dialog box.

Files needed: None

1. **In Word, with the document still open from the previous exercise, choose File ⇨ Save As.**

2. **Click *Your Name*'s SkyDrive or Computer, depending on where you want to save your work from the exercises in this book.**

    See Figure 1-39.

3. **Click the Browse button.**

    The Save As dialog box opens, as shown in Figure 1-40.

Places bar   Address bar

EXTRA INFO

The bar at the left is the navigation pane. It provides shortcuts for various places where you can save files. The bar across the top is the address bar. It shows the current location.

Figure 1-40

4. **Scroll through the navigation pane to see the available locations for saving files.**

5. **In the navigation pane, click Computer.**

   A list of drives appears.

6. **Double-click the C: drive.**

   A list of folders on the C: drive appears.

7. **Scroll up in the navigation pane to locate the Documents shortcut and double-click it.**

   The Documents folder's content appears.

8. **Right-click an empty spot in the right pane of the dialog box, point to New, and click Folder.**

   A new folder appears with the name highlighted, ready for you to name it.

9. **Type** Dummies Kit **and press Enter to name the folder.**

   You've just created a folder that you can use to store all the work that you do for this class, as shown in Figure 1-41.

New folder

Figure 1-41

10. **Double-click the Dummies Kit folder to open it.**

11. **In the address bar, click the right-pointing arrow to the left of Dummies Kit.**

   A list of all the other folders in the Documents folder appears.

   TIP

   In the address bar, the parts of a path are separated by right-pointing triangles rather than by slashes. You can click any of the triangles to open a drop-down list containing all the *subfolders* (that is, the folders within that folder).

12. **Click any of the folders on that list to switch to that folder.**

13. **In the address bar, click Documents.**

   The Documents folder reappears.

14. **In the address bar, click Libraries.**

   A list of the libraries appears: Documents, Music, Pictures, and Videos, as shown in Figure 1-42.

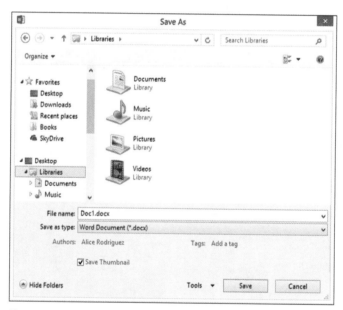

Figure 1-42

15. **Scroll up near the top of the navigation pane and click Desktop.**

    You can save directly to your desktop by saving to this location.

16. **In the navigation pane, click Documents and then double-click Dummies Kit.**

    The Dummies Kit folder reappears.

17. **In the File Name text box, type** Lesson 1 Practice.

18. **Open the Save as Type drop-down list and select Word Document (.docx), as shown in Figure 1-43.**

19. **Click Save.**

    The file is saved.

20. **Choose File ⇨ Close to close the document without exiting Word.**

Figure 1-43

Opening a document

When you open a file, you copy it from your hard drive (or other storage location) into the computer's memory, where Word can access it for viewing and modifying it.

The Open dialog box's navigation controls are almost exactly the same as those in the Save As dialog box, so you can browse to a different storage location if needed.

If you want to reopen a recently used file, there's an even quicker way than using the Open dialog box. Choose File ⇨ Open and then click the file's name on the Recent Files list.

In this exercise, you open a saved file.

Files needed: Any saved Word document, such as the Lesson 1 Practice file you saved in the previous exercise

1. **In Word, choose File ⇨ Open.**

2. **Click either *Your Name's* SkyDrive or Computer, depending on where you chose to save in the previous exercise.**

3. **Click the Browse button.**

   The Open dialog box appears. The location shown is the Dummies Kit folder because it was the last folder you accessed during this session.

4. **Select the Lesson 1 Practice folder, as shown in Figure 1-44.**

5. **Click Open.**

   The file opens in Word.

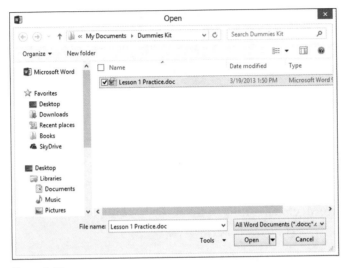

Figure 1-44

6. **Choose File ⇨ Close to close the document without exiting Word.**

7. **Choose File ⇨ Open.**

   A list of recently opened files appears on the right side of the screen.

8. **Click Lesson 1 Practice.**

   That file reopens.

9. **Choose File ⇨ Close to close the document again.**

Recovering lost work

Computers lock up occasionally, and applications sometimes crash in the middle of important projects. When that happens, any work that you haven't saved is gone.

To minimize the pain of those situations, Word, Excel, and PowerPoint all have an AutoRecover feature that silently saves your drafts as you work, once every ten minutes or at some other interval you specify. These drafts are saved in temporary hidden files that are deleted when you close the application successfully (that is, not abruptly due to a lockup, crash, or power outage). If the application crashes, those temporary saved files appear for your perusal when the program starts back up. You can choose to do either of the following:

✔ Save them if their versions are newer than the ones you have on your hard drive.

✔ Discard them if they contain nothing you need.

In this exercise, you change the interval at which Word saves backup drafts for AutoRecover.

Files needed: None

1. **In Word, choose File ⇨ Options.**

   The Word Options dialog box opens.

2. **Click the Save category on the left.**

3. **Make sure that the Save AutoRecover Information Every XX Minutes check box is selected.**

4. **If desired, change the value in the Minutes box to another number.**

   For example, to save every 5 minutes, type **5** there, as shown in Figure 1-45.

AutoRecover interval

Figure 1-45

5. Click OK.

Exit Word without saving your changes to any open files.

Summing Up

Excel, Word, and PowerPoint are all very similar in their basic functionality and appearance. In this chapter, you explored several different applications and learned how to start and exit the programs, create and save your work, and insert text and graphics.

- The Ribbon and Backstage view provide a consistent interface for managing files and issuing commands in each application.

- Word, Excel, and PowerPoint all start a new blank document when they open. (Access it by pressing Esc at the app's Start screen.) You can use this document, or you can open an existing one. Excel documents are called workbooks; PowerPoint documents are called presentations.

- To enter text in a document, click where you want to place it; that moves the insertion point there. Then type.

- To insert a picture, click the Insert tab on the Ribbon and then click the Pictures button. It works the same in Word, Excel, and PowerPoint.

- Scroll bars enable you to scroll to different parts of a document. You can also move around by clicking where you want to go or by using the arrow keys to move the insertion point.

- Each application has a different set of views for working with data in different ways. You can switch among them on the View tab.

- The Zoom feature increases or decreases the magnification of the data displayed onscreen. Use the Zoom slider and controls in the lower-right corner of the application window.

- To save your work, use the Save command on the File menu, or press Ctrl+S, or click the Save button on the Quick Access Toolbar.

- To open a file, use the Open command on the File menu. You can also select a recently used file from the Open category in Backstage view.

Try-it-yourself lab

For more practice with the features covered in this chapter, try the following exercise on your own:

1. **Start Excel and, in a new blank workbook, in cell A1, type** Grocery List.

2. **Starting in cell A3, type a grocery shopping list of at least six items, with each item appearing in a different cell in column A.**

3. **Save the file as Lesson 1 Grocery List in the Dummies Kit folder you created earlier.**

4. **Close Excel.**

Know this tech talk

application: A program that performs a useful user task, such as creating a word processing document or calculating a number.

Backstage view: The section of an Office application that appears when the File menu is open. It contains commands for working with files, options, importing, exporting, and printing.

cell cursor: In Excel, the dark outline around the active cell.

cloud: A generic term for secure, Internet-based storage and applications.

data file: A file in which the information you enter in an application is stored for later reuse.

document: A data file in a word processing program. Can also refer generically to any data file.

file extension: The code following the period at the end of a file name, indicating the file's type. Some file extensions are hidden by default in Windows.

folder: An organizing container on a hard drive in which to store files.

insertion point: In a text-editing application, a flashing vertical line indicating where text will be inserted when typed.

presentation: A data file in a presentation program such as PowerPoint.

Quick Access Toolbar: The customizable toolbar that appears above the Ribbon.

scroll bar: A bar along the right and/or bottom side of a window that can be used to change the viewing area.

scroll box: The movable box inside the scroll bar.

suite: A collection of programs with complementary functions and common user interface elements

workbook: A data file in a spreadsheet program such as Excel.

Chapter 2
Creating a Word Document

✔ Starting new documents based on templates can *save time and provide guidance as to what content to insert and where to place it.* Many templates are available for free via Office.com.

✔ Selecting text before issuing a command enables you to *act on large blocks of text at a time.* You can select text either with the keyboard or the mouse.

✔ Formatting text *makes your documents more attractive and readable.* You can apply different fonts, sizes, and colors, as well as use style sets and themes to automate the process of formatting an entire document.

✔ Check your spelling and grammar in order to *avoid embarrassing errors* in documents you distribute to others. Word can help you check both individual words and the entire document easily.

✔ You can *share your documents with other people* via e-mail or by printing them. You can begin sending a document via e-mail from within Word, and your default e-mail program opens to send the message.

1. **How do you start a document based on an online template?**

Find out on page 59

2. **How can you change a document's margins?**

Find out on page 63

3. **How do you set the paper size and page orientation?**

Find out on page 65

4. **What are two ways to change the font size?**

Find out on page 73

5. **What kinds of formatting does a theme affect?**

Find out on page 80

6. **What does it mean when text has a wavy red underline?**

Find out on page 85

7. **How do you send Word documents via e-mail?**

Find out on page 88

icrosoft Word is the most popular of the Office applications because nearly everyone needs to create text documents of one type or another. With Word, you can create everything from fax cover sheets to school research papers to family holiday letters.

In this chapter, I explain how to create, edit, format, and share simple documents. By the end of this chapter, you'll have a good grasp of the entire process of document creation, from start to finish, including how to share your work with others via print or e-mail. Later chapters will then build on this knowledge, adding in the fancier aspects such as using styles, graphics, and multiple sections.

Creating a New Document Using a Template

As you learned in Chapter 1, you can create a blank new document, or you can base a new document on a template. Each Office application has some templates that are stored locally on your hard drive and many more that are available via the Internet. After starting a new document, you can adjust the paper size and orientation if needed.

REMEMBER

Even when you start a blank document, you're still (technically) using a template. It's a template called Normal, and it specifies certain default settings for a new blank document, such as the default fonts (Calibri for body text and Cambria for headings), default font sizes (11 point for body text), and margins (1 inch on all sides).

When you create a new document by clicking the Blank Document icon or by pressing Ctrl+N, the resulting document is based on the Normal template. If you stick with the default values for the Normal template's definition, the Normal template doesn't exist as a separate file. It's built into Word itself. You won't find it if you search your hard drive for it. However, if you make a change to one or more of the Normal template's settings, Word saves them to a file called `Normal.dotm`. If Word at any point can't find `Normal.dotm`, it reverts to its internally stored copy and goes back to the default values.

That's important to know because if you ever accidentally redefine the Normal template so that it produces documents with unwanted settings, or if it ever gets corrupted, all you have to do is find and delete `Normal.dotm` from your hard drive, and you go back to a fresh-from-the-factory version of the default settings for new blank documents. The template is stored in `C:\Users\user\AppData\Roaming\Microsoft\Templates`, where *user* is the logged-in username.

In this exercise, you start a new Word document using a template.

Files needed: None

1. In Word, choose File➪New.

Icons for creating new documents appear, as shown in Figure 2-1.

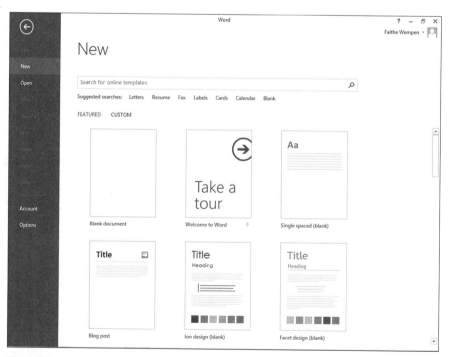

Figure 2-1

2. **Click in the Search for Online Templates box and type** Brochures. **Then press Enter.**

   Word uses your Internet connection to retrieve a list of available brochure templates.

3. **In the Category list at the right, click Business.**

   The list is filtered to show only templates that have business as a keyword.

4. **In the Category list at the right, click Tri-Fold.**

   An X appears next to Tri-Fold, and the list is further filtered to show templates that have both keywords. See Figure 2-2.

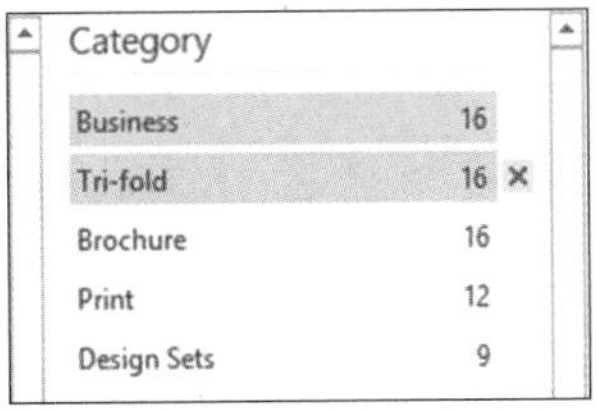

5. **Point the mouse pointer at the Business category on the list at the right.**

   An X appears to the right of the Business category.

6. **Click the X to remove the Business category filter.**

7. **Click the Tri-Fold Brochure (Red Design) template.**

   A preview of it appears, as shown in Figure 2-3.

Category	
Business	16
Tri-fold	16 ✕
Brochure	16
Print	12
Design Sets	9

Figure 2-2

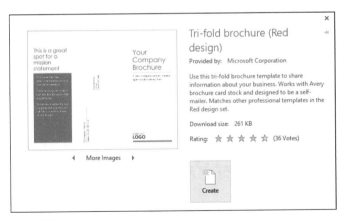

Figure 2-3

8. **Click the Create button below the preview.**

   The template is downloaded, and a new document appears based on it.

9. **Examine the document to see what types of content the template provided.**

10. **Choose File⇨Close to close the document.**

    If prompted to save your changes, click Don't Save.

11. **Choose File⇨New.**

    The icons reappear for new document types.

12. **In the search box, type** urban report **and press Enter.**

13. **Click the Report (Urban theme) template.**

    If there are two copies, click either copy. A sample of the template appears.

14. **Click the Create button.**

    A new document opens based on the selected template.

15. **Scroll through the new document and notice the placeholders ready for you to fill in to create your own version of the report.**

16. **Save the document as Lesson 2 Practice.**

Leave Word and the document file open for the next exercise.

For more practice, create several more new documents by using different templates. Don't save any of them.

Adjusting Page Settings

A template might not always use the page settings for the work you want to create. If you want to change the page margins, orientation, or size, you can use the Page Layout tab.

Setting page margins

Word provides several easy-to-use margin presets. You can also individually specify the margins for each side of the page if you prefer.

In this exercise, you change the page margins in two ways: using a preset and using an exact value.

Files needed: Lesson 2 Practice, created in the previous exercise

1. **In Word, with the Lesson 2 Practice document still open from the previous exercise, click the Page Layout tab on the Ribbon.**

2. **Click the Margins button.**

   A Margins drop-down list opens, as shown in Figure 2-4.

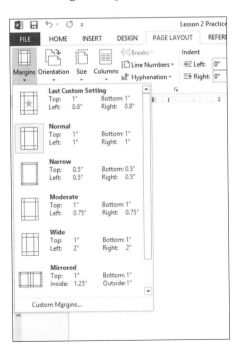

Figure 2-4

LINGO

The **margins** are the amounts of blank space that Word reserves on each side of the paper. In most cases, you want them to be roughly the same on all sides, or at least the same at both the right/left, so the document looks symmetrical. In special cases, though, such as when you're going to bind the document on the left or at the top, you want to leave more blank space on one particular side.

EXTRA INFO

The Mirrored margin choice enables you to specify different margins for right and left depending on whether the page number is odd or even. This option allows you to print pages for a two-sided booklet with the extra space on whichever side of the page will be in the binding.

3. **Click the Narrow option.**

   Presets for narrow margins are applied to the top, bottom, right, and left margins for the document.

4. **Click the Margins button again and then click Custom Margins.**

   The Page Setup dialog box opens.

5. **In the Top, Bottom, Right, and Left boxes, type** 1.3, **as in Figure 2-5.**

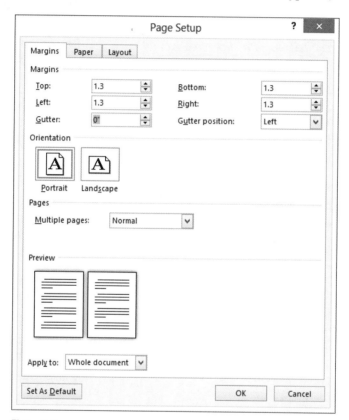

Figure 2-5

6. **Click OK.**

   The margins change. You can tell the margins change because the sample text is positioned differently on the pages.

7. **Save your work.**

   Leave Word and the document file open for the next exercise.

Setting paper size and orientation

The standard paper size in the U.S. is 8.5 x 11 inches, also known as Letter. Most of the templates available through Word use this paper size, although some exceptions exist. For example, an envelope template might use a page size that matches a standard business envelope, or a legal brief template might use legal-size paper (8.5 x 14 inches).

In this exercise, you set the page orientation of a document to Landscape and change its paper size.

Files needed: Lesson 2 Practice, created earlier in this lesson

LINGO

A document's **orientation** can be either portrait or landscape.

Portrait is a standard page in which the tall part of the paper runs along the left and right sides.

Landscape is a rotated page in which the tall part of the paper runs along the top and bottom.

1. **In Word, with the Lesson 2 Practice document still open from the previous exercise, click the Page Layout tab on the Ribbon if it isn't already displayed.**

2. **Click the Orientation button.**

   A drop-down list opens and gives you two options: Portrait and Landscape.

3. **Click the Landscape option.**

   The page changes to Landscape mode.

4. **Change the orientation back to Portrait.**

5. **Click the Size button.**

   A list of common paper sizes appears, as shown in Figure 2-6.

Look online for websites that explain the paper sizes common in various countries. Here's one such site to start you out:

www.cl.cam.ac.uk/~mgk25/iso-paper.html

6. **Click the option A4 8.27" x 11.69". You may need to scroll down the list to find it.**

   The paper size changes.

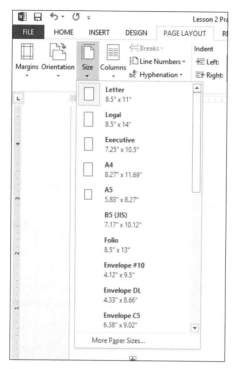

Figure 2-6

Changing the paper size in Word doesn't change the paper size in your printer, of course, so if you print on a different size paper than you tell Word you're using, the printing may not be centered on the paper.

For more practice, click More Paper Sizes at the bottom of the Size menu and set up a custom paper size by entering a width and height on the Paper tab of the Page Setup dialog box.

7. Save your work.

Leave Word and the document file open for the next exercise.

Editing Text

After creating a document and setting its basic properties (such as margins, orientation, and page size), you're ready to start editing its content. Editing can include adding text, deleting text, modifying text, and moving and copying blocks of text from one location to another.

If you used a template to get started, you may already have some sample content in the document (text and/or graphics). You can edit this content, or you can delete it and start from scratch.

Filling text placeholders

Some templates include placeholders to guide you in creating content in a specific format. You aren't required to use the placeholders; you can delete them if you like. However, if you aren't sure how to get started with a particular type of document, the template's placeholders can be helpful guides.

In this exercise, you edit a document's text by filling in placeholders.

Files needed: Lesson 2 Practice, created earlier in this lesson

1. **In Word, with the Lesson 2 Practice document still open from the previous exercise, triple-click the Report (Urban design) placeholder text to select it.**

    The placeholder becomes highlighted, as shown in Figure 2-7.

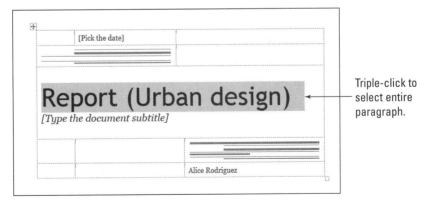

Figure 2-7

2. **Type** Mountain Vista Vacations.

The text appears in the placeholder box.

3. **Click in the [Type the document subtitle] placeholder and type** Affordable Family Fun.

4. **Click in the [Pick the date] placeholder.**

The text becomes highlighted, and a drop-down arrow appears to its right.

5. **Click the arrow to open a date picker, as shown in Figure 2-8.**

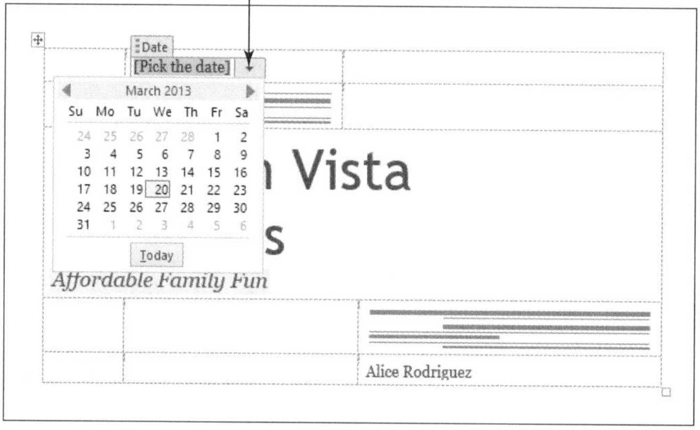

Figure 2-8

6. **Click the Today button to select today's date.**

The date picker closes.

7. **Click the name below the green horizontal lines.**

By default, it's the name of the registered user of this copy of Word.

8. **Type your own name to replace the default name.**

The cover page information is now complete, as shown in Figure 2-9.

9. **Save your work and close the document.**

Leave Word open for the next exercise.

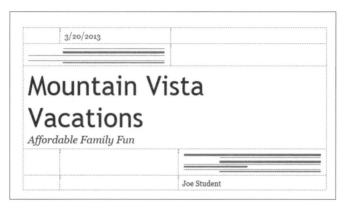

Figure 2-9

Typing and editing text

Most documents don't contain text placeholders, so you're on your own in deciding what to type. Fortunately, it's easy to type and edit text in Word.

To delete text, press Delete (to delete the character to the right of the insertion point) or Backspace (to delete the character to the left of the insertion point). To delete more than one character at once, select the block of text to delete and then press Delete or Backspace.

You can also select some text and then type over it. When you type after selecting text, the selected text is replaced by what you type.

In this exercise, you type some text in a new document and then edit it using several different editing techniques.

Files needed: None

1. **In Word, press Ctrl+N to start a new blank document.**

2. **Type the following text in the document:**

Dear Karen:

Florida is certainly a long way from home, and although we are enjoying our trip, we are looking forward to being home again with our good friends.

We are having a wonderful time on our vacation. The weather has been perfect. Elroy and George have been collecting shells, and Judy and I have been enjoying the pool.

3. **Triple-click the last paragraph to select it.**

4. **Drag the paragraph up and drop it between the other two paragraphs (between the salutation and the first body paragraph).**

See Figure 2-10.

5. **Double-click the name *Karen* in the first paragraph and type** Rosie.

6. **Click to move the insertion point after the word Florida in the last paragraph. Press Backspace until the entire word is deleted.**

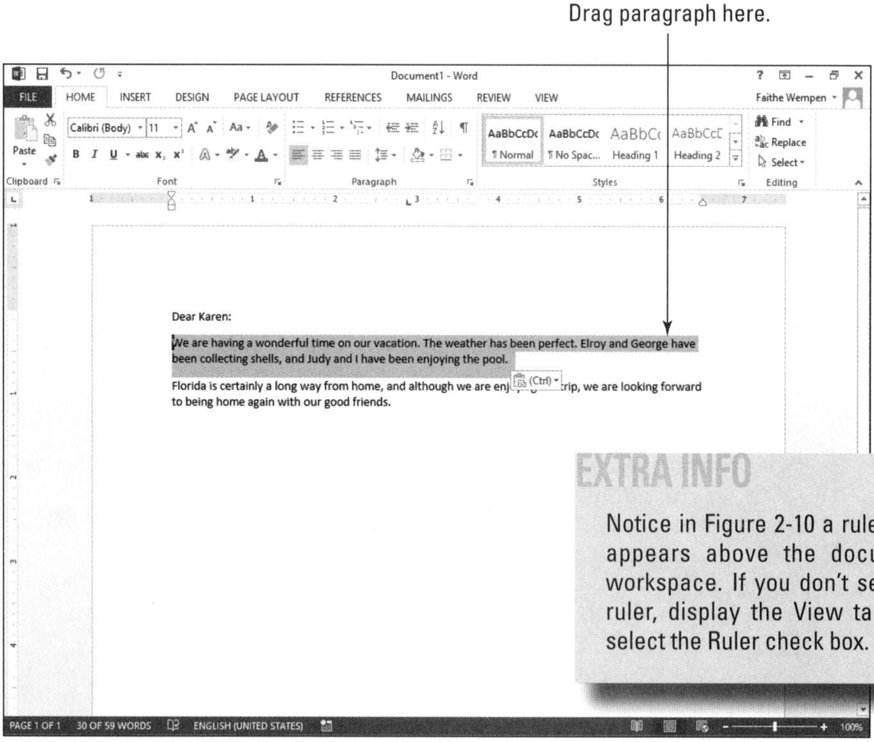

Drag paragraph here.

EXTRA INFO

Notice in Figure 2-10 a ruler that appears above the document workspace. If you don't see the ruler, display the View tab and select the Ruler check box.

Figure 2-10

7. **Type** California.

8. **Use the arrow keys to move the insertion point before *shells* in the first paragraph and then type** sea.

The document resembles Figure 2-11.

Dear Rosie:

We are having a wonderful time on our vacation. The weather has been perfect. Elroy and George have been collecting seashells, and Judy and I have been enjoying the pool.

California is certainly a long way from home, and although we are enjoying our trip, we are looking forward to being home again with our good friends.

Figure 2-11

9. **Save the document as Lesson 2 Vacation.**

Leave the document open for the next exercise.

Selecting Text

Selecting blocks of text before you issue an editing or formatting command allows you to act on the entire block at once. For example, you can select multiple paragraphs before applying new line spacing or indentation settings, and those settings will apply to every paragraph in the selection.

You have many ways to select text:

- ✔ You can drag across the text with the mouse (with the left mouse button pressed) to select any amount of text.
- ✔ You can move the insertion point to the beginning of the text and then hold down the Shift key while you press the arrow keys to extend the selection.
- ✔ You can press the F8 key to turn on Extend mode, and then you can use the arrow keys to extend the selection.
- ✔ You can double-click a word to select it or triple-click within a paragraph to select it.
- ✔ You can press Ctrl+A to select the entire document.
- ✔ You can click to the left of a line to select that line.

In this exercise, you practice selecting parts of a document.

Files needed: Lesson 2 Vacation, created in the previous exercise

1. **In Word, in the Lesson 2 Vacation file, triple-click within the second paragraph to select it.**

2. **Hold down the Shift key and press the down-arrow key twice to extend the selection to the next paragraph.**

   See Figure 2-12.

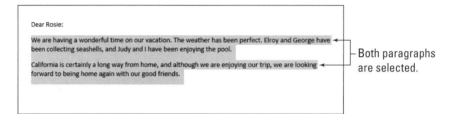

Dear Rosie:

We are having a wonderful time on our vacation. The weather has been perfect. Elroy and George have been collecting seashells, and Judy and I have been enjoying the pool.

California is certainly a long way from home, and although we are enjoying our trip, we are looking forward to being home again with our good friends.

Both paragraphs are selected.

Figure 2-12

PRACTICE

For more practice, click away from the selected paragraphs to deselect them and then double-click several words to select them. Then try double-clicking one word and holding down the Shift key while you double-click a different word. Try it again with the Ctrl key instead of Shift.

3. **Press Ctrl+A to select the entire document.**

4. **Click away from the selected text to deselect it.**

5. **Drag the mouse across the word *wonderful* in the second paragraph to select it.**

6. **Position the mouse pointer to the left of the first line in the second paragraph.**

   The mouse pointer turns into a white arrow that points diagonally up and to the right.

   If you don't see the arrow, make sure you're in Print Layout view. On the View tab, click the Print Layout button.

7. **Click to select the line.**

   See Figure 2-13.

Line is selected.

Dear Rosie:

We are having a wonderful time on our vacation. The weather has been perfect. Elroy and George have been collecting seashells, and Judy and I have been enjoying the pool.

California is certainly a long way from home, and although we are enjoying our trip, we are looking forward to being home again with our good friends.

Figure 2-13

Leave the document open for the next exercise. You don't have to save your work because you didn't make any changes.

Formatting Text

Text formatting can make a big difference in the readability of a document. By making certain text larger, boldface, or a different font, you can call attention to it and add interest for your readers.

You can apply each type of character formatting individually, or you can use style sets or themes to apply multiple types of formatting at once.

Choosing text font, size, and color

Each font is available in a wide variety of sizes. The sizes are measured in **points**, with each point being ½ of an inch on a printout. (The size it appears onscreen depends on the display zoom. You learn about zoom in Chapter 1.) Text sizes vary from very small (6 points) to very large (100 points or more). An average document uses body text that's between 10 and 12 points, and headings between 12 and 18 points.

You can also color each font by using either a **standard color**, which doesn't change when you change document themes, or a **theme color**, which does change. Later in the lesson, you learn how to change themes, and you see what happens to the text colors you've applied when the theme colors change.

You can apply fonts, sizes, and colors either from the Home tab of the Ribbon or from the Mini toolbar.

In this exercise, you format some text by applying different fonts, sizes, and colors to it.

Files needed: Lesson 2 Vacation, from the previous exercise

1. **In Word, in the Lesson 2 Vacation file, move the insertion point to the beginning of the document and press Enter to create a new line.**

2. **Press the up-arrow key once to move the insertion point into the new line and then type** Our Vacation.

3. **Triple-click** *Our Vacation* **to select the entire paragraph.**

4. **Point the mouse pointer at the selected paragraph so that the Mini toolbar appears, as shown in Figure 2-14.**

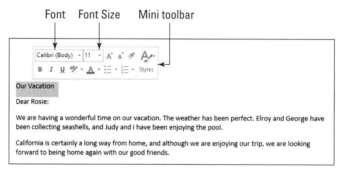

Figure 2-14

5. **Open the Font drop-down list on the Mini toolbar and click Arial Black.**

6. **Open the Font Size drop-down list on the Mini toolbar and click 14.**

   If the Mini toolbar is no longer visible, right-click the text to make the Mini toolbar reappear.

For more practice, change the font and font size by using the controls in the Font group on the Ribbon.

7. **On the Ribbon, click the Increase Font Size button to increase the font size of the selected text to 16 points, as shown in Figure 2-15.**

Increase Font Size   Font Color

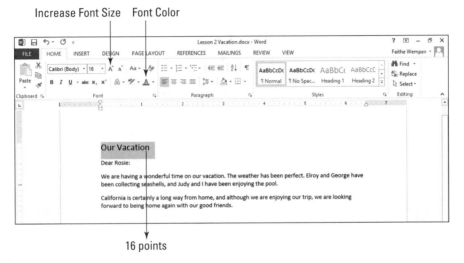

16 points

Figure 2-15

8. **Click the face of the Font Color button.**

Whatever color was already displayed on the button is applied to the text. (The color that appears depends on the most recently used font color.)

9. **Click the down arrow to the right of the Font Color button.**

A palette of colors appears, as shown in Figure 2-16.

10. **Click the red square under Standard Colors.**

The text becomes red.

11. **Click the down arrow on the Font Color button again to reopen the color palette.**

12. **Click the Orange, Accent 2 square on the top row of the Theme Colors section. (See Figure 2-16.)**

Orange, Accent 2

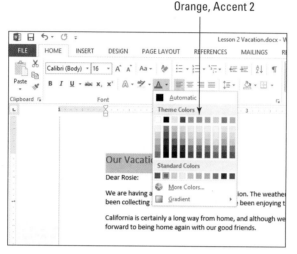

Figure 2-16

Pointing at a square makes its name appear in a ScreenTip.

For more practice, try some of the tints and shades below the theme colors. A **tint** is a lighter version of a color, and a **shade** is a darker version of it.

Leave the document open for the next exercise.

Applying text attributes and effects

Figure 2-17 shows samples of some of these attributes. Table 2-1 summarizes the keyboard shortcuts for them.

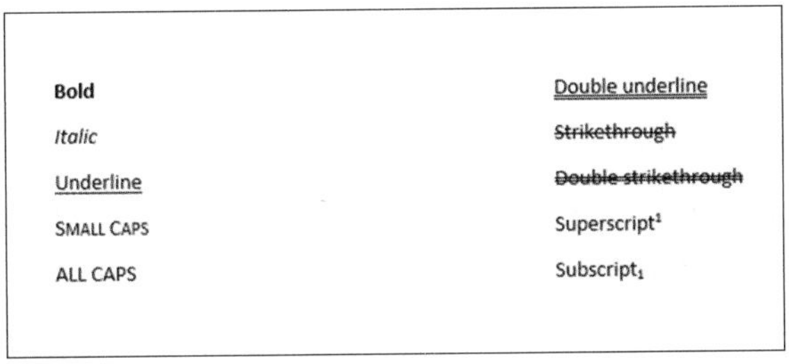

Bold	Double underline
Italic	~~Strikethrough~~
Underline	~~Double strikethrough~~
SMALL CAPS	Superscript[1]
ALL CAPS	Subscript[1]

Figure 2-17

LINGO

You can modify text with a variety of **attributes**, such as bold, italics, underlining, and so on. You can apply some of these attributes from the Mini toolbar and/or the Font group on the Home tab. Others are available in the Font dialog box. Some of them also have keyboard shortcuts.

Table 2-1	Keyboard Shortcuts for Applying Text Attributes
Attribute	*Keyboard Shortcut*
Bold	Ctrl+B
Italic	Ctrl+I
Underline	Ctrl+U
Subscript	Ctrl+=
Superscript	Ctrl+Shift++ (plus sign)
Underline words but not space	Ctrl+Shift+W
Double underline text	Ctrl+Shift+D
Small caps	Ctrl+Shift+K
All caps	Ctrl+Shift+A

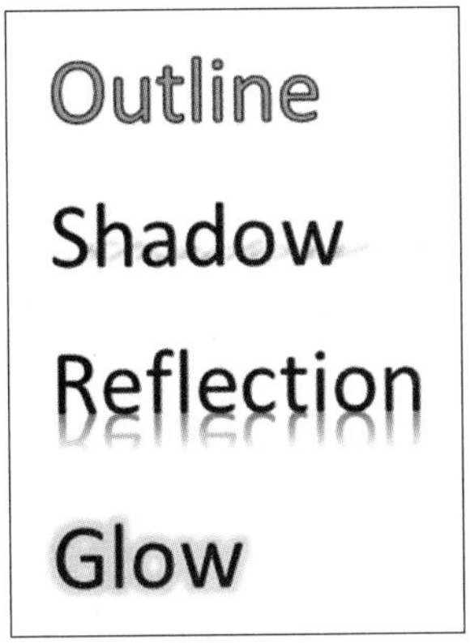

Outline

Shadow

Reflection

Glow

Figure 2-18

LINGO

You can apply **text effects**, also called **WordArt effects**. The available text effects include Outline, Shadow, Reflection, and Glow. Figure 2-18 shows some examples of these effects, accessed from the Text Effects and Typography button's menu on the Home tab. The Text Effects button's menu also includes a number of presets that combine color fills, outlines, and other effects in a single operation.

In this exercise, you format some text by applying some attributes and effects to it.

Files needed: Lesson 2 Vacation, from the previous exercise

1. **In Word, in the Lesson 2 Vacation file, triple-click the title *(Our Vacation)* to select it.**

2. **On the Home tab of the Ribbon, click the Text Effects and Typography button and click the second sample in the second row, as shown in Figure 2-19.**

   The text becomes blue with a blue reflection.

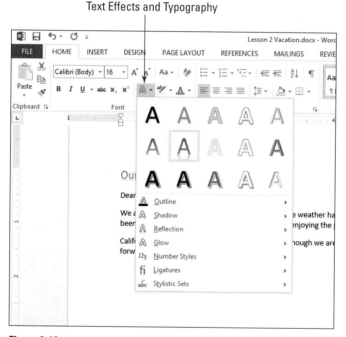

Figure 2-19

3. **Click the Text Effects button again, point to Glow, and click the first effect in the Glow Variations section, as shown in Figure 2-20.**

4. **Click the Italic button on the Home tab.**

   The text is italicized.

5. **Click the dialog box launcher in the lower-right corner of the Font group on the Home tab.**

   The Font dialog box opens, as shown in Figure 2-21.

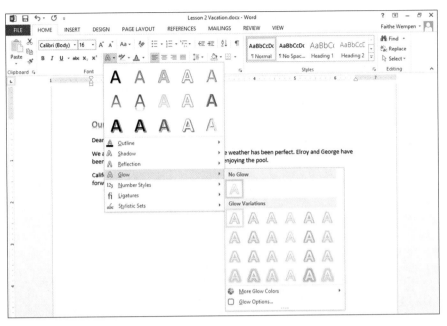

Figure 2-20

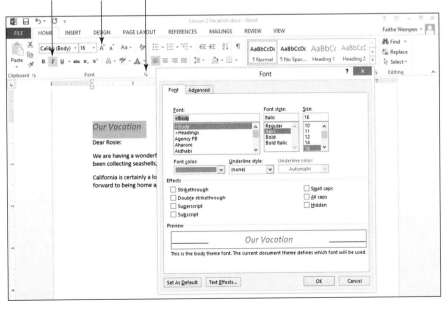

Figure 2-21

6. **Select the Small Caps check box. Then click OK.**
7. **Click the Increase Font Size button two times to increase the font size to 20 pt.**
8. **Save your work.**

Leave the document open for the next exercise.

Working with themes

All the Office applications use the same set of themes, so themes can help you standardize the look of your work across multiple applications. For example, you could make the fonts and colors on a brochure you create in Word similar to a presentation you create in PowerPoint.

LINGO

A **theme** is a file that contains settings for fonts (heading and body), colors, and object formatting effects (such as 3D effects for drawn shapes and SmartArt diagrams, both of which you learn about in later lessons). Themes enable you to dramatically change the look of a document quickly.

In a Word document that contains only text, you won't notice the effect changes when you switch to a different theme, but the font and color changes will be apparent.

You can also apply color themes, font themes, and/or effect themes separately. This ability is useful when none of the available themes exactly match what you want. After you make the selections you want to create the right combination of colors, fonts, and effects, you can save your choices as a new theme to use in other documents (including in Excel and PowerPoint as well as in Word).

Themes affect only text that hasn't had manual formatting applied that overrides the defaults. For example, if you've specified a certain font or font color for some text, that text doesn't change when you change the theme. You can strip off manual formatting with the Clear Formatting button on the Home tab.

In this exercise, you change a document's formatting by applying a different theme, theme fonts, and theme colors.

Files needed: Lesson 2 Vacation, from the previous exercise

1. **In Word, in the Lesson 2 Vacation file, click the Design tab on the Ribbon and then click the Themes button.**

   A list of themes appears, as shown in Figure 2-22.

2. **Click the Damask theme.**

   The colors and fonts in the document change to match the theme.

3. **Click the Theme Fonts button on the Ribbon.**

   A list of available theme font sets appears, as shown in Figure 2-23.

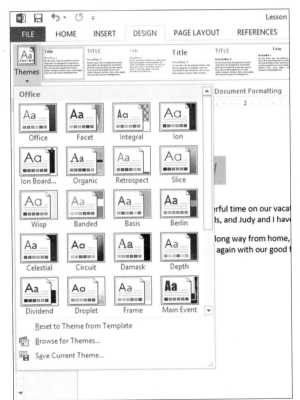

Figure 2-22

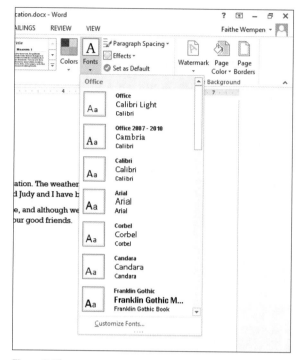

Figure 2-23

Before selecting a font theme, point the mouse cursor at several other font themes and see their effects in the text behind the open menu.

4. **Click the Calibri Light-Constantia font theme.**

   The fonts in the document change.

5. **Click the Theme Colors button on the Ribbon.**

   A list of available theme color sets appears, as shown in Figure 2-24.

6. **Click the Green Yellow color theme.**

   The color of the heading changes to blue.

7. **Save your work and close the document.**

Leave Word open for the next exercise.

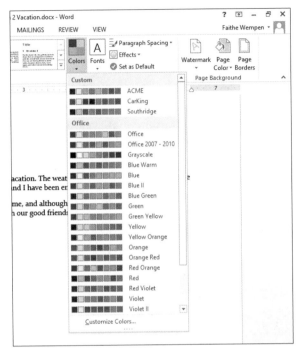

Figure 2-24

Applying style sets

At the top of the Font list on the Home tab are two entries: one designated for Headings and one for Body. If you use these settings rather than specifying individual fonts, you can reformat the document by choosing a different style set.

LINGO

A **style set** is a preset combination of fonts, paragraph line spacing, character spacing, and indentation. Style sets enable you to quickly change the look of the document without manually reformatting each paragraph.

WARNING!

If you've manually applied specific fonts, as in the preceding exercise when formatting the *Our Vacation* text, you won't see a change when you apply a different style set. If you don't get the results you expect with a style set, select the entire document (Ctrl+A) and then clear the formatting by clicking the Clear Formatting button on the Home tab or by pressing Ctrl+spacebar.

In this exercise, you format some text by applying different fonts, sizes, and colors to it.

Files needed: Lesson 2 Vacation, from the previous exercise

1. **In Word, in the Lesson 2 Vacation file, triple-click the title *(Our Vacation)* to select it if it isn't already selected.**

2. **Click the Clear All Formatting button on the Ribbon's Home tab to remove all the formatting you've applied to the selected text.**

   See Figure 2-25.

Clear All Formatting

Figure 2-25

3. **Open the Font drop-down list and select Calibri Light (Headings) at the top of the list.**

4. **Select the rest of the document (everything except the *Our Vacation* paragraph). Then open the Font drop-down list and select Constantia (Body) at the top of the list.**

5. **Click the Design tab on the Ribbon and then click the More button in the Document Formatting group.**

   A list of available style sets appears, as shown in Figure 2-26.

PRACTICE

Pointing to an item previews it. Point to each of the style sets on the Style Set menu, one by one, and watch the document's formatting change.

6. **Select the Lines (Distinctive) option.**

   The Lines (Distinctive) style set is applied.

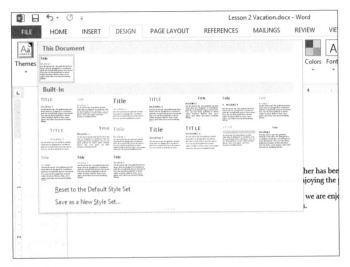

Figure 2-26

7. **Triple-click the *Our Vacation* paragraph and change the font size to 18 point by selecting 18 from the Font Size drop-down list. Then click away from the text to deselect it.**

The document should look like Figure 2-27.

Our Vacation

Dear Rosie:

We are having a wonderful time on our vacation. The weather has been perfect. Elroy and George have been collecting seashells, and Judy and I have been enjoying the pool.

California is certainly a long way from home, and although we are enjoying our trip, we are looking forward to being home again with our good friends.

Figure 2-27

8. **Save your work.**

Leave the document open for the next exercise.

Checking Spelling and Grammar

Spelling and grammar errors in your documents can leave a bad impression with your audience, and can be the cause of lost customers, jobs, and opportunities. Fortunately, Word can help save you from the consequences of such errors, whether they're errors due to carelessness or errors due to lack of knowledge of spelling and grammar.

Word automatically checks your spelling and grammar as you type. Wavy red underlines indicate possible spelling errors, and wavy blue underlines indicate possible grammar errors. To correct one of these errors on the fly, right-click the underlined text and choose a quick correction from the shortcut menu.

You can also run the full-blown Spelling and Grammar utility within Word to check the entire document at once. One by one, each potential error appears in a dialog box, and you click buttons to decide how to deal with each one.

One of the choices when dealing with a potentially misspelled word is to add the word to the dictionary so that it isn't flagged as misspelled in any future spell check in any document. The dictionary file is common to all the Office applications, so any word you add to the dictionary in Word will also no longer be flagged as misspelled in Excel, PowerPoint, or Outlook.

Word has a more robust and powerful Spelling and Grammar checker than the other Office applications do, but they all have similar functionality. After you learn how to check spelling in Word, you can also do it in the other Office apps.

In this exercise, you correct spelling and grammar errors in a document.

Files needed: `Lesson 2 Spelling.docx`

1. **In Word, open the Lesson 2 Spelling file and save it as Lesson 2 Spelling Corrected.**

2. **Right-click the misspelled word *eerors* and, on the shortcut menu, click the correct spelling, *errors,* as shown in Figure 2-28.**

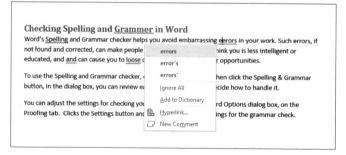

Figure 2-28

3. Click at the beginning of the first body paragraph (after the document title) to move the insertion point there.

4. On the Review tab of the Ribbon, click Spelling & Grammar.

The Grammar task pane opens, with the first mistake highlighted, as shown in Figure 2-29. If the first mistake found had been a spelling error, the Spelling task pane would have appeared instead.

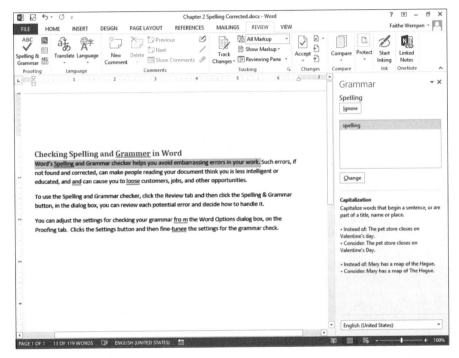

Figure 2-29

5. Click Ignore to ignore the first grammar error found.

The title of the task pane changes to Spelling, and the next error it finds is a double usage of the word *and*.

6. Click Delete to delete the duplicate instance.

The next mistake found is an improper usage of *loose*.

7. Click Change to change the word to *lose*.

The next error that appears is an extra space in the word *from*.

8. **Click Change to remove the blank space in the word.**

   The next mistake that appears is an extra e at the end of the word *tune.*

9. **Click Change to correct the word.**

   The next mistake that appears is a misspelling of *grammar.*

10. **Click Change All to change all instances of *grammer* to *grammar.***

11. **If the Readability Statistics dialog box appears, click OK to close it.**

    This dialog box may or may not appear depending on your settings.

12. **Save your work.**

Leave the document open for the next exercise.

Sharing Your Document with Others

If the people with whom you want to share your work are also Office 2013 users, sharing with them is easy. Just give them your data file. You can transfer a data file to someone else via a USB drive, a portable disc such as writeable CD or DVD, or an e-mail. Users of Office 2007 and 2010 can also work freely with your Office 2013 data files because the file formats are identical.

To share with people who don't have Office 2007 or higher, you can save in other formats. Word (and the other Office apps) supports a variety of saving formats, so you're sure to find a format that bridges the distance between Office and the program that your recipient has to work with.

E-mailing your document to others

Some versions of Office include Microsoft Outlook, an e-mail, calendar, and contact management program. If you don't have Outlook, you might have some other e-mail program, such as Outlook.com (Microsoft's free online mail service), Windows Mail (which comes with Windows Vista and is available for free download for Windows 7), Outlook Express (which comes with Windows XP), or some non-Microsoft program such as Eudora. When you send a document via e-mail from within Word,

LINGO

One way to distribute your work to others is to send it to them via e-mail. Your document piggybacks on an e-mail as an **attachment**. An attachment is a file that's separate from the body of the e-mail, traveling along with the e-mail to its destination.

Word calls up your default e-mail application, whatever that may be. The steps in this book assume Outlook 2013 is your default e-mail application; your steps might be different if you have something else.

WARNING!

If you use a web-based e-mail application, such as Hotmail, Gmail, or Yahoo! Mail, you can't follow along with the steps in this section. You can still send Word files as e-mail attachments, but you can't initiate the process from within Word. You start a new e-mail message from within the web interface and then attach the file from there.

In this exercise, you send a document to yourself as an e-mail attachment. These steps assume that Outlook is your default e-mail program and that your e-mail account is already set up in it.

Files needed: `Lesson 2 Spelling.docx`, *from the previous exercise*

1. **In Word, with Lesson 2 Spelling open, choose File⇨Share.**

   File sharing options appear.

2. **Click the Email button and then click the Send As Attachment button.**

   A new message opens in Outlook (or your default e-mail application) with the `Lesson 2 Spelling.docx` file already attached. The filename also appears in the Subject line, as shown in Figure 2-30.

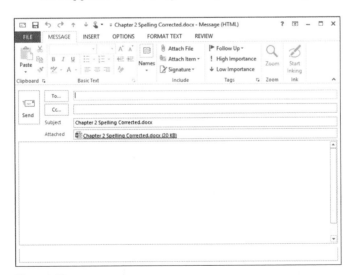

Figure 2-30

3. **Click in the To box and type your own e-mail address there.**

4. **Click the Send button.**

   The file is sent to you.

> If the e-mail doesn't come immediately, issue the Send command in your mail program. Its exact name will vary depending on the mail program; in Outlook, it's called Send/Receive All Folders.

5. **Close Outlook and return to Word.**

6. **Close the document (but not Word), saving your changes if prompted.**

Leave Word open for the next exercise.

Sharing your document in other formats

If your intended recipients use earlier versions of Office or don't have Office at all, you must save your work in another format before transferring the file to them. All the Office programs allow you to export your work in other formats, so you can transfer just about any data to just about any other application.

> The farther away you get from the original version of the file, the more formatting features you lose. For example, saving in Word 2013 format preserves the most features, and saving in Word 97–2003 format loses some features. RTF loses still more, and plain text loses all formatting.

In this exercise, you save a file in two different formats.

Files needed: Lesson 2 Distribution.docx

1. **In Word, open the Lesson 2 Distribution file.**

2. **Choose File⇨Save As. Click your SkyDrive or click Computer and then click the Browse button.**

   The Save As dialog box opens.

3. **Navigate to the location where you want to save the file.**

4. **Open the Save As Type drop-down list and select Word 97–2003 Document, as shown in Figure 2-31.**

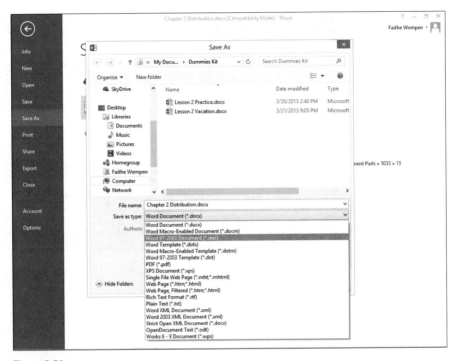

Figure 2-31

5. Click Save.

Your document is saved in a format that's compatible with earlier Word versions (Word 97 through Word 2003). It's also usable in Word 2007 and higher.

6. Choose File⇨Save As.

7. Open the Save As Type drop-down list and select Rich Text Format.

8. Click Save.

Your document is saved in Rich Text Format. This format is useful for exchanging data with someone who has a different brand of Word processor, such as WordPerfect.

Leave the document open for the next exercise.

Printing Your Work

Another way to distribute your work is by printing it, provided you have access to a printer. You can do a quick print with the default settings, or you can specify a certain printer, number of copies, page range, and other settings.

In this exercise, you print a document.

Files needed: `Lesson 2 Distribution.docx`, *or any other document file*

1. **In Word, with** `Lesson 2 Distribution.docx` **open, choose File➪Print.**

2. **In the Copies box, click the up arrow once to change the number to 2. Then click the down arrow to change it back to 1.**

3. **Open the Printer drop-down list and select the printer you want to use, as shown in Figure 2-32.**

EXTRA INFO

Some of the items on the list of printers are not actually printers, such as Microsoft XPS Document Writer, or Send to OneNote 2013. Word outputs to some external formats by treating the converter utilities as printers. You "print" to the driver, which then generates a file of the document in a different format.

Figure 2-32

For more practice, check out the additional print options. For example, you can change the page range, orientation, paper size, margins, and duplex setting (that is, print one-sided or two-sided). The settings for duplex and collation, as well as for printing only specific pages, don't apply to the document used in this exercise because it has only one page.

4. **Click the Print button.**

The document prints.

Want more help learning the basics of Word document creation and editing? Go to this address and click any of the Word tutorials listed there:

`http://office.microsoft.com/en-us/word-help/`
`CH010369478.aspx`

Summing Up

Word makes it easy to create a basic document. You can either start typing in the blank document that opens automatically at startup or choose one of the templates provided. Here are the key points this lesson covered:

- ✔ To start a new blank document, press Ctrl+N, or choose File➪New and then click Blank Document.

- ✔ To start a document based on a template, choose File➪New, pick the template you want (using the Search feature to locate it if needed), and then click Create.

- ✔ To set page margins, click the Margins button on the Page Layout tab.

- ✔ To change the paper size, click the Size button on the Page Layout tab.

- ✔ Portrait and Landscape are the two page orientations. Portrait is the default. To switch, click the Orientation button on the Page Layout tab.

- ✔ Fonts, or typefaces, are lettering styles. Choose a font from the Home tab or the Mini toolbar.

- ✔ Font sizes are measured in points. A point is $\frac{1}{72}$ of an inch. Choose font sizes from the Home tab or from the Mini toolbar.

- ✔ A style set applies a different appearance to a document including fonts, paragraph spacing, character spacing, and indentation. To change the style set, click the Design tab, click the More button, and then click the desired style set.

- ✔ Some text attributes and effects can be applied from the Mini toolbar or the Font group on the Home tab. Others must be applied from the Font dialog box. To open the Font dialog box, click the dialog box launcher in the Font group.

- ✔ A theme is a file that contains settings for fonts, colors, and object formatting effects. Apply a theme by clicking the Page Layout tab and then the Themes button.

✔ Word checks spelling and grammar automatically, and underlines errors with red wavy underline (for spelling) or blue wavy underline (for grammar).

✔ You can also launch a full spelling and grammar check by clicking the Review tab and then the Spelling & Grammar button.

✔ To e-mail your document to others, choose File⇨Share⇨Email⇨ Send As Attachment.

✔ To print your document, choose File⇨Print.

Try-it-yourself lab

For more practice with the features covered in this lesson, try the following exercise on your own:

1. **Start Word and write a description of a funny or embarrassing incident that happened recently to you or someone you know.**

2. **Add a new paragraph at the beginning of the document and type a title there (such as** My Most Embarrassing Day Ever**).**

3. **Format the title with an eye-catching font, font size, and color. Use one of the theme colors.**

4. **Apply a different style set to the document.**

5. **Apply a different theme to the document.**

6. **Check your spelling and grammar and make any corrections needed.**

7. **E-mail the document to yourself or to a friend you want to share it with.**

8. **Print one copy of the document.**

9. **Close Word.**

Know this tech talk

attachment: A file attached to an e-mail so that the file is sent along with the message.

attributes: Formatting options such as bold, italics, and underline.

character formatting: Formatting that affects individual characters, such as font choices. (Contrast this to paragraph formatting, such as indentation and line spacing, that affects entire paragraphs.)

font: Also called a *typeface.* A style of lettering, such as Arial, Times New Roman, or Calibri.

insertion point: In a text editing application, a flashing vertical line indicating where text will be inserted when typed.

landscape: A page orientation in which the wide part of the paper forms the top and bottom.

margins: The space between the edge of the paper and the text.

orientation: The direction the text runs on a piece of paper where one dimension is greater than the other. See also *portrait* and *landscape.*

point: A unit of measure that's $\frac{1}{72}$ of an inch. Font size is measured in points.

portrait: A page orientation in which the narrow part of the paper forms the top and bottom.

standard color: A fixed color that doesn't change when you change to a different theme.

style set: A set of font, indentation, and line spacing options.

template: An example file on which new documents may be based.

text effects: Special WordArt-style effects applied to text such as glow, reflection, and shadowing.

theme: A set of font, color, and graphic effect settings stored in a separate file, accessible to all Office applications.

theme color: A set of color choices that are applied to color placeholders in a document.

typeface: See *font.*

Chapter 3

Paragraph and Page Formatting in Word

- ✔ Paragraph formatting enables you to *control the indentation, line spacing, and horizontal alignment* of a paragraph.

- ✔ *Indenting a paragraph can set it off visually* from the rest of the document for greater emphasis.

- ✔ *To make a text-heavy document easier to read,* increase its line spacing so that more space appears between each line.

- ✔ Create a numbered list to *organize a list in which the order of the items is significant;* use a bulleted list when the order is not significant.

- ✔ Apply styles to paragraphs that have similar functions, such as headings or quotations, to *ensure formatting consistency throughout the document.*

- ✔ Headers and footers allow you to *repeat elements at the top or bottom of each page.*

1. What is justified alignment?

Find out on page 100

2. How do you create a hanging indent?

Find out on page 102

3. How do you double-space a document?

Find out on page 105

4. How do you create a numbered list that uses Roman numerals?

Find out on page 118

5. How can you make changes to a style?

Find out on page 125

6. How do you number the pages of a document?

Find out on page 133

Paragraphs are essential building blocks in a Word document. Each time you press Enter, you start a new paragraph. If you've ever seen a document where the author didn't use paragraph breaks, you know how important paragraphs can be. They break up the content into more easily understandable chunks, which helps the reader both visually and logically.

In this chapter, you learn how to apply various types of formatting to paragraphs and how to simplify and automate paragraph formatting by using text formatting presets called styles. You also learn how to control the headers and footers that appear on each page of your document and use them to display information, such as a page number or copyright notice.

Formatting Paragraphs

If you apply paragraph formatting when no text is selected, the formatting applies to the paragraph in which the insertion point is currently located.

If you apply paragraph formatting when text is selected, the formatting applies to whatever paragraphs are included in that selection, even if only one character of the paragraph is included. Being able to format paragraphs this way is useful because you can select multiple paragraphs at once and then format them as a group.

LINGO

Paragraph formatting is formatting that affects whole paragraphs and cannot be applied to individual characters. For example, line spacing is a type of paragraph formatting, along with indentation and alignment.

TIP To set the paragraph formatting for the entire document at once, press Ctrl+A to select the entire document and then issue the paragraph formatting commands.

Applying horizontal alignment

The horizontal alignment choices are Align Text Left, Center, Align Text Right, and Justify. Figure 3-1 shows an example of each of the alignment types.

Each of those is pretty self-evident except the last one. *Justify* aligns both the left and right sides of the paragraph with the margins, stretching out or compressing the text in each line as needed to make it fit. The final line in the paragraph is exempt and appears left-aligned.

LINGO

Horizontal alignment refers to the positioning of the paragraph between the right and left margins.

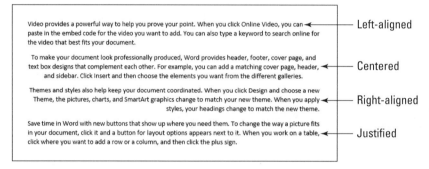

Video provides a powerful way to help you prove your point. When you click Online Video, you can paste in the embed code for the video you want to add. You can also type a keyword to search online for the video that best fits your document. — Left-aligned

To make your document look professionally produced, Word provides header, footer, cover page, and text box designs that complement each other. For example, you can add a matching cover page, header, and sidebar. Click Insert and then choose the elements you want from the different galleries. — Centered

Themes and styles also help keep your document coordinated. When you click Design and choose a new Theme, the pictures, charts, and SmartArt graphics change to match your new theme. When you apply styles, your headings change to match the new theme. — Right-aligned

Save time in Word with new buttons that show up where you need them. To change the way a picture fits in your document, click it and a button for layout options appears next to it. When you work on a table, click where you want to add a row or a column, and then click the plus sign. — Justified

Figure 3-1

If you apply Justify alignment to a paragraph that contains only one line, it looks like it is left-aligned. However, if you then type more text into the paragraph so it wraps to additional lines, the Justify alignment becomes apparent.

In this exercise, you apply horizontal alignment changes to a business letter.

Files needed: Lesson 3 Time Out.docx

1. **In Word, open** Lesson 3 Time Out.docx **from the data files for this chapter and save it as Lesson 3 Time Out Letter.**

2. **Select the first three lines (the facility's name and address), as shown in Figure 3-2, and click the Center button on the Ribbon's Home tab or press Ctrl+E.**

Center

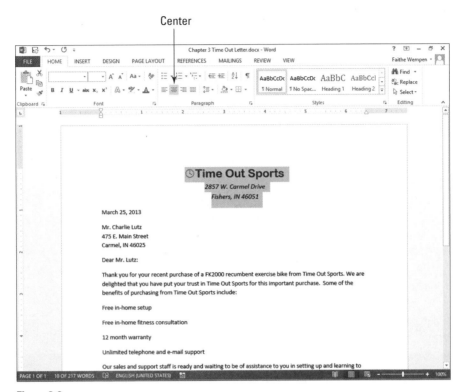

Figure 3-2

3. **Click in the first body paragraph (the paragraph that starts with "Thank you . . .") and click the Justify button on the Home tab, labeled in Figure 3-3.**

   The paragraph changes to Justify alignment.

4. **Select the last four body paragraphs of the document (starting with "Our sales and support staff . . .") and click the Justify button again.**

   Those paragraphs change to Justify alignment. Figure 3-3 shows the results.

5. **Save the changes to the document.**

Leave Word and the document file open for the next exercise.

Justify

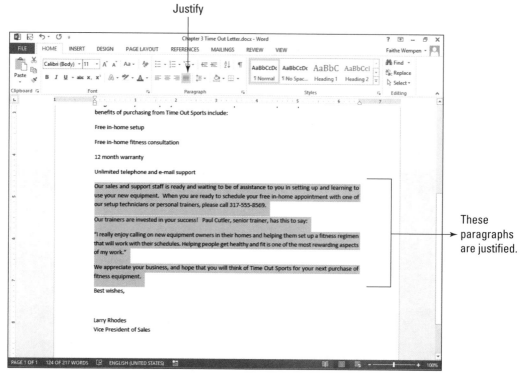

Figure 3-3

Indenting a paragraph

When a paragraph has no indentation, it's allowed to take up the full range of space between the left and right margins. When you set indentation for a paragraph, its left and/or right sides are inset by the amount you specify. Many people like to indent quotations to set them apart from the rest of the text for emphasis, for example.

First-line indents are sometimes used in reports and books to help the reader's eye catch the beginning of a paragraph. In layouts where there is vertical space between paragraphs, first-line indents are less useful because it's easy to see where a new paragraph begins without that help.

LINGO

The **indentation** of a paragraph refers to how its left and/or right sides are inset.

In addition to a left and right indent value, each paragraph can optionally have a special indent for the first line. If the first line is indented more than the rest of the paragraph, it's known as a **first-line indent**. (Clever name.) If the first line is indented less than the rest of the paragraph, it's called a **hanging indent**.

Hanging indents are typically used to create listings. In a bulleted or numbered list, the bullet or number hangs off the left edge of the paragraph, in a hanging indent. However, in Word, when you create bulleted or numbered lists (covered later in this chapter), Word adjusts the paragraph's hanging indent automatically, so you don't have to think about it.

In this exercise, you apply indents to paragraphs in a letter.

Files needed: `Lesson 3 Time Out Letter.docx`

1. **In Word, with the `Lesson 3 Time Out Letter.docx` document still open from the previous exercise, triple-click the paragraph containing the quotation to select it (the paragraph that begins with "I really enjoy . . .").**

2. **Click the Increase Indent button on the Home tab of the Ribbon.**

   The left indent increases by 0.5 inch, as shown in Figure 3-4.

Increase Indent   Dialog box launcher

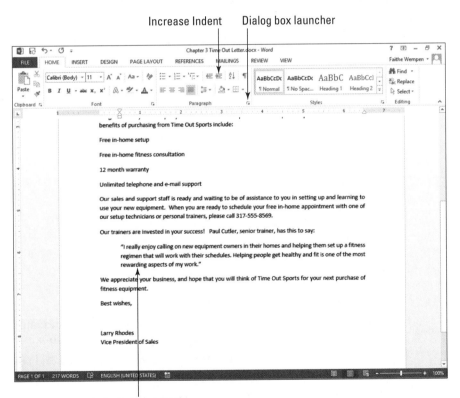

Indented paragraph

Figure 3-4

3. **Click the dialog box launcher in the Paragraph group to open the Paragraph dialog box.**

4. **Under Indentation, click the up increment arrow on the Right text box to increase the right indent to 0.5 inch.**

   See Figure 3-5.

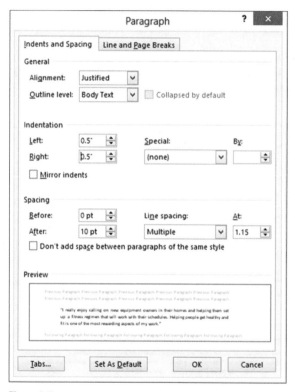

Figure 3-5

5. **Click OK.**

   Now the paragraph is indented 0.5 inch on each side.

6. **Click in the paragraph that begins "Our sales . . ." and click the dialog box launcher again to reopen the Paragraph dialog box.**

7. **Under Indentation, open the Special drop-down list and select First Line, as shown in Figure 3-6.**

   A first line indent default value of 0.5 inch appears.

8. **Click OK.**

   That paragraph is now first-line indented by 0.5 inch.

For more practice, try setting a hanging indent for one of the remaining paragraphs. Choose Hanging from the Special drop-down list in the Paragraph dialog box. When you're finished, press Ctrl+Z to undo your change.

9. Save the changes to the document.

Leave Word and the document file open for the next exercise.

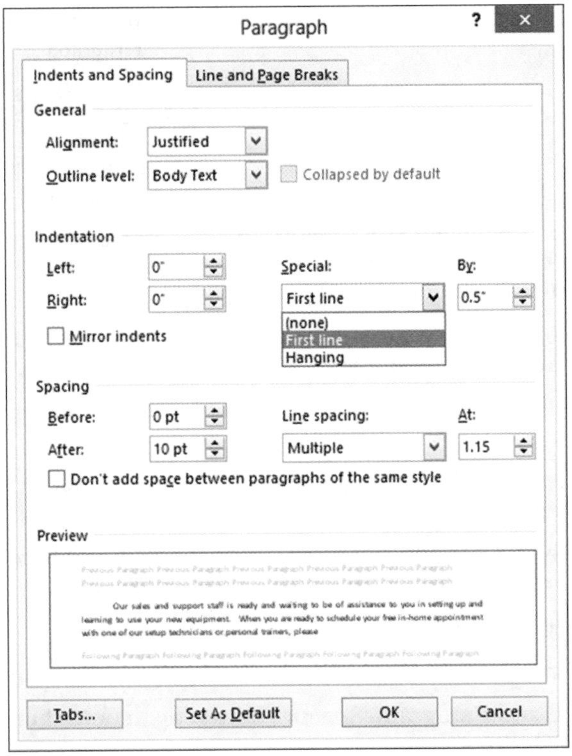

EXTRA INFO

You can also create a first-line indent by positioning the insertion point at the beginning of a paragraph and pressing the Tab key. Normally this would place a 0.5-inch tab at the beginning of the paragraph, but the Word AutoCorrect feature immediately converts it to a real first-line indent for you.

Figure 3-6

Changing vertical spacing

You can set line spacing to any of several presets, such as Single, Double, and 1.5 Lines, or to an exact value, measured in points. You may remember from Chapter 2 that a point is $1/72$ of an inch. Space before and after a paragraph is specified in points, too.

If you specify an exact amount of space per line and you change the font size, the text may not look right anymore. For example, if you change the font size to a larger size than the exact spacing is set for, the lines might overlap vertically. If you aren't sure what font sizes you need, don't use exact spacing.

In this exercise, you change the line spacing for paragraphs in a letter.

Files needed: `Lesson 3 Time Out Letter.docx`

1. **In Word, with the `Lesson 3 Time Out Letter.docx` document still open from the previous exercise, press Ctrl+A to select the entire document.**

2. **Click the Line Spacing button on the Ribbon's Home tab, opening its menu, and choose 1.0, as shown in Figure 3-7.**

   The line spacing in every paragraph changes to single-spacing. See Figure 3-7.

3. **Select the paragraph beginning with "Free in-home setup . . ." and the next two paragraphs following it.**

4. **Click the Line and Paragraph Spacing button again and then choose Remove Space After Paragraph, as shown in Figure 3-8.**

   The extra vertical space between paragraphs is eliminated.

5. **Select the Time Out Sports heading at the top of the document.**

6. **Click the Line and Paragraph Spacing button again and then choose Line Spacing Options.**

   The Paragraph dialog box opens.

You can click the dialog box launcher for the Paragraph group to open the Paragraph dialog box if you prefer that method.

7. **Decrease the value in the After text box to 6 pt, as shown in Figure 3-9.**

8. **Click OK to accept the new setting.**

LINGO

Vertical spacing refers to the amount of space (also known as the **leading**) between each line. A paragraph has three values you can set for its spacing:

Line spacing: The space between the lines within a multi-line paragraph

Before: Extra spacing added above the first line of the paragraph

After: Extra spacing added below the last line of the paragraph

Line Spacing

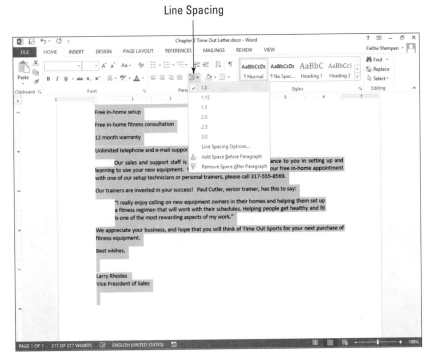

Figure 3-7

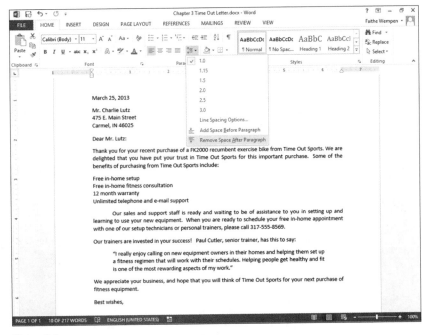

Figure 3-8

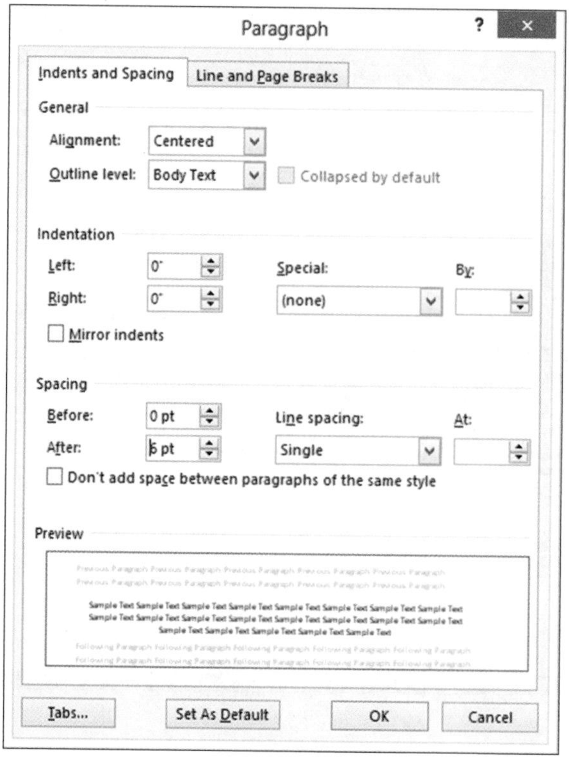

Paragraph dialog box

Paragraph   ?   ✕

Indents and Spacing   Line and Page Breaks

General

Alignment: Centered ⌄

Outline level: Body Text ⌄   ☐ Collapsed by default

Indentation

Left: 0" ⬍   Special: By:

Right: 0" ⬍   (none) ⌄   ⬍

☐ Mirror indents

Spacing

Before: 0 pt ⬍   Line spacing: At:

After: 6 pt ⬍   Single ⌄   ⬍

☐ Don't add space between paragraphs of the same style

Preview

Tabs...   Set As Default   OK   Cancel

Figure 3-9

9. **Triple-click the quotation paragraph to select it.**

10. **Click the Line Spacing button again and choose Line Spacing Options.**

    The Paragraph dialog box opens again.

11. **Under Spacing, open the Line Spacing drop-down list and choose Exactly and then type 15 in the At text box to its right, as shown in Figure 3-10.**

12. **Click OK to accept the new setting.**

PRACTICE

For more practice, set the font size for the paragraph you just formatted to 24 points and watch what happens to the line spacing. It stays at 15 points, and the lines overlap. Press Ctrl+Z to undo your change when you're finished experimenting.

Figure 3-10

13. Save the changes to the document.

Leave Word and the document file open for the next exercise.

Adding Borders and Shading

By default, a paragraph has no border or shading. You can add either or both to a single paragraph or any group of paragraphs to make them stand out from the rest of the document. You can use any border thickness, style, and color you like, and any color of shading.

Placing a border around a paragraph

A paragraph border appears around the outside of a single paragraph. If the paragraph is indented, the border will also be indented (left and right only; the indent doesn't change for hanging or first-line indents).

If you place the same border around two or more consecutive paragraphs, the border surrounds them as a group. That way you can create groups of paragraphs that appear "boxed" together for special emphasis.

In this exercise, you add a border around a paragraph.

Files needed: `Lesson 3 Time Out Letter.docx`, *open from the preceding exercise.*

1. **In the Lesson 3 Time Out Letter document, click anywhere within the quotation paragraph.**

2. **On the Home tab of the Ribbon, in the Paragraph group, open the Border button's drop-down list and select Outside Borders.**

   A plain black border appears around the quotation paragraph, as shown in Figure 3-11. You could stop here if you wanted a plain border, but the next steps show you how to format the border in different ways.

3. **From the Border button's drop-down list, select Borders and Shading.**

   The Borders and Shading dialog box opens.

4. **Click the Shadow button (under Settings on the left).**

   The border in the Preview area becomes thicker at the bottom and right sides, simulating a shadow.

5. **Click the Box button.**

   The border in the Preview area once again has the same thickness on all sides.

Border button

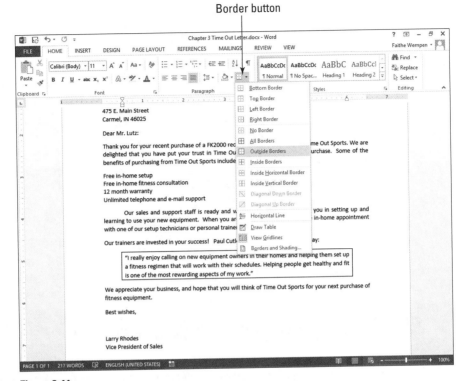

Figure 3-11

6. **From the Color drop-down list, select the Blue, Accent 1 theme color (the fifth button in the top row); from the Width drop-down list, select 1½pt; in the Style area, click one of the dashed lines; and in the Preview area, click the buttons that represent the right and left sides, turning off those sides.**

Figure 3-12 shows the completed dialog box.

7. **Click OK to apply the border to the paragraph.**

8. **Save the document.**

Leave the document open for the next exercise.

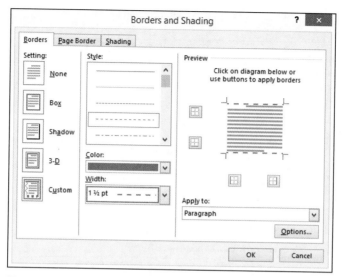

Figure 3-12

Shading a paragraph's background

Shading a paragraph helps it stand out from the rest of the document and adds visual interest to the text. You can use shading with or without a border.

As with a border, shading follows along with any indent settings you may have specified for the paragraph. If the paragraph is indented, the shading is also.

Word applies only solid-color shading to paragraphs. If you want a gradient shading behind a paragraph or you want some other special shading effect such as a pattern, texture, or graphic, place a text box (choose Insert⇨Text Box) and then apply the desired shading to the text box as a Fill, like you would with a graphic.

In this exercise, you add shading to a paragraph.

Files needed: `Lesson 3 Time Out Letter.docx,` *open from the preceding exercise*

1. **In the Lesson 3 Time Out Letter document, click anywhere within the quotation paragraph.**

2. **On the Home tab of the Ribbon, in the Paragraph group, open the Shading drop-down list and choose Blue, Accent 1, Lighter 80%, as shown in Figure 3-13.**

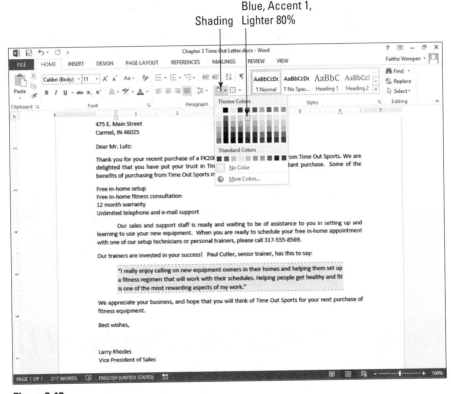

Figure 3-13

3. **Reopen the Shading drop-down list and choose More Colors.**

The Colors dialog box opens.

4. **Click the Standard tab, click a light yellow square (see Figure 3-14), and then click OK to accept the new color choice.**

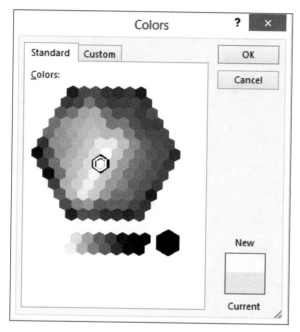

Figure 3-14

5. **Save the document.**

Leave the document open for the next exercise.

Creating Bulleted and Numbered Lists

Word makes it easy to create bulleted and numbered lists in your documents. You can create a list from existing paragraphs, or you can turn on the list feature and type the list as you go. Either way, you're working with the Bullets button or the Numbering button on the Home tab.

Creating a basic numbered or bulleted list

In this exercise, you convert some paragraphs into a numbered list and then change it to a bulleted list.

Files needed: `Lesson 3 Time Out Letter.docx`

1. **In Word, with the `Lesson 3 Time Out Letter.docx` document still open from the previous exercise, select the list of four benefits, starting with "Free in-home setup . . .".**

2. **Click the Numbering button on the Home tab of the Ribbon.**

   The list becomes numbered.

3. **Click the Bullets button.**

   The list switches to a bulleted list, as shown in Figure 3-15.

Leave Word and the document file open for the next exercise.

Changing the bullet character

You can use any character you like for the bullets in a bulleted list; you're not limited to the standard black circle. Word offers a choice of several common characters on the Bullets button's palette, and you can also select any picture or character from any font to use.

In this exercise, you change the bullet character to several different text-based and graphical bullets.

Files needed: `Lesson 3 Time Out Letter.docx`

1. **In Word, with the `Lesson 3 Time Out Letter.docx` document still open from the previous exercise, select the four bulleted paragraphs.**

2. **Click the down arrow on the Bullets button, opening its palette, as shown in Figure 3-16.**

Bullets   Numbering

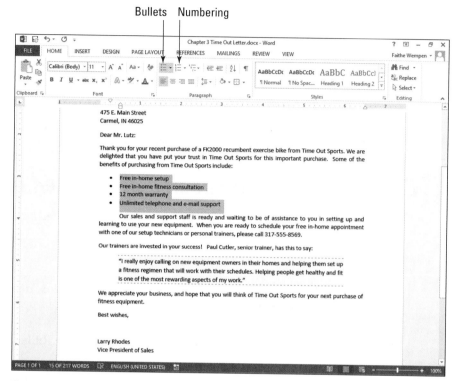

Figure 3-15

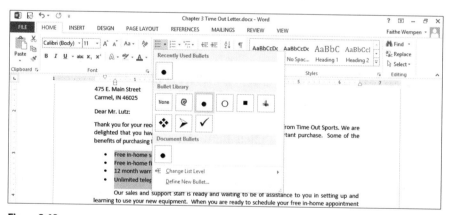

Figure 3-16

3. **Click the check mark bullet.**

   The list changes to use that character.

4. **Click the down arrow on the Bullets button again, reopening its palette.**

5. **Choose Define New Bullet.**

   The Define New Bullet dialog box opens.

6. **Click the Symbol button.**

   The Symbol dialog box opens.

7. **Open the Font drop-down list and select Wingdings if it isn't already selected, as shown in Figure 3-17.**

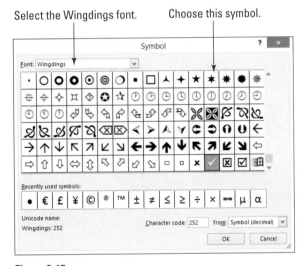

Figure 3-17

8. **Find and click a six-pointed black star.**

9. **Click OK to close the Symbol dialog box.**

10. **Click OK to close the Define New Bullet dialog box.**

    The bulleted list appears with the new star bullets.

11. **Click the down arrow on the Bullets button again, reopening its palette.**

12. **Choose Define New Bullet.**

    The Define New Bullet dialog box opens.

13. **Click the Picture button.**

    The Insert Pictures dialog box opens, as shown in Figure 3-18.

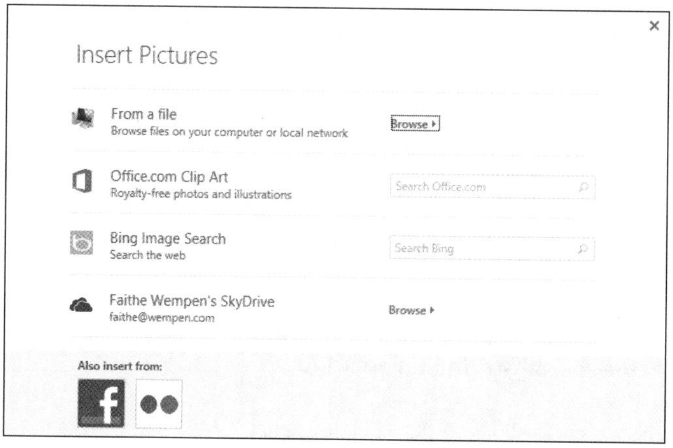

Figure 3-18

14. **Click in the Office.com Clip Art text box and type** bullet, **and then press Enter.**

15. **Click any of the picture bullets that appeals to you and then click Insert.**

    Choose one of the simple graphics, not one of the photos of gun bullets.

16. **Click OK to close the Define New Bullet dialog box.**

    The picture bullets appear in the document.

17. **Save the changes to the document.**

Leave Word and the document file open for the next exercise.

Changing the numbering style

Changing the numbering style is much like changing the bullet character, except you have a few extra options, like choosing a starting number. You can select from various styles of numbering that include uppercase or lowercase letters, Roman numerals, or Arabic (regular) numerals.

In this exercise, you change the numbering format for a numbered list.

Files needed: Lesson 3 Time Out Letter.docx

1. **In Word, with the** Lesson 3 Time Out Letter.docx **document still open from the previous exercise, select the four bulleted paragraphs if they aren't already selected.**

2. **Click the down arrow on the Numbering button on the Ribbon's Home tab, opening its palette.**

3. **In the Numbering Library section of the palette, click the numbering style that uses uppercase letters (A, B, C).**

See Figure 3-19.

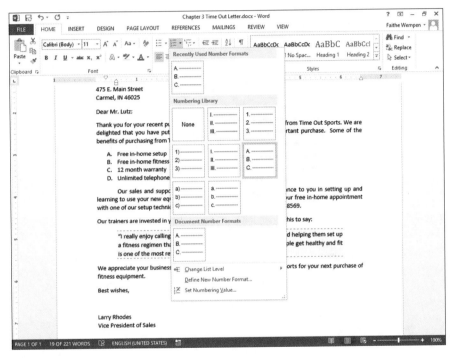

Figure 3-19

4. **Click the down arrow on the Numbering button on the Home tab and then click Define New Number Format.**

5. **In the Number Format text box, delete the period following the shaded A and type a colon (:), as shown in Figure 3-20.**

6. **Click the Font button.**

The Font dialog box opens.

7. **Set the Font Size to 14 points, as shown in Figure 3-21.**

8. **Click OK to return to the Define New Number Format dialog box and then click OK to accept the new format.**

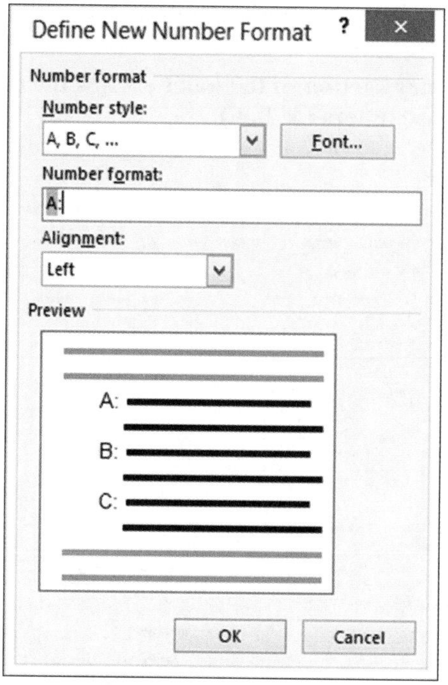

Figure 3-20

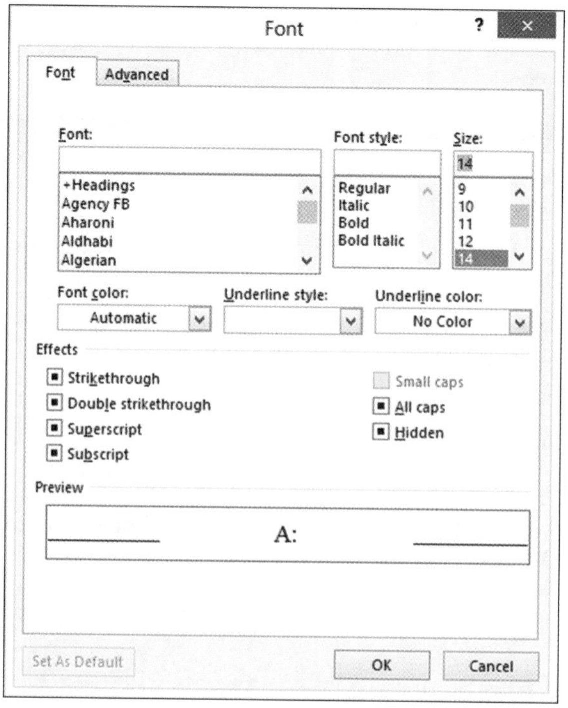

Figure 3-21

The list now appears with extra-large letters, followed by colons, as shown in Figure 3-22.

9. **Save the changes to the document and close it.**

Leave Word open for the next exercise.

A:	Free in-home setup
B:	Free in-home fitness consultation
C:	12 month warranty
D:	Unlimited telephone and e-mail support

Figure 3-22

Working with Styles

Using a style makes it easy to apply consistent formatting throughout a document. For example, you might apply the Heading 1 style to all headings in the document and the Normal style to all the regular body text. Here are the advantages of this approach:

LINGO

A **style** is a named set of formatting specifications.

- ✔ **Ease:** Applying a style is easier than manually applying formatting. And changing a style's formatting is a snap. If you want the headings to look different, for example, you can modify the Heading 1 style to change them all at once.

- ✔ **Consistency:** You don't have to worry about all the headings being formatted consistently; because they're all using the same style, they're automatically all the same.

By default, each paragraph is assigned a Normal style. The template in use determines the styles available and how they're defined.

TIP

In Word 2013 in documents that use the default blank (Normal) template, the Normal style uses Calibri 11 point font and left-aligns the text, with no indentation.

You can redefine the styles in a document, and you can even create your own new styles.

Applying a style

In the Styles group on the Home tab is a Styles gallery. The first row appears on the Ribbon itself, and you can see the rest of it by clicking the More button to open the full gallery.

LINGO

The **Styles gallery** on the Home tab contains shortcuts for commonly used styles.

Not all styles appear in the Styles gallery — only the ones that are designated to appear there in their definition. The rest of them appear only in the Styles pane. To open the Styles pane, click the dialog box launcher on the Styles group.

To apply a style, select the paragraph(s) that you want to affect or move the insertion point into the paragraph. Then click the style you want to apply, either in the Styles gallery or in the Styles pane. Some styles also have keyboard shortcuts assigned to them for quick applying.

In this exercise, you apply styles to the paragraphs in a document.

Files needed: `Lesson 3 Syllabus.docx`

1. **In Word, open** `Lesson 3 Syllabus.docx` **and save it as** `Lesson 3 Syllabus Formatted.docx`.

2. **Click in the first paragraph** *(CIT 233)*. **Then on the Home tab, in the Styles group, click the More button (see Figure 3-23) to open the Styles gallery.**

More button

Figure 3-23

3. **Click the Title style. (See Figure 3-24.)**

The style is applied to the first paragraph.

Title style

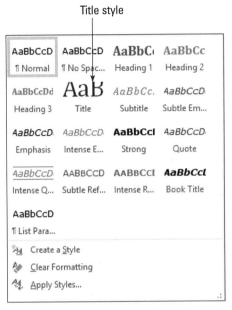

Figure 3-24

4. Using the same procedure as Steps 2 and 3, apply the Subtitle style to the second paragraph.

5. Select one of the orange paragraphs and then apply the Heading 1 style by clicking Heading 1 in the Styles gallery. Repeat for all the remaining orange paragraphs.

TIP

Here's a shortcut: Click to the left of the first orange paragraph to select it and then hold down the Ctrl key and do the same for each of the remaining orange paragraphs. After they're all selected, apply the style to them all at once.

6. Click the dialog box launcher on the Styles group to open the Styles pane.

7. Scroll through the Styles pane and locate the Heading 2 style; then click in one of the green paragraphs near the end of the document and click the Heading 2 style in the Styles pane to apply it.

8. **Apply the Heading 2 style to all the remaining green paragraphs.**

The last page of the document resembles Figure 3-25.

Styles pane

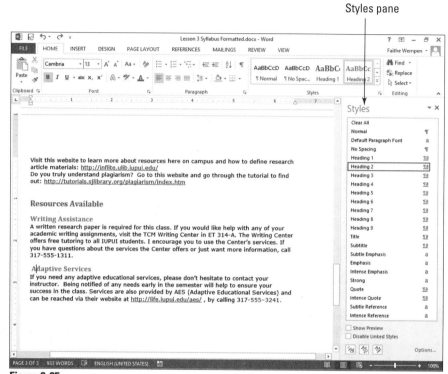

Figure 3-25

LINGO

Scroll through the Styles pane's list and look at the symbols to the right of each style. Most of the styles in the Styles pane have a paragraph symbol (¶) to their right. This means that they are **paragraph styles** — they apply to entire paragraphs at once. They may include both paragraph and character formatting in their definitions, but if you click in a paragraph and then apply the style, the style will be applied to the whole paragraph. In contrast, some styles may have a lowercase *a* to their right on the list; these are **character styles**, or text-level styles, and they apply only to the text that you select before applying them. A character style can contain only character-based formatting.

9. **Save the changes to the document.**

Leave the document open for the next exercise.

Modifying a style

You can modify a style in two ways: by example or by manually changing the style's definition. The by-example method is much easier, but somewhat less flexible. The following exercise shows both methods.

In this exercise, you change the definitions of some styles.

Files needed: Lesson 3 Syllabus Formatted.docx, *open from the preceding exercise*

1. **Triple-click the document subtitle (the second paragraph) to select it and then change the font size to 18 point from the Font Size drop-down list.**

2. **In the Styles pane, click the down arrow to the right of the Subtitle style or right-click the Subtitle style.**

3. **In the menu that appears, choose Update Subtitle to Match Selection, as shown in Figure 3-26.**

   The style is updated with the new font size.

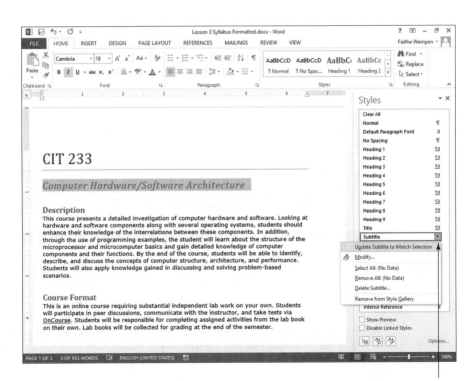

Click here to open menu.

Figure 3-26

4. Reopen the Subtitle style's menu and choose Modify.

The Modify Style dialog box opens.

For more practice, make other changes to the style's definition using the font controls in the Modify Style dialog box. The buttons and lists in the dialog box correspond to the tools in the Font and Paragraph groups on the Home tab.

5. In the bottom-left corner of the dialog box, click the Format button and choose Font, as shown in Figure 3-27.

The Font dialog box appears.

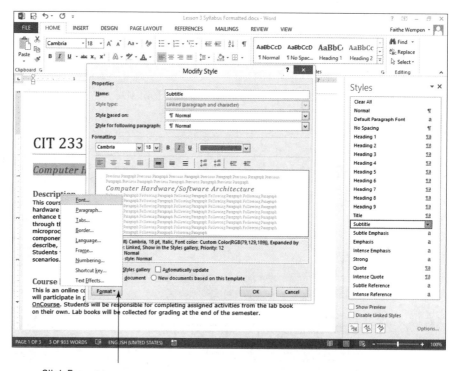

Click Format to open menu.

Figure 3-27

6. Select the Small Caps check box, as shown in Figure 3-28, and then click OK to return to the Modify Style dialog box.

Select Small Caps.

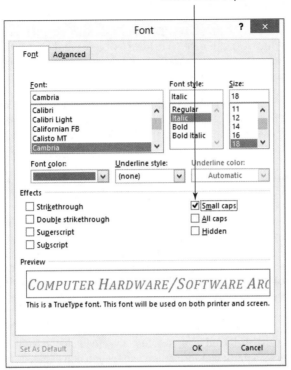

Figure 3-28

Notice the Add to the Styles Gallery check box in the bottom-left corner of the Modify Style dialog box. This check box's status determines whether a particular style appears in the Styles gallery.

7. Click OK to close the Modify Style dialog box.

The style definition is updated.

8. Save the changes to the document.

Leave the document open for the next exercise.

Because the Subtitle style is used only once in this document, you don't get to see one of the biggest benefits of styles in this exercise: the fact that when you update a style, all text that has that style applied to it updates immediately. For more practice, change the definition of the Heading 1 or Heading 2 style, and watch all the instances change.

Creating a new style

You can also create your own styles. This is especially useful if you want to build a template that you can give to other people to make sure that everyone formats documents the same way, such as in a group where each person assembles a different section of a report.

When you create your own styles, you can name them anything you like. Most people like to name styles based on their purposes, to make it easier to choose which style to apply. For example, *Figure Caption* would be a good name; *Style13* would not.

Just like when modifying a style, you can create a new style either by example or by manually specifying a style definition.

If you go with the definition method, you can specify some additional options that aren't available with the by-example method, such as defining which style follows this style. (In other words, if someone types a paragraph using this style and then presses Enter, what style will the next new paragraph be? The paragraph that follows a heading style is usually a body paragraph style. The paragraph that follows a body paragraph is usually another body paragraph.)

Each new style is based on an existing style (usually the Normal style) so that if there's a particular formatting aspect you don't specify, it trickles down from the parent style.

For example, suppose you create a new style named Important, and you base it on the Normal style. The Important style starts out with identical formatting to the Normal style, which is Calibri 11-point font. You might then modify it to have bold, red text. The definition of Important is Normal+bold+red.

That's significant if you later change the definition of Normal to 12-point font. That font size change trickles down to Important automatically, and all text formatted with the Important style becomes 12 points in size.

In this exercise, you create a new style.

Files needed: `Lesson 3 Syllabus Formatted.docx`, *open from the preceding exercise*

1. **Under the Topics heading, triple-click the first bulleted item** (*CPUs and Assembly language*) **to select it.**

2. **At the bottom of the Styles pane, click the New Style button, labeled in Figure 3-29.**

   The Create New Style from Formatting dialog box opens, as shown in Figure 3-29.

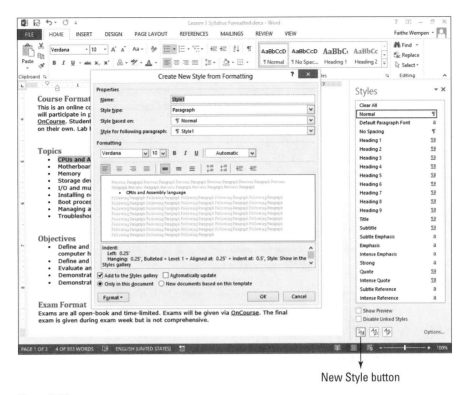

New Style button

Figure 3-29

3. **In the Name text box, type**
Bulleted List. **Then click the**
Format button in the lower-left
corner of the dialog box and
choose Numbering.

The Numbering and Bullets
dialog box appears.

4. **Click the Bullets tab (see**
Figure 3-30), click the white
circle bullet character, and then
click OK.

5. **Click the Format button again**
and choose Shortcut Key.

The Customize Keyboard dialog
box opens.

6. **Press Ctrl+Q.**

That key combination appears
in the Press New Shortcut Key
text box.

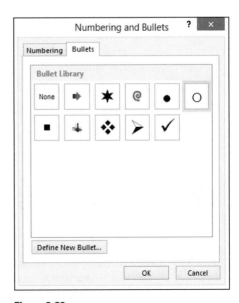

Figure 3-30

7. Open the Save Changes In drop-down list and select **Lesson 3 Syllabus Formatted.docx**, as shown in Figure 3-31.

Figure 3-31

8. Click the Assign button to assign the keyboard shortcut to the style, click Close to close the Customize Keyboard dialog box, and then click OK to accept the new style definition.

9. Using any method (for example, the Ctrl+Q shortcut), apply the new style, Bulleted List, to all the remaining bulleted paragraphs in the document.

10. Click the Close (X) button on the Styles pane to close it.

11. Save the changes to the document.

Leave the document open for the next exercise.

Copying Formats with Format Painter

When many different blocks of text need to be formatted the same way, it can be tedious to select and format each block. As a shortcut, Word offers the Format Painter feature. Format Painter picks up the formatting from one block of text and applies it to another.

If you select the destination text, Format Painter copies only *character-based formatting* (that is, the type of formatting created by the commands in the Font group of the Home tab). If you click in a paragraph as the destination, rather than selecting, Word copies both character and paragraph settings. Paragraph settings include things like left and right indents, tab stops, and spacing between lines.

In this exercise, you copy the formatting from one block of text to another.

Files needed: Lesson 3 Syllabus Formatted.docx, *from the previous exercise*

1. **Triple-click the first bulleted paragraph (CPUs and Assembly language) to select it.**

2. **On the Home tab of the Ribbon, open the Font Color button's palette and click the Green standard color.**

3. **Click the Italics button on the Home tab.**

4. **Click the Format Painter button on the Home tab, as shown in Figure 3-32.**

   The mouse pointer turns into a paintbrush.

Format Painter

Figure 3-32

5. **Click and drag across the bulleted paragraphs immediately below the one you formatted.**

   The formatting is copied to those paragraphs, and then the Format Painter feature turns itself off automatically.

6. **With the text still selected that you just copied the formatting to, double-click the Format Painter button.**

   Double-clicking Format Painter rather than clicking it turns it on so that it remains on until you turn it off.

7. **Drag across each of the other bulleted paragraphs to copy the formatting to them.**

   The formatting is copied to each of those paragraphs, as shown in Figure 3-33.

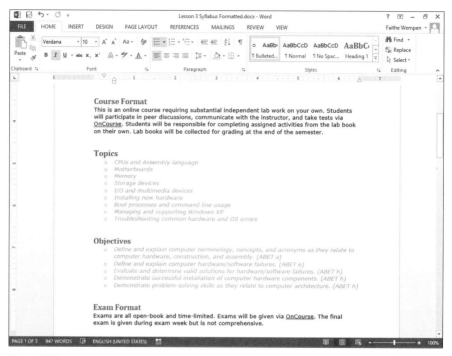

Figure 3-33

8. **Click the Format Painter button to turn off the feature and then save your work.**

Leave the document open for the next exercise.

Using Headers and Footers

Every document has a header and footer area, which are both empty by default. The header and footer appear in Print Layout view, Read Mode, and Web Layout view, and also on the printed page. (If you're in Draft view, you might want to switch to Print Layout view to follow along in this section more easily.)

LINGO

Headers and **footers** contain content that repeats at the top and bottom of each page, respectively, outside of the top and bottom margins.

You can place text in the header and footer that repeats on every page, and you can insert a variety of codes in them that display information such as page numbers, dates, and times.

Numbering the pages

Have you ever dropped a stack of papers that needed to stay in a certain order? If the pages were numbered, putting them back together was fairly simple. If not, what a frustrating, time-consuming task.

Fortunately, Word makes it very easy to number your document pages. And you can choose from a variety of numbering styles and formats. When you number pages in Word, you don't have to manually type the numbers onto each page. Instead, you place a code in the document that numbers the pages automatically. Sweet!

When you use the Page Numbering feature in Word, it automatically inserts the proper code in either the header or the footer so that each page is numbered consecutively.

Page numbers are visible only in Print Layout view, Read Mode, Print Preview, and on the printouts themselves. You don't see the page numbers if you're working in Draft view or Web Layout view, even though they're there.

In this exercise, you place a page numbering code in a document's footer.

Files needed: `Lesson 3 Syllabus Formatted.docx`, *open from the previous exercise*

1. **Choose Insert⭢Page Number⭢Bottom of Page⭢Plain Number 3. (See Figure 3-34.)**

   A page number code is placed at the right side of the footer, and the footer becomes active, as shown in Figure 3-35.

You can't edit the body of the document while you're in this mode. To resume working within the main part of the document, double-click the main document (anywhere below the header or above the footer).

The page number code is gray when you select it; that's your clue that it's a code and not regular text.

Figure 3-34

3. Double-click anywhere in the main part of the document to leave the footer.

The body of the document becomes editable again and the actual page numbers appear at the bottoms of the pages.

For more practice, choose Insert⇨Page Number⇨Remove Page Numbers to undo the page number insertion and then choose a different preset from the Bottom of Page submenu. Not all the presets are plain; some of them add formatting.

Leave the document open for the next exercise.

Notice in Figure 3-34 the other page number position options instead of Bottom of Page:

- ✔ **Top of Page:** Places the page number code in the *header* (at the top of the page). The page numbers appear on every page.

- ✔ **Page Margins:** Places the page number code on the side of the page. The page numbers appear on every page.

- ✔ **Current Position:** Places the page number code at the insertion point in the document (as a one-time thing). Because the code is not in the

Page number code

Figure 3-35

header or footer, it doesn't repeat on each page. You might use this to create a cross-reference to content that's on another page, for example.

✔ **Format Page Numbers:** Opens a dialog box where you can fine-tune the formatting of the page numbering code, such as using Roman numerals or letters instead of digits.

✔ **Remove Page Numbers:** Removes existing page numbering code(s).

Using a header or footer preset

In addition to a page number, you can put other content in the header and footer areas of your document. For example, if you're typing the minutes of a club meeting, you might want to put the club's name in the header so that it appears across the top of each page.

Here are two ways of putting content into them: You can use presets to insert codes and formatting, or you can type text and insert codes manually into the headers and footers.

In this exercise, you use a header preset.

Files needed: Lesson 3 Syllabus Formatted.docx, open from the preceding exercise

1. **In the Lesson 3 Syllabus Formatted document, choose Insert⇨Header⇨ Banded.**

   Placeholder text and a colored bar appear in the Header section, and the Header section becomes active.

TIP

Some of the presets for headers and footers also include a page-numbering code. This saves you the step of inserting the page-numbering code separately.

2. **Click in the *[DOCUMENT TITLE]* placeholder and then type** CIT 233 Syllabus. **See Figure 3-36.**

Type in the shaded text box.

Figure 3-36

3. **Choose Header & Footer Tools Design⇨Close Header and Footer.**

   This is an alternative way of returning to normal editing mode.

Leave the document open for the next exercise.

Creating a custom header or footer

The header and footer presets are great if they happen to match what you want to place there, but you can also create your own custom headers and footers that contain the exact combination of text and codes that you need. To do so, open the header or footer, click in it, and then type the text you want. Use the buttons on the Header & Footer Tools Design tab to insert codes.

In this exercise, you create a custom footer that uses a combination of date/time codes, page numbers, and typed text.

Files needed: `Lesson 3 Syllabus Formatted.docx`, open from the preceding exercise

1. **In the Lesson 3 Syllabus Formatted document, double-click at the bottom of the first page to open the footer and move the insertion point into it.**

2. **Select the page number that's already there and press the Delete key.**

3. **Press the Backspace key twice to move the insertion point to the left side of the footer.**

4. **Choose Header & Footer Tools Design⇨Date & Time.**

   The Date and Time dialog box opens, as shown in Figure 3-37.

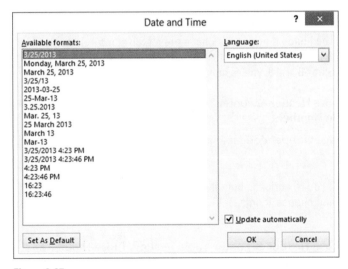

Figure 3-37

5. **Make sure that the Update Automatically check box is selected, click the first date format on the list, and then click OK.**

A code for the date appears in the footer.

You can tell it's a code rather than plain text because when you point to it, it appears with a gray background.

6. **Right-click the date code and choose Toggle Field Codes.**

This lets you see the code that creates the date, as shown in Figure 3-38.

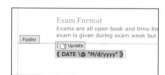

7. **Click in the date code and click the Update text that appears above it.**

Figure 3-38

The date code is updated and returns to showing the date itself rather than the code.

8. **Click to the right of the date code to move the insertion point there and then press the Tab key to move to the center of the footer.**

9. **Type** Lawrence College **and press Tab to move to the right of the footer.**

The headers and footers have preset tab stops — a center-aligned one in the center, and a right-aligned one at the right. When you press Tab in Steps 8 and 9, you're moving to those existing tab stops.

10. **Choose Header & Footer Tools Design⇨Page Number⇨Current Position⇨ Plain Number.**

A page number code is inserted.

If you're curious about the code behind the page number, right-click it and choose Toggle Field Codes, as you did with the date in Step 6.

11. **Choose Header & Footer Tools Design⇨Close Header and Footer and then choose File⇨Print and check the preview at the right.**

Notice that the codes in the footer produce today's date and the current page number on each page.

12. **Press Esc to leave Backstage view without printing.**

In a complex document, you can get very fancy with headers and footers. For example, you can choose to have a different header and footer on the first page, and you can have different headers and footers on odd and even pages. That's handy when you're printing a double-sided booklet, for example, so the page numbers can always be on the outside edges. To set either of those options, select their check boxes on the Header & Footer Tools Design tab, shown in Figure 3-39.

Figure 3-39

You can also create section breaks and have a different header and footer in each section. When you use multiple headers and footers in a document, you can move between them by clicking the Previous and Next buttons on the Header & Footer Tools Design tab.

To adjust the header and footer size and positioning, use the settings in the Position group on the Header & Footer Tools Design tab, shown in Figure 3-39. You can specify a Header from Top and Footer from Bottom position there. For example, if you want a taller header section, increase the Header from Top setting.

Summing Up

Word provides several ways to format paragraphs and tables and to help automate formatting. Here are the key points from this chapter:

- ✔ To apply horizontal alignment, use the buttons in the Paragraph group on the Home tab. Your choices are Align Text Left, Align Text Right, Center, and Justify.

- ✔ You can indent a paragraph at the left or right (all lines). You can also apply a first-line or hanging indent.

- ✔ To indent the entire paragraph at the left, you can use the Increase Indent button in the Paragraph group on the Home tab.

✔ To set other indentation, open the Paragraph dialog box by clicking the dialog box launcher in the Paragraph group.

✔ You can set vertical spacing from the Line and Paragraph Spacing button on the Home tab or from the Paragraph dialog box.

✔ To create a default numbered or bulleted list, use their respective buttons on the Home tab. Each button has a drop-down list from which you can select other bullet or numbering styles.

✔ Styles are named formatting combinations that are stored in the template. You can apply them to paragraphs to quickly format the paragraphs with standardized settings.

✔ Some styles are available on the Styles gallery on the Home tab; others must be applied from the Styles task pane.

✔ You can redefine a style by example or by manually editing a style's definition.

✔ To access the document's header and footer areas, double-click at the top or bottom of the page in Print Layout view or choose Insert⇨Header or Insert⇨Footer.

✔ Use the tools on the Header & Footer Tools Design tab to insert page numbers, dates, and other codes in a header or footer.

Try-it-yourself lab

For more practice with the features covered in this chapter, try the following exercise on your own:

1. **Use the Internet to research a new technology or medical advance that interests you.**

2. **Using Word, write a report that summarizes what you learned. Use Word's built-in styles to format the report (Title, Heading 1, Heading 2, and so on).**

3. **Create a new style and name it Body. Format it using a different font than Normal style uses. Apply the Body style to all the body paragraphs in your document.**

4. **Center the document title at the top of the document.**

5. **Write your name above the title. Format it with the Subtitle style and right-align it.**

6. **Add a footer that contains your name, today's date (as a code), and a page numbering code.**

7. **Save your document with a name of your choice and close Word.**

Know this tech talk

border: A line placed on top of a table gridline (or on the outside of some other object) to make its outline appear with certain formatting and to make the outline appear on printouts.

bulleted list: A list in which the order of items is not important and each paragraph is preceded by the same symbol.

character style: A style that can be applied to individual characters in a paragraph, not necessarily the entire paragraph.

first-line indent: An indent that affects the first line of the paragraph only. When it's a reverse indent of the first line (that is, the first line is indented less than subsequent lines), it's called a *hanging indent*.

footer: The area at the bottom of each page that contains information that repeats on multiple pages.

hanging indent: An indent where the first line of the paragraph is indented less than the other lines in the paragraph. Compare to *first-line indent.*

header: The area at the top of each page that contains information that repeats on multiple pages.

horizontal alignment: The positioning of a paragraph between the right and left margins.

indentation: The amount that a paragraph is offset from the left or right margin.

justified: A horizontal alignment that stretches the text out so that it touches both the right and left margins.

leading: Vertical spacing between the lines of text.

numbered list: A list in which the order of the items is important and each paragraph is preceded by a consecutive number.

paragraph formatting: Formatting that affects whole paragraphs and cannot be applied to individual characters.

paragraph style: A style that applies to the entire paragraph, not just individual characters.

point: A measure of $\frac{1}{72}$ of an inch.

style: A named set of formatting specifications stored with a template or document.

Styles gallery: A short list of commonly used styles appearing on the Home tab.

vertical spacing: The amount of space (leading) between each line.

Chapter 4

Working with Tables and Graphics in Word

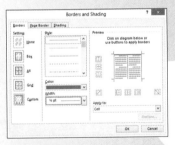

- Using tables allows you to *organize complex sets of data* in an orderly fashion.

- Find and insert artwork from the Microsoft online collection to *use professionally designed artwork* without paying royalties or usage fees.

- Insert your own photos and other artwork in a Word document to *personalize your work and make it more interesting to view*.

- Change the text wrap settings for graphics to *fine-tune the way that the text in the document wraps* around and interacts with the graphics.

1. How do you draw a table by dragging with the mouse?

Find out on page 145

2. How do you convert existing text to a table?

Find out on page 147

3. How do you resize a row or column in a table?

Find out on page 150

4. What's the difference between borders and gridlines?

Find out on page 153

5. How do you access free artwork online?

Find out on page 156

6. How do you make text wrap around a picture?

Find out on page 162

Tables help you present rows and columns of data in an orderly way. You can draw tables or create them by using a preset grid.

You can dress up Word documents with a variety of graphics. You can import pictures from online sources, use pictures from your collection, or create artwork inside of Word with drawing tools (which is beyond the scope of this chapter). Graphics can make a document more interesting and can explain visual concepts more easily than text alone. You know the old saying . . . a picture is worth a thousand words.

In this chapter, you learn how to insert and format tables and images and how to position and format pictures in a document. You also learn about the drawing tools, which are available not only in Word but also in Excel and PowerPoint.

Creating a Table

Tables are useful for displaying information in multicolumn layouts, such as address lists and schedules. You may be surprised at all the uses you can find for tables in your documents!

In this chapter, you learn how to insert tables in a Word document in several ways. You also learn how to modify a table and how to apply formatting to it that makes it easier to read and understand.

To create a table in Word, you can either insert a table as a whole or draw one line by line. In most cases, if you want a standard-looking table (that is, one with equally sized rows and columns), your best bet is to insert it. If you want an unusual-looking table, such as with different numbers of columns in some rows, you may be better off drawing the table.

When inserting a new table, you can specify a number of rows and columns to create a blank grid and then fill in the grid by typing. Press the Tab key to move to the next cell. When you reach the end of the last row, you can press Tab to add a row to the table.

In the following exercise, you create a new table in two ways.

Files needed: None

1. **Start a new blank document in Word and save it as Lesson 4 Table.**

2. **Choose Insert⇨Table and, in the menu that appears with a grid, drag across the grid to select three rows and three columns, as shown in Figure 4-1. Then release the mouse button to create the table.**

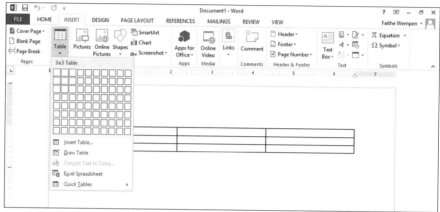

Figure 4-1

For extra practice, delete the table you just inserted (press Ctrl+Z to undo the last action) and then insert the table by choosing Insert⇨Table⇨ Insert Table. In the dialog box that opens, enter the number of rows and columns as digits and click OK.

3. **In the first cell of the first row, type Name and then press Tab to move to the next column.**

4. **Type Position, press Tab, type Active?, and press Tab.**

   The insertion point moves to the first cell in the next row.

5. **Type the rest of the entries shown in Figure 4-2 into the table. Be sure to press Tab after each entry. When you reach the bottom-right cell, press Tab again.**

   A new blank row appears at the bottom of the table.

Name	Position	Active?
Sheldon Peterson	Catcher	Yes
Brendon Lowe	Pitcher	Yes
Peter Fitzgerald	First Base	Yes
John Wilson	Second Base	No

Figure 4-2

6. **Click below the table to move the insertion point and then choose Insert⇨Table⇨Draw Table.**

   The mouse pointer turns into a pencil symbol.

7. **Drag to draw a box that is approximately the same height and width as the table you created earlier.**

   A box appears, and the mouse pointer remains a pencil.

8. **Drag within the box to draw two vertical lines and two horizontal lines.**

   After you draw each line, remember to release the mouse button.

9. **Draw an additional vertical line that spans only the bottom two rows, as shown in Figure 4-3.**

Rightmost column divider
spans only two rows.

Figure 4-3

10. **Type the text shown in Figure 4-4 into the new table.**

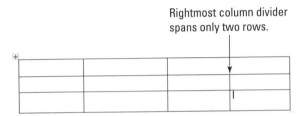

Shift	Location	Worker	
Day	Clermont	Tom	Jones
Day	Clermont	Alice	Little

Figure 4-4

11. **Save the changes to the document and close it.**

Leave Word open for the next exercise.

Converting text to a table

If you already have some text that's separated into rows and columns with tabs, commas, or some other consistent character, you can convert that text to a table with a few simple clicks.

For conversion to work, the existing text must be delimited with a consistent character to separate the columns. Tab stops and commas are the two most common ways that data is delimited. For example, the text in Figure 4-5 shows some of the data from the preceding exercise as a delimited text file in Notepad (a text editor), three columns with commas marking where each column should break.

In the following exercise, you convert some existing delimited text in a Word document into a table.

Figure 4-5

Files needed: `Lesson 4 Schedule.docx`

1. **Open Lesson 4 Schedule and save it as Lesson 4 Schedule Table.**
2. **Select all the text in the document and then choose Insert⇨Table⇨Convert Text to Table.**

You can press Ctrl+A to select all the text in the document.

The Convert Text to Table dialog box opens, as shown in Figure 4-6.

3. **Click OK.**

The text converts to a five-column table.

4. **Save the changes to the document.**

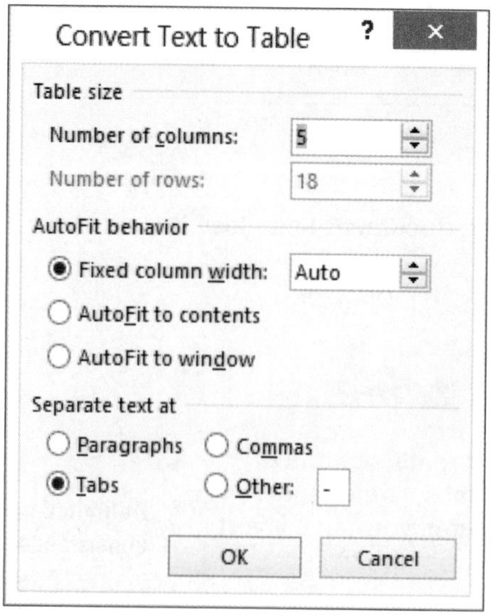

Figure 4-6

Leave the document open for the next exercise.

 If you don't get the results you expect when converting text to a table, the problem is probably that not all rows have the same number of delimiters in them. You may be missing a tab, for example, or have two tabs in a row. Press Ctrl+Z to undo the table creation, check your column markers, and try again. You can turn on the display of hidden characters by clicking the Home tab's Show/Hide (¶) button to make it easier to see where the tabs are.

Selecting rows and columns

Working with a table often involves selecting one or more cells, rows, or columns. Here are the many ways to do this:

- ✔ Drag across the cells you want to select.

- ✔ Click in the upper-left cell you want to select and then hold down the Shift key and press arrow keys to extend the selection.

- ✔ Click outside of the table on the left side to select an entire row.

- ✔ Click outside of the table above the table to select an entire column.

- ✔ Click the table selector icon (the four-headed arrow in a box; see Figure 4-7) in the upper-left corner of the table to select the entire table.

- ✔ On the Table Tools tab, click the Select button and then choose what you want to select from the menu that appears.

Table Selector

Week	Begins	Read	Do Labs
1	8-23	Chapters 1 and 2	1.1, 1.3, 1.4, 2.1, 2.2, 2.3, 2.4
2	8-30	Chapter 4	4.1, 4.3, 4.4, 4.5

Figure 4-7

In the following exercise, you practice selecting various parts of a table.

Files needed: `Lesson 4 Schedule Table.docx`, *open from the preceding exercise*

1. **In Lesson 4 Schedule Table, click inside any cell of the table and then click the table selector icon. (Refer to Figure 4-7.)**

   The entire table is selected.

2. **Click away from the table to deselect it.**

3. **Position the mouse pointer to the left of the table, next to the second row, and click.**

   That row becomes selected, as shown in Figure 4-8.

Week	Begins	Read	Do Labs	What's Due
1	8-23	Chapters 1 and 2	1.1, 1.3, 1.4, 2.1, 2.2, 2.3, 2.4	Introduce yourself to your classmates in the Forum area
2	8-30	Chapter 4	4.1, 4.3, 4.4, 4.5	
3	9-6	Chapter 5	5.1, 5.2, 5.6	
4	9-13	Chapter 6	6.2, 6.4	Take Test #1 (1, 2, 4, 5)

Figure 4-8

In Figure 4-8, notice the plus sign near the mouse pointer. If you click the plus sign, a new row is added to the table at that position.

4. **Drag the mouse downward to row 4.**

   Rows 3 and 4 also become selected.

5. **Position the mouse pointer above the first column so the pointer becomes a black down-pointing arrow and then click.**

   The first column becomes selected.

6. **Click in the first cell and hold down the Shift key. Press the right-arrow key twice to extend the selection and then press the down-arrow key once to extend the selection.**

   Three cells in each of the first two rows are selected.

7. **Click in the first cell again and drag down to the third cell in the third row to extend the selection.**

Leave the document open for the next exercise.

Resizing rows and columns

Word handles row height automatically for you, so you usually don't have to think about it. The row height changes as needed to accommodate the font size of the text in the cells of that row. Text in a cell wraps automatically to the next line when it runs out of room horizontally, so you can expect your table rows to expand in height as you type more text into them.

If you manually resize a row's height, the ability to auto-resize to fit content is turned off for that row. Therefore, if you add more text to that row later, Word doesn't automatically expand that row's height to accommodate it, and some text may be truncated.

In contrast, column width remains fixed until you change it, regardless of the cell's content. If you want the width of a column to change, you must change it yourself.

In the following exercise, you resize the rows and columns of a table.

Files needed: Lesson 4 Schedule Table.docx, *open from the preceding exercise*

1. **In Lesson 4 Schedule Table, hover the mouse pointer over the column divider between the first and second columns.**

   The mouse pointer becomes a double-headed arrow, as shown in Figure 4-9.

Week	Begins
1	8-23
2	8-30

Figure 4-9

2. **Drag to the right slightly to increase the width of the first column by about ¼ inches.**

   Notice that the second column's text now wraps unattractively, as shown in Figure 4-10.

3. **Press Ctrl+Z to undo the column width change; while pressing the Shift key, repeat Steps 1–2.**

   This time the other columns shift to the right to make room for the new width.

Week	Begins
1	8-23
2	8-30

Figure 4-10

4. **Select the cells containing 1 and 2 in the first column.**

5. **Drag the column divider within the selected area between the first and second columns to the left about ¼ inch, dragging that column back to its original position.**

   Only the two rows where cells were selected are affected, as shown in Figure 4-11.

Week	Begins
1	8-23
2	8-30

Figure 4-11

6. **Press Ctrl+Z to undo the column change; click to move the insertion point inside any cell in the first column.**

7. **Choose Table Tools Layout⇨AutoFit⇨ AutoFit Contents. (See Figure 4-12.)**

   All the column widths are adjusted in the table to fit the content.

8. **Position the mouse pointer over the horizontal divider between the heading row at the top and the first data row.**

   The mouse pointer becomes a two-headed arrow, as shown in Figure 4-13.

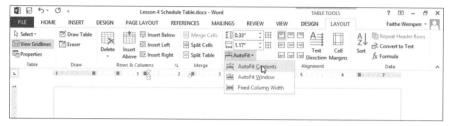

Figure 4-12

9. **Drag downward to increase the height of the heading row by about ¼ inch.**

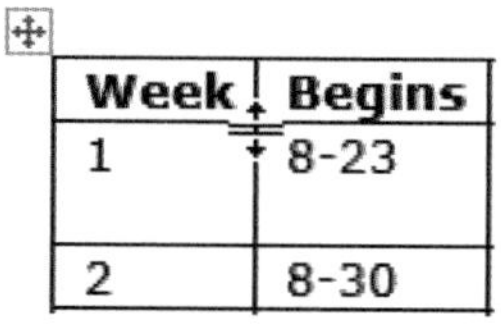

10. **Select the heading row and choose Table Tools Layout⇨Align Bottom Left.**

The headings are bottom-aligned in their cells, as shown in Figure 4-14. Vertical alignment was not an issue previously because the height of the row was autofitted to the content.

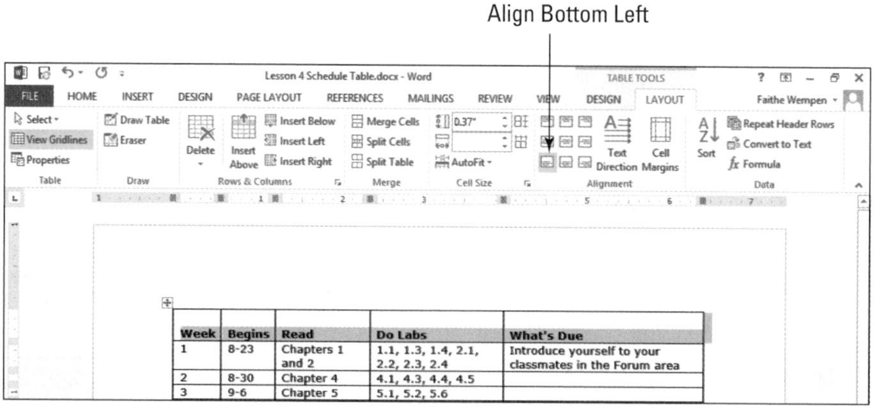

Week	Begins
1	8-23
2	8-30

Figure 4-13

Align Bottom Left

Week	Begins	Read	Do Labs	What's Due
1	8-23	Chapters 1 and 2	1.1, 1.3, 1.4, 2.1, 2.2, 2.3, 2.4	Introduce yourself to your classmates in the Forum area
2	8-30	Chapter 4	4.1, 4.3, 4.4, 4.5	
3	9-6	Chapter 5	5.1, 5.2, 5.6	

Figure 4-14

11. **Click the table selector icon in the upper-left corner of the table to select the entire table.**

12. **Choose Table Tools Layout⇨Distribute Columns to evenly distribute the space among all the columns. (See Figure 4-15.)**

13. **Press Ctrl+Z to undo the resizing.**

14. **Save the changes to the document.**

Leave the document open for the next exercise.

Distribute Columns

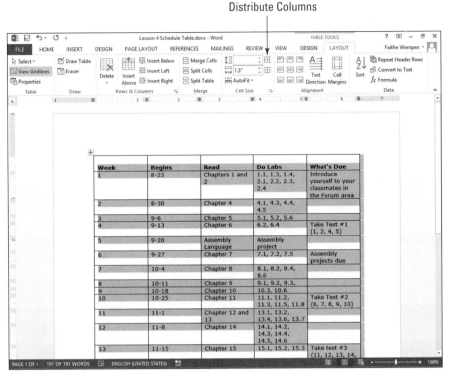

Figure 4-15

Formatting table borders

Gridlines can be displayed or hidden onscreen (via Table Tools Layout⇨View Gridlines). Gridlines do not print, and when displayed onscreen, they appear as thin blue or gray dashed lines.

You probably won't see the gridlines in most tables because they're covered by borders. By default, table gridlines have a plain black ½-pt border.

You can change the borders to different colors, styles (such as dotted or dashed), and thicknesses or remove the borders altogether.

In the following exercise, you apply formatting to table borders.

Files needed: `Lesson 4 Schedule Table.docx`, *open from the preceding exercise*

1. **In Lesson 4 Schedule Table, select the entire table and then choose Table Tools Design⇨Borders⇨No Border. (See Figure 4-16.)**

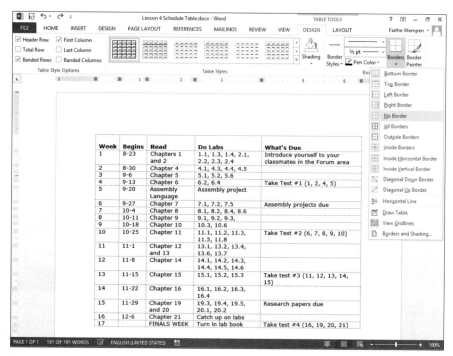

Figure 4-16

2. **If the gridlines don't display already, choose Table Tools Layout⇨View Gridlines.**

   Dashed lines appear for the table's row and column dividers, as shown in Figure 4-17.

3. **Select the header row of the table and then choose Table Tools Design⇨Line Weight⇨2¼ pt. (See Figure 4-18.)**

4. **Choose Table Tools Design⇨Pen Color and click a red square.**

5. **Choose Table Tools Design⇨Borders⇨Bottom Border.**

   A red bottom border with 2¼-pt thickness appears on the header row only.

6. **Select all the rows in the table *except* the header row and then click the dialog box launcher for the Borders group on the Table Tools Design tab.**

View Gridlines

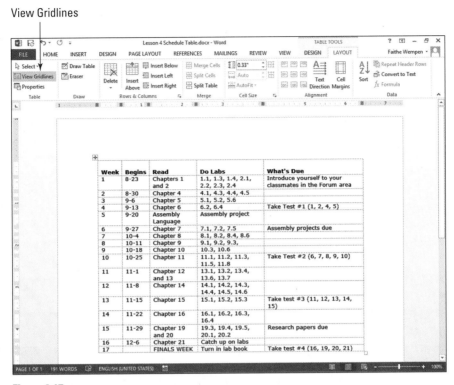

Figure 4-17

The Borders and Shading dialog box opens with the Borders tab displayed. A red border shows in the sample for the top of the selection; when you applied the red border, the first row was selected, and the border was at its bottom. The new selection has that same border as its top.

7. **From the Width drop-down list, choose ½ pt.**

8. **In the Preview area, click the areas where vertical borders might appear (see Figure 4-19) and then click OK.**

Line Weights

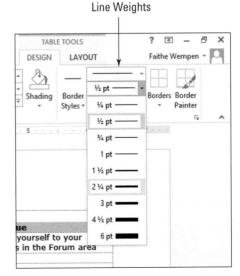

Figure 4-18

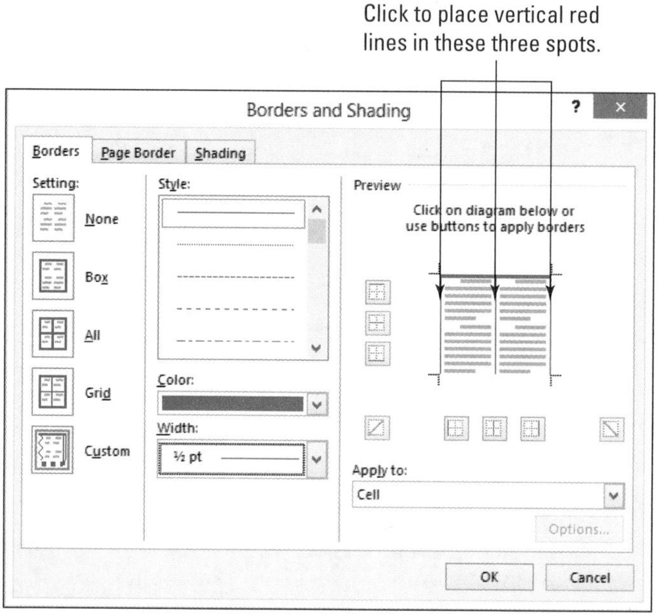

Click to place vertical red
lines in these three spots.

Figure 4-19

9. **Click away from the table to deselect it. Then turn off the gridlines again by choosing Table Tools Layout⇨View Gridlines.**

   The table now has a thick, top border separating the header from the rest of the table, and red vertical lines separate the columns, as shown in Figure 4-20.

10. **Save the changes to the document.**

Close the document. Leave Word open for the next exercise.

Inserting Pictures from the Web

When you buy any of the Office applications, you get free access to a large online library of clip art maintained by Microsoft at Office.com. Each of the main Office applications has an Online Pictures command that opens a dialog box in which you can search this library and insert images from it into your documents. This image library contains not only clip art but also royalty-free stock photography.

Office.com is only one of the possible sources of online images you can explore. You can also

LINGO

Clip art is generic artwork. In the days before computers, companies would buy large books of line drawings, and when they needed an image, they would clip it out of the book and glue it to a paste-up layout. Today, clip art refers to line-based drawings such as the ones you can get from Office.com.

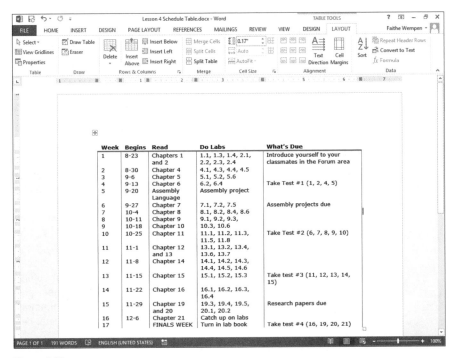

Figure 4-20

retrieve files via a Bing Image Search on the web. Bing (www.bing.com) is a search engine sponsored by Microsoft, and the Bing Image Search feature in Office applications enables you to easily locate images from all over the Internet.

Understanding vector and raster graphics

There are two types of computer graphics: vector and raster. They're very different from one another, and each is best suited for a different purpose.

Clip art is a type of **vector graphic**. A vector graphic is created behind the scenes by using math formulas; if you've taken a geometry class where you plotted a function on graph paper, you get the idea. Computerized clip art builds images by layering and combining individual lines and shapes, each one constructed via a math formula. As a result, the clips can be resized without losing any quality because resizing simply changes the math formula. Clip art files are also very small compared with raster graphics. The main drawback of clip art is that the images don't look real — they look like drawings.

Photos from digital cameras are examples of **raster graphics**. A raster graphic is a densely packed collection of colored dots that together form an image. If you zoom in on a photo on a computer, you can see these dots individually. In a raster graphic, each dot is called a **pixel**, and its color is represented by a numeric code (usually 24 or 32 binary digits in length per pixel). Raster graphics can be photorealistic, but because so much data is required to define each pixel, the file sizes tend to be large.

Finding and inserting pictures from the web

In the following exercise, you practice searching for online pictures by using both Office.com and a Bing image search and inserting them in a document.

Files needed: Lesson 4 Breton.docx

1. **Open** Lesson 4 Breton.docx **and save it as** Lesson 4 Breton Art.docx.

2. **Position the insertion point at the beginning of the first body paragraph ("This week...").**

TIP The picture will be placed wherever the insertion point is. If the insertion point is in the middle of a paragraph, the picture will split the paragraph in two, possibly creating an awkward look that you didn't intend. For best results in most cases, position the insertion point on its own line, between two paragraphs, or at least at the beginning or end of a paragraph.

3. **Choose Insert⇨Online Pictures.**

   The Insert Pictures dialog box opens.

4. **Click in the Office.com Clip Art search box, type** poinsettia, **and press Enter.**

   A selection of pictures that have *poinsettia* as a keyword appear in the task pane. See Figure 4-21.

5. **Scroll through the resulting clips.**

   Notice that the results are a mixture of line drawings and photographs.

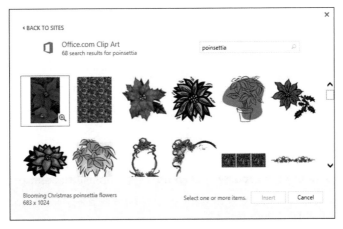

Figure 4-21

6. **Click one of the clips and then click the Insert button to insert it.**

   The clip appears in the document, as in Figure 4-22.

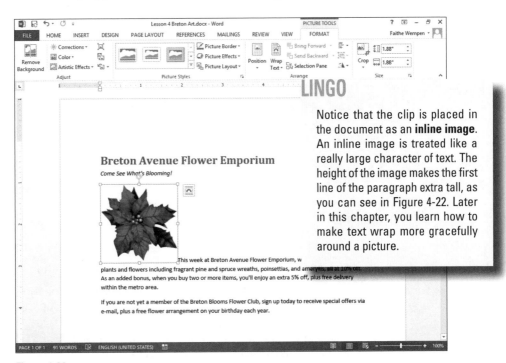

LINGO

Notice that the clip is placed in the document as an **inline image**. An inline image is treated like a really large character of text. The height of the image makes the first line of the paragraph extra tall, as you can see in Figure 4-22. Later in this chapter, you learn how to make text wrap more gracefully around a picture.

Figure 4-22

7. **Press Delete to remove the inserted clip.**

8. **Press Enter to create a new paragraph and then press the up-arrow key once to move the insertion point into that new paragraph.**

9. **Repeat Steps 2–5 to insert a different picture.**

   This time the clip appears on its own line.

10. **Press Delete to remove the inserted clip.**

11. **Choose Insert⇨Online Pictures.**

   The Insert Pictures dialog box opens.

12. **Click in the Bing Image Search box, type** poinsettia, **and press Enter.**

   A selection of pictures that have *poinsettia* as a keyword appear in the task pane. See Figure 4-23.

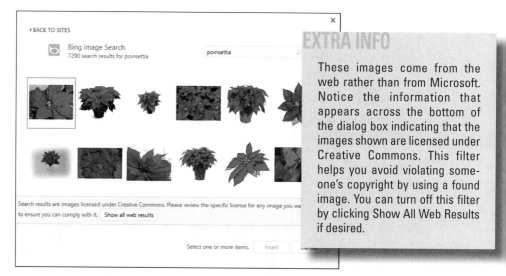

Figure 4-23

13. **Click one of the pictures and then click the Insert button to insert it.**

   The clip appears in the document. Depending on the picture you chose, the image may be small, as in Figure 4-22, or may take up the entire page width.

14. **Press Delete to remove the inserted clip and press Delete again to delete the blank line you created earlier.**

15. **Save the changes to the document.**

Leave the document open for the next exercise.

Inserting Photos from Files

The clips available online are generic. Sometimes, you might want to insert a more personal picture, such as a digital photo you took or a picture that a friend or co-worker sent you via e-mail.

In the following exercise, you insert a photograph from a file stored on your hard drive.

Files needed: `Lesson 4 Breton Art.docx`, *already open from the previous exercise*

1. **In `Lesson 4 Breton Art.docx`, click at the end of the document and press Enter to start a new paragraph.**

2. **Choose Insert⇨Pictures.**

   The Insert Picture dialog box opens.

3. **Navigate to the folder containing the data files for this chapter and select `04graphic01.jpg`, as shown in Figure 4-24.**

4. **Click the Insert button.**

   The picture is inserted in the document.

5. **Save the changes to the document.**

Leave the document open for the next exercise.

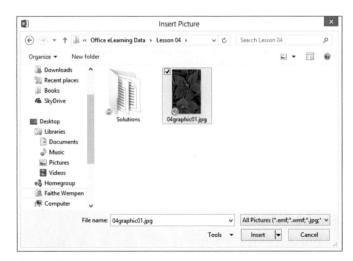

Figure 4-24

Managing Picture Size and Placement

After you insert a graphic in a document, you may decide you want to move it or change how the text around it interacts with it. For example, you might want the text to wrap around the graphic or even run on top of it.

You can size and position a graphic in several ways. You can manually size or move by dragging; you can specify exact values for height, width, and/or position on the page; or you can use the Word placement commands to place the image in relation to other content.

Changing the text wrap setting for a picture

By default, as I mention earlier, a picture is inserted as an inline image, which means it's treated like a text character. That's not usually the best way for an image to interact with the text, though. More often you want the text to flow around the image so that, if the text moves (due to editing), the graphic stays where you put it. You can change a picture's **text wrap** setting to control this.

In the following exercise, you change the text wrap setting for a picture.

Files needed: `Lesson 4 Breton Art.docx`*, already open from the previous exercise*

1. **In `Lesson 4 Breton Art.docx`, select the picture that you inserted in the previous exercise.**

   The Picture Tools Format tab becomes available.

2. **Choose Picture Tools Format⇨Wrap Text to open a menu of text wrap settings.**

   See Figure 4-25.

3. **Choose Square.**

4. **Drag the picture upward and drop it at the left margin so that it top-aligns with the top of the first body paragraph, as shown in Figure 4-26.**

For extra practice, try each of the other Wrap Text settings and compare their results. You don't have to select each of the settings; just pointing at a setting shows a preview of it in the document.

The photo currently in the document is rectangular, so you don't see any difference between some of the settings. To understand the differences between them, you must use a piece of clip art with a transparent background for your experiments.

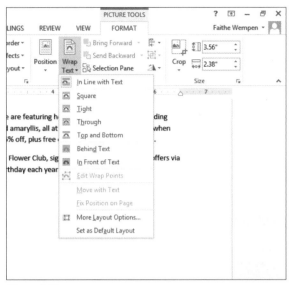

Figure 4-25

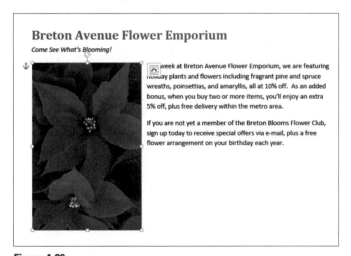

Figure 4-26

5. Press Delete to delete the picture.

6. Reposition the insertion point at the beginning of the first body paragraph.

7. **Using the Online Pictures command, locate and insert a clip art image (a drawing, not a photograph) that has a white (transparent) background.**

   You learned about the Online Pictures command earlier, in the section "Finding and inserting pictures from the web."

8. **Choose Picture Tools Format⇨Wrap Text and choose Square.**

   The text wraps around the clip art with a rectangular border, as shown in Figure 4-27.

This icon opens a menu that mirrors the Text Wrap button's menu.

EXTRA INFO

Notice the icon next to the selected picture that looks like an arch? You can click that button to open a floating version of the Wrap Text button's menu, as an alternative to clicking the Text Wrap button on the Ribbon.

Figure 4-27

9. **Click the Wrap Text button again and choose Tight.**

   The text wraps around the image itself, not its rectangular frame, as in Figure 4-28.

Text wraps into the graphic's frame.

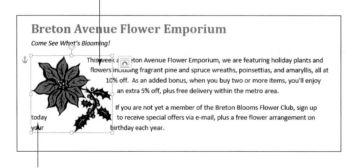

Some text may wrap into the frame in odd places.

Figure 4-28

Notice in Figure 4-28 that some stray bits of text appear below and to the left of the image. You can fix the stray text by adjusting the image's wrap points.

10. **Click the Wrap Text button again and choose Edit Wrap Points.**

Black squares and a dotted red outline appear around the clip art image.

These usually invisible points determine where the text is allowed to flow when text is set to Tight (that is, to wrap tightly around the image). See Figure 4-29.

11. **Drag one or more of the black squares outward to block out the space where the stray text appears so that it can't flow there anymore.**

See Figure 4-30 for an example.

Figure 4-29

12. **Click away from the image to deselect it and finalize the change in its wrap points.**

13. **Save the changes to the document.**

Leave the document open for the next exercise.

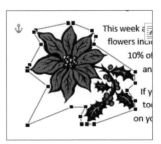

Moving a picture

You can move a picture by dragging it where you want it to go. The way a picture moves when you drag it varies depending on the text wrap setting you've chosen for the picture. If the default setting of In Line with Text is in effect, you can drag a picture only to a spot where you can also drag text:

Figure 4-30

✔ Within existing paragraphs

✔ Before or after existing paragraphs

You can't place a picture outside of the document margins or below the end-of-document marker. If any other text wrapping setting is in effect, you can drag a picture anywhere on the page.

You can also move a picture by specifying an exact position for it, from the Layout dialog box, or by using one of the presets in the Position drop-down list on the Format tab under Picture Tools.

In the following exercise, you move a picture.

Files needed: `Lesson 4 Breton Art.docx`, *already open from the previous exercise*

1. In `Lesson 4 Breton Art.docx`, select the picture that you worked with in the previous exercise.

2. Choose Picture Tools Format⇨Position button to open a menu of positions. Choose the position that shows the picture in the upper-right corner of the document.

   See Figure 4-31.

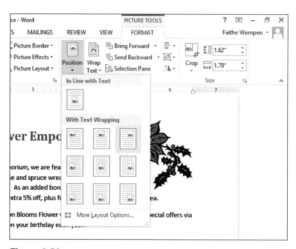

Figure 4-31

3. Drag the picture downward slightly so that its top aligns with the top of the first body paragraph.

4. Click the Position button again and choose More Layout Options.

   The Layout dialog box opens with the Position tab displayed.

5. In the Horizontal section, in the Absolute Position text box, enter 5.

6. In the Vertical section, in the Absolute Position text box, enter 1.

   Figure 4-32 shows the dialog box with these settings.

7. Click OK to close the dialog box.

   The picture's position is adjusted according to the settings you entered.

But what if you want the picture to move with the text, if you add or delete more text in the document so the text that's next to the picture now might not later be? The following steps show how to set that up.

8. **Click the Position button and choose More Layout Options to reopen the Layout dialog box.**

9. **In the Vertical section, for the Absolute Position setting, change the setting in the Below drop-down list to Paragraph.**

10. **Change the value in the Absolute Position text box to 0.2".**

11. **Make sure that the Move Object with Text check box is selected.**

Figure 4-33 shows the dialog box with these settings.

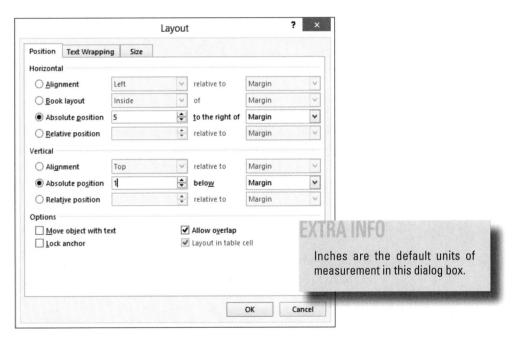

Figure 4-32

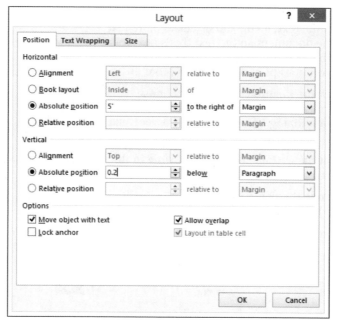

Figure 4-33

12. **Click OK.**

13. **Click at the beginning of the paragraph that contains the document subheading ("Come see . . .") and press Enter twice.**

Notice that the picture moves with the paragraph to which it is adjacent.

14. **Press Backspace twice to delete the extra paragraphs just created.**

15. **Save the changes to the document.**

Leave the document open for the next exercise.

Resizing a picture

You can resize a picture by dragging its selection handles or by specifying an exact height and width for the picture from the Layout dialog box.

TIP

Most image types maintain the aspect ratio automatically if you drag a corner selection handle. If the aspect ratio doesn't stay constant when you drag a corner selection handle, hold down Shift as you drag to force it to do so.

WARNING!

Raster images look fuzzy if you enlarge them past their original size. That's one advantage of vector images: They remain crisp and sharp at any size.

LINGO

When you resize a picture, its **aspect ratio** can change. The aspect ratio is the proportion of width to height. A photo may not look right if you don't maintain the aspect ratio; clip art is less likely to suffer from small differences in the ratio. When you drag a corner selection handle, the aspect ratio is maintained; when you drag a side selection handle, it is not.

In the following exercise, you resize a picture.

Files needed: `Lesson 4 Breton Art.docx`, *already open from the previous exercise*

1. **In** `Lesson 4 Breton Art.docx`, **select the clip art image that you worked with in the previous exercise if it isn't already selected.**

2. **Hover the mouse pointer over the lower-left selection handle.**

   The mouse pointer becomes a double-headed diagonal arrow, as shown in Figure 4-34.

Mouse pointer

Figure 4-34

3. Drag out and downward, enlarging the image by about ½ inch.

Use the onscreen ruler to gauge the distance. If the ruler doesn't appear, select the Ruler check box on the View tab.

4. Right-click the picture and choose Size and Position.

The Layout dialog box opens with the Size tab displayed.

5. In the Height section, set the Absolute setting to 2".

The Width automatically changes because the aspect ratio is locked. See Figure 4-35.

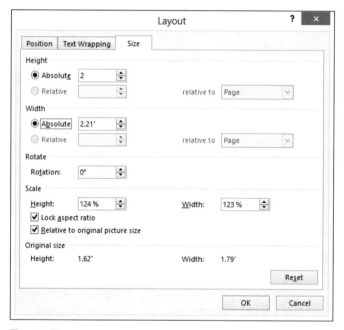

Figure 4-35

6. Click OK.

7. Save the changes to the document and close it.

Exit Word.

Summing Up

Here are the key points from this chapter:

- ✔ You can create a new table from the Insert tab, either by specifying a number of rows and columns or by drawing the table.

- ✔ You can convert existing delimited text into a table with the Convert Text to Table command.

- ✔ Drag the borders of a table to resize rows and columns.

- ✔ Tables have gridlines (nonprinting lines that show where the rows and columns are) and, optionally, borders (formatting applied to the gridlines).

- ✔ You can format a table's borders from the Table Tools Design tab.

- ✔ To insert an online picture from Office.com or a Bing image search, click the Online Pictures button on the Insert tab.

- ✔ To insert your own pictures, click the Pictures button on the Insert tab.

- ✔ A picture's text wrap setting determines whether it will be an inline image or will interact with surrounding text (and in what manner).

- ✔ To move a picture, drag it with the mouse. You can also specify an exact position for it in the Layout dialog box.

- ✔ To resize a picture, drag one of its selection handles. Drag a corner to resize it proportionally (that is, maintaining its aspect ratio).

Try-it-yourself lab

For more practice with the features covered in this chapter, try the following exercises on your own.

To practice working with tables:

1. **In a new document, create a table with two columns and ten rows.**

2. **In the left column, type a list of items you want to purchase for your home.**

3. **In the right column, type the approximate price for each item.**

4. Add a new row at the top of the table and, in the new row, type the columns' headings.

5. Format the table attractively.

6. Save your document with a name of your choice and then close Word.

To practice working with graphics:

1. Start Word and begin creating a flyer that advertises a yard sale. Type appropriate text, including a location, date, time, and list of items to be sold.

2. Find and insert two online pictures that would be appropriate for this flyer.

3. Set the text wrapping on the pictures so that the text wraps around them and then position and size the pictures attractively.

4. Save your document with the name of your choice and then close Word.

Know this tech talk

aspect ratio: The proportion of height to width of an image.

border: Formatting applied to the outer edge or gridline of a table cell or other object.

clip art: Generic artwork, available from third-party sources or from the Microsoft Office.com collection.

delimited: Multicolumn data where the columns are separated using a consistent character, such as a tab.

graphic: Any picture file. Also called an *image.*

gridlines: The nonprinting lines that (optionally) show onscreen where the edges of a table's rows and columns are.

illustration: A vector image. Also called *clip art.*

image: Any picture file. Also called a *graphic.*

inline image: A picture that is placed within the document's paragraph structure and is treated as a character of text.

photograph: A raster image.

pixel: An individual dot or data point in a raster graphic.

raster graphic: A type of graphic that defines the color of each pixel (dot) that makes up the image individually.

table: A grid of rows and columns for storing and displaying information in a multicolumn layout.

text wrap: The setting that determines how the surrounding text interacts with an image if it isn't an inline image.

vector graphic: A type of graphic that defines each line or fill with a math formula.

Chapter 5

Creating Basic Worksheets in Excel

▶ Selecting ranges enables you to *apply a single command to multiple cells at once.*

▶ You can *edit the content of a cell* either in the cell itself or in the Formula bar.

▶ Moving and copying data between cells *saves data-entry time and effort.*

▶ Dragging the fill handle *copies cell content quickly into many cells at once.*

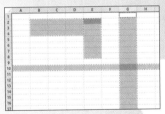

▶ Inserting and deleting rows and columns in a worksheet *changes its structure without moving content.*

▶ Renaming a worksheet tab enables you to *assign a more meaningful title to a sheet.*

▶ Inserting new worksheets into a workbook enables you to *expand a workbook's capacity.*

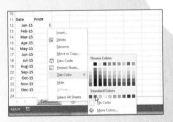

1. How do you move the cell cursor quickly back to cell A1?

Find out on page 182

2. How do you select a noncontiguous range?

Find out on page 183

3. How do you clear a cell's content?

Find out on page 188

4. How do you move and copy cell content with the Clipboard?

Find out on page 190

5. How can you quickly fill a set of increasing values into a large range?

Find out on page 192

6. How do you insert new rows and columns?

Find out on page 195

7. How can you change the color of a worksheet tab?

Find out on page 197

xcel has many practical uses. You can use its orderly row-and-column worksheet structure to organize multicolumn lists, create business forms, and much more. Excel provides more than just data organization, though; it enables you to write formulas that perform calculations on your data. This feature makes Excel an ideal tool for storing financial information, such as checkbook register and investment portfolio data.

In this chapter, I introduce you to the Excel interface and teach you some of the concepts you need to know. You learn how to move around in Excel, how to type and edit data, and how to manipulate rows, columns, cells, and sheets.

Understanding the Excel Interface

Excel is very much like Word and other Office applications. Excel has a File tab that opens a Backstage view, a Ribbon with multiple tabs that contain commands you can click to execute, a Quick Access toolbar, a status bar, scroll bars, and a Zoom slider. Figure 5-1 provides a quick overview.

The next several sections walk you through the Excel interface, including both the commands and the work area, and show you how to move around. After you get your bearings in Excel, you're ready to start creating worksheets.

Quick Access
toolbar
Tab

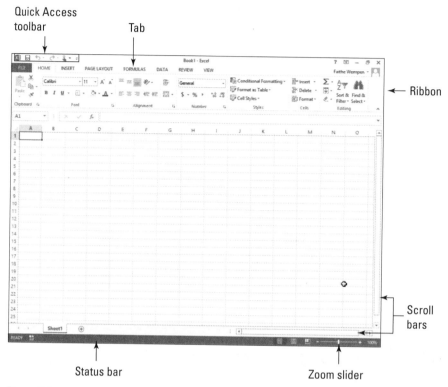

Ribbon

Scroll
bars

Status bar

Zoom slider

Figure 5-1

Touring the Excel interface

The best way to learn about a new application is to jump in and start exploring. Work through this exercise to see how Excel is set up. You learned some basics about Office apps in Chapter 1, but this exercise goes into more depth on Excel specifically.

In the following exercise, you start Excel and explore its interface.

LINGO

Starting out with some basic terminology is a good idea. A **spreadsheet** is a grid composed of rows and columns. At the intersection of each row and column is a **cell.** You can type text, numbers, and formulas into cells to build your spreadsheet. In Excel, spreadsheets are dubbed **worksheets** or just **sheets.** Worksheets are stored in data files, or **workbooks,** and each workbook can contain multiple worksheets. **Worksheet tabs** at the bottom of a workbook window enable you to switch quickly between worksheets.

Files needed: None

1. **Start Excel 2013 from the Start screen (Windows 8) or Start menu (Windows 7).**

   You learned to start Office applications in Chapter 1.

You might want to pin the Excel 2013 tile to the taskbar in Windows 8 to save yourself some time in opening it. Right-click the Excel 2013 tile on the Start screen and then click Pin to Taskbar in the command bar that appears at the bottom of the screen. From that point on, you can start Excel by clicking the Excel icon on the taskbar from the desktop. This trick works with all the Office apps, by the way.

An opening screen appears, as shown in Figure 5-2, providing shortcuts to recently used workbook files and thumbnails of some available templates. One of the templates is Blank Workbook.

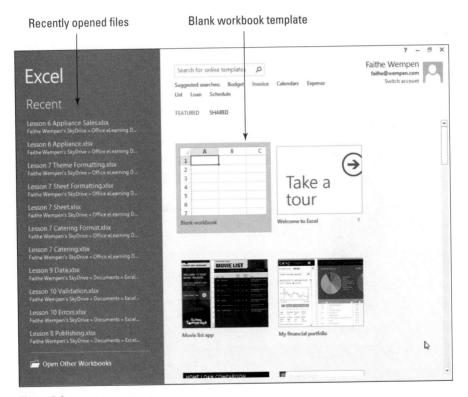

Figure 5-2

2. Click the Blank Workbook thumbnail image to start a new blank workbook.

Alternatively, you can also press the Esc key to go to a new blank workbook from the opening screen.

A new workbook appears.

3. Click the File tab to open Backstage view and then click Info.

Information about the active document appears, as shown in Figure 5-3.

4. Click the Back arrow, or press the Esc key, to return to the new blank workbook. (See Figure 5-4.)

The Back arrow is the left-pointing arrow in the upper-left corner.

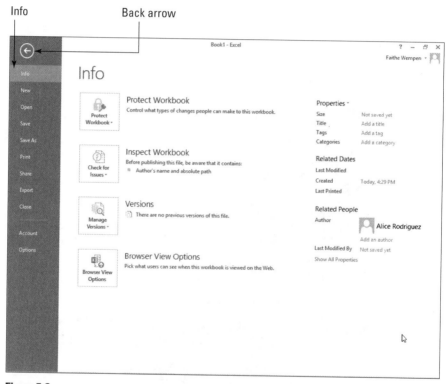

Figure 5-3

Name box shows address of active cell.

View tab

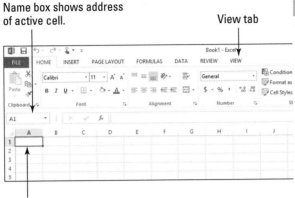

Active cell (A1) is the cell with the cell cursor around it.

Figure 5-4

Figure 5-4 shows a worksheet in Excel. Each row has a unique number, and each column has a unique letter. The combination of a letter and a number forms a **cell address.** The letter comes first. For example, the cell in the upper-left corner is A1. When you type in Excel, your typing is entered into the **active cell,** which features the **cell cursor,** or a thick green outline. The active cell's ~~name~~ address appears in the **Name box.**

5. **Click the View tab on the Ribbon and then click the Zoom button so that the Zoom dialog box opens. (See Figure 5-5.)**

6. **Select 200% and then click OK.**

   The dialog box closes, and the magnification changes to show each cell in a more close-up view.

7. **At the bottom-right corner of the Excel window, drag the Zoom slider left to 100%, changing the zoom back to its original setting. (See Figure 5-6.)**

Leave the workbook open for the next exercise.

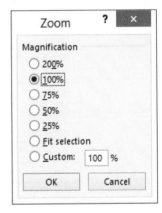

Figure 5-5

Zoom slider

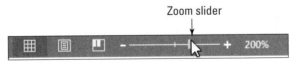

Figure 5-6

Moving the cell cursor

To type in a cell, you must first make it active by moving the cell cursor there. As shown earlier in Figure 5-4, the cell cursor is a thick green outline. You can move the cell cursor by pressing the arrow keys on the keyboard, by clicking the desired cell, or by using one of the Excel keyboard shortcuts. Table 5-1 provides some of the most common keyboard shortcuts for moving the cell cursor.

Table 5-1	Movement Shortcuts
Press This . . .	*To Move . . .*
Arrow keys	One cell in the direction of the arrow
Tab	One cell to the right
Shift+Tab	One cell to the left
Ctrl+arrow key	To the edge of the current data region (the first or last cell that isn't empty) in the direction of the arrow
End	To the cell in the lower-right corner of the window*
Ctrl+End	To the last cell in the worksheet, in the lowest used row of the rightmost used column
Home	To the beginning of the row containing the active cell
Ctrl+Home	To the beginning of the worksheet (cell A1)
Page Down	One screen down
Alt+Page Down	One screen to the right
Ctrl+Page Down	To the next sheet in the workbook
Page Up	One screen up
Alt+Page Up	One screen to the left
Ctrl+Page Up	To the previous sheet in the workbook

* This works only when the Scroll Lock key has been pressed on your keyboard to turn on the Scroll Lock function.

In the following exercise, you move the cell cursor in a worksheet.

Files needed: None

1. From any blank worksheet, such as the one from the preceding section, click cell C3 to move the cell cursor there.

2. **Press the right-arrow key to move to cell D3 and then press the down-arrow key to move to cell D4.**

3. **Press the Home key to move to cell A4.**

   Pressing Home moves the cursor to the beginning of the current row, which in this case is row 4.

4. **Press the Page Down key.**

The cell cursor moves to a cell that is one screenful down from the preceding position. Depending on the window size and screen resolution, the exact cell varies, but you are still in column A.

5. **Use the vertical scroll bar to scroll the display up so that cell A1 is visible.**

   Notice that the cell cursor does not move while you scroll. The Name box still displays the name of the cell you moved to previously.

6. **Press Ctrl+Home to move to cell A1.**

Leave the workbook open for the next exercise.

Selecting ranges

Range names are written with the upper-left cell address, a colon, and the lower-right cell address, as in the example A1:F3. Here A1:F3 means the range that begins in the upper-left corner with A1 and ends in the lower-right corner with F3.

When a range contains noncontiguous cells, the pieces are separated by commas, like this: B8:C14,D8:G14. The range name B8:C14,D8:G14 tells Excel to select the range from B8 through C14, plus the range from D8 through G14.

You can select a range by using either the keyboard or the mouse. Table 5-2 provides some of the most common range selection shortcuts.

LINGO

You might sometimes want to select a multicell **range** before you issue a command. For example, if you want to format all the text in a range a certain way, select that range and then issue the formatting command. Technically, a range can consist of a single cell; however, a range most commonly consists of multiple cells.

A range is usually **contiguous,** or all the cells are in a single rectangular block, but they don't have to be. You can also select **noncontiguous** cells in a range by holding down the Ctrl key while you select additional cells.

Table 5-2	Range Selection Shortcuts
Press This . . .	**To Extend the Selection To . . .**
Ctrl+Shift+arrow key	The last nonblank cell in the same column or row as the active cell; or if the next cell is blank, to the next nonblank cell
Ctrl+Shift+End	The last used cell on the worksheet (lower-right corner of the range containing data)
Ctrl+Shift+Home	The beginning of the worksheet (cell A1)
Ctrl+Shift+Page Down	The current and next sheet in the workbook
Ctrl+Shift+Page Up	The current and previous sheet in the workbook
Ctrl+spacebar	The entire column where the active cell is located
Shift+spacebar	The entire row where the active cell is located
Ctrl+A	The entire worksheet

In the following exercise, you practice selecting ranges.

Files needed: None

1. **On any blank worksheet, such as the one from the preceding exercise, click cell B2 to move the cell cursor there.**

2. **While holding down the Shift key, press the right-arrow key twice and the down-arrow key twice, extending the selection to the range B2:D4. (See Figure 5-7.)**

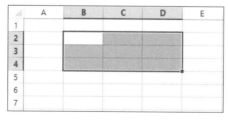

EXTRA INFO

The row and column headers turn bold when cells within them are selected.

Figure 5-7

3. **Hold down the Ctrl key and click cell E2 to add only that cell to the selected range.**

4. **While still holding down the Ctrl key, hold down the left mouse button and drag from cell E2 to cell E8 so that the range is B2:D4,E2:E8, as shown in Figure 5-8.**

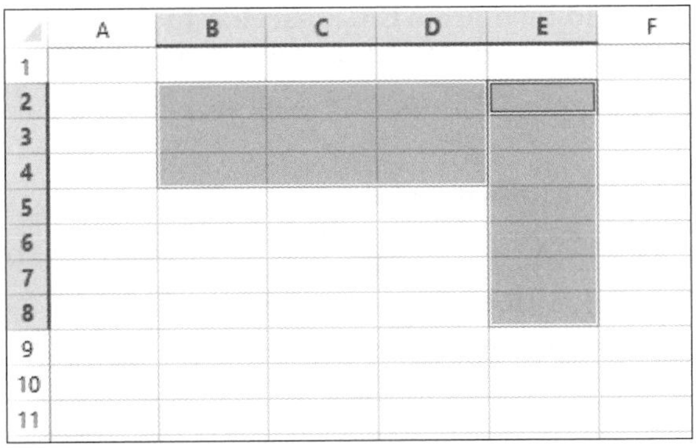

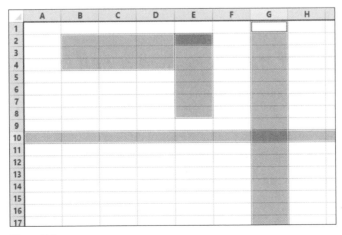

Figure 5-8

EXTRA INFO

Notice that the active cell is E2. Its name appears in the Name box, and the selection box appears around the cell in Figure 5-9. That's because cell E2 is the cell you most recently clicked — the starting point of the most recent addition to the range. This points out the difference between the active cell and a multicell range. When you type text, it goes into the active cell only. When you apply formatting or some other command, it applies to all the cells in the selected range.

5. **Hold down the Ctrl key and click row 10's row header (the number 10 at the left edge of the row) to add that entire row to the selected range.**
6. **Hold down the Ctrl key and click column G's column header (the letter G at the top of the column) to add that entire column to the selected range.**

   Your selection should look like Figure 5-9 at this point.
7. **Click any cell to cancel the range selection.**

   Only that cell you clicked is selected.

Figure 5-9

8. **Click in cell C4 and then press Ctrl+spacebar to select the entire column and then click any cell to cancel the range selection.**

9. **Click in cell C4 again and press Shift+spacebar to select the entire row.**

10. **Click the Select All button (labeled in Figure 5-10) in the upper-left corner of the spreadsheet grid — where the row numbers and the column letters intersect — to select the entire worksheet, as shown in Figure 5-10.**

Select All

Instead of clicking the Select All button, you can press Ctrl+Shift+spacebar or Ctrl+A.

11. **Click any cell to cancel the range selection.**

Leave the workbook open for the next exercise.

Figure 5-10

Typing and Editing Cell Content

Up to this point in the chapter, I've introduced you to some spreadsheet basics. Now it's time to actually do something: Enter some text and numbers into cells.

Typing text or numbers into a cell

To type in a cell, simply select the cell and begin typing. When you finish typing, you can leave the cell in any of these ways:

- ✔ **Press Enter:** Moves you to the next cell down.
- ✔ **Press Tab:** Moves you to the next cell to the right.
- ✔ **Press Shift+Tab:** Moves you to the next cell to the left.

   ✔ **Press an arrow key:** Moves you in the direction of the arrow.

   ✔ **Click in another cell:** Moves you to that cell.

If you make a mistake when editing, you can press the Esc key to cancel the edit before you leave the cell. If you need to undo an edit after you leave the cell, press Ctrl+Z or click the Undo button on the Quick Access toolbar.

In the following exercise, you enter text into a worksheet.

Files needed: None

   1. **On any blank worksheet, such as the one from the preceding exercise, click cell A1.**

   2. **Type** Mortgage Calculator **and press Enter.**

   3. **Click cell A1 again to reselect it and notice that the cell's content appears in the Formula bar, as shown in Figure 5-11.**

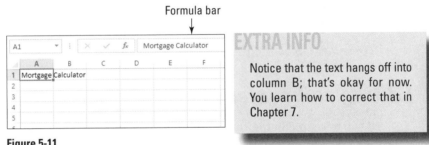

Formula bar

EXTRA INFO

Notice that the text hangs off into column B; that's okay for now. You learn how to correct that in Chapter 7.

Figure 5-11

   4. **Click cell A3, type** Loan Amount, **and press Tab so the cell cursor moves to cell B3.**

   5. **Type** 250000 **and press Enter so the cell cursor moves to cell A4.**

   6. **In cell A4, type** Interest, **and press Tab so the cell cursor moves to cell B4.**

   7. **Type** .05 **and press Enter so the cell cursor moves to cell A5.**

8. **Type** Periods **and press Tab so the cell cursor moves to cell B5.**

9. **Type** 360 **and press Enter so the cell cursor moves to cell A6.**

10. **Type** Payment **and press Enter so the cell cursor moves to cell A7.**

The worksheet looks like Figure 5-12 at this point.

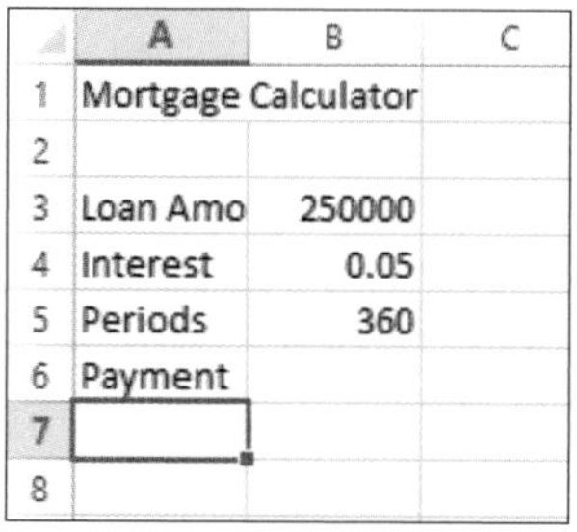

	A	B	C
1	Mortgage Calculator		
2			
3	Loan Amo	250000	
4	Interest	0.05	
5	Periods	360	
6	Payment		
7			
8			

Figure 5-12

11. **Save the file as** Lesson 5 Mortgage. xlsx.

Leave the workbook open for the next exercise.

LINGO

The **Formula bar** is the text area immediately above the worksheet grid, to the right of the Name box. This bar shows the active cell's contents. When the content is text or a number, what appears in the cell and what appears in the Formula bar are identical. When the content is a formula or function, the Formula bar shows the actual formula/function, and the cell itself shows the result of it.

Editing cell content

If you need to edit the content in a cell, you can

- Click the cell to select it, and then click the cell again to move the insertion point into it. Edit just as you would in any text program.

- Click the cell to select it and then type a new entry to replace the old one.

If you decide you don't want the text you typed in a particular cell, you can get rid of it in several ways:

- Select the cell; then right-click the cell and choose Clear Contents from the menu that appears.

- Select the cell; then choose Home⇨Clear⇨Clear Contents.

✔ Select the cell, press the spacebar, and then press Enter. This technically doesn't clear the cell's content, but it replaces it with a space.

✔ Select the cell and press the Delete key.

EXTRA INFO

Don't confuse the Delete key on the keyboard (which issues the Clear command) with the Delete command on the Ribbon. The Delete command doesn't *clear* the cell content; instead, it *removes* the entire cell. You find out more about deleting cells in the upcoming section, "Changing the Worksheet Structure."

And while I'm on the subject, don't confuse Clear with Cut, either. The Cut command works in conjunction with the Clipboard. Cut moves the content to the Clipboard, and you can then paste it somewhere else. Excel, however, differs from other applications in the way this command works: Using Cut doesn't immediately remove the content. Instead, Excel puts a flashing dotted box around the content and waits for you to reposition the cell cursor and issue the Paste command. If you do something else in the interim, the cut-and-paste operation is canceled, and the content that you cut remains in its original location. You learn more about cutting and pasting in the section "Copying and moving data between cells" later in this chapter.

In the following exercise, you edit text in a worksheet.

Files needed: `Lesson 5 Mortgage.xlsx`

1. **In the Lesson 5 Mortgage file from the preceding exercise, click in cell A3.**

2. **Click in the Formula bar to move the insertion point there, double-click the word *Loan* to select it, press the Delete key, and then press the Delete key again to delete the space before the remaining word *Amount*.**

3. **Press Enter to finalize the edit.**

   The cell cursor moves to cell A4.

4. **Click in B3, type** 300000, **and press Enter.**

   The new value replaces the old one.

5. **Right-click cell B4 and choose Clear Contents. Then type** 0.0635 **and press Enter.**

6. **Click cell B5 to select it and then double-click in B5 to move the insertion point there. Position the insertion point to the right of the 6, press the Backspace key twice, and type** 18, **changing the value in the cell to 180. Press Enter.**

The worksheet looks like Figure 5-13.

7. **Click the Save button on the Quick Access toolbar to save the changes to the workbook.**

◢	A	B
1	Mortgage Calculator	
2		
3	Amount	300000
4	Interest	0.0635
5	Periods	180
6	Payment	
7		

Figure 5-13

Leave the workbook open for the next exercise.

Copying and moving data between cells

When you're creating a spreadsheet, it's common not to get everything in the right cells on your first try. Fortunately, moving content between cells is easy.

Here are the two methods you can use to move content:

- ✔ **Mouse method:** Point at the dark outline around the selected range and then drag to the new location. If you want to copy rather than move, hold down the Ctrl key while you drag.

- ✔ **Clipboard method:** Choose Home⇨Cut or press Ctrl+X. (If you want to copy rather than simply move, choose Home⇨Copy rather than Cut or press Ctrl+C.) Then click the destination cell and choose Home⇨Paste or press Ctrl+V.

If you're moving or copying a multicell range with the Clipboard method, you can either select the same size and shape of range for the destination, or you can select a single cell, in which case the paste occurs with the selected cell in the upper-left corner.

In the following exercise, you move and copy cell content by using two methods.

Files needed: Lesson 5 Mortgage.xlsx

1. **In the Lesson 5 Mortgage file from the preceding exercise, select the range A1:B6.**

To do so, click A1, hold down the left mouse button, and drag to cell B6. Then release the mouse button.

2. Point at the border of the selection so the mouse pointer shows a four-headed arrow along with the arrow pointer.

3. Drag the selection to C1:D6.

   An outline shows the selection while you drag the selection, and a ScreenTip shows the cell address of the destination, as shown in Figure 5-14.

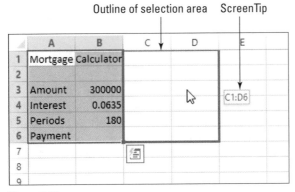

Figure 5-14

4. Click cell C1 and press Ctrl+X to cut.

   A dotted outline appears around C1.

5. Click cell B1 and press Ctrl+V to paste.

   The text moves from C1 to B1.

6. Select C3:D6 and then choose Home⇨Cut.

7. Click cell B3 and then choose Home⇨Paste.

   The completed worksheet is shown in Figure 5-15.

8. Click the Save button on the Quick Access toolbar to save the changes to the workbook.

Leave the workbook open for the next exercise.

	A	B	C	D
1		Mortgage Calculator		
2				
3		Amount	300000	
4		Interest	0.0635	
5		Periods	180	
6		Payment		
7				
8				

Figure 5-15

Using AutoFill to fill cell content

When you have a lot of data to enter and that data consists of some type of repeatable pattern or sequence, you can save time by using AutoFill. To use AutoFill, you select the cell or cells that already contain an example of what you want to fill and then drag the fill handle.

LINGO

The **fill handle** is the little black square in the lower-right corner of the selected cell or range.

Depending on how you use it, AutoFill can either fill the same value into every cell in the target area, or it can fill in a sequence (such as days of the month, days of the week, or a numeric sequence such as 2, 4, 6, 8). Here are the general rules for how it works:

- ✔ When AutoFill recognizes the selected text as a member of one of its preset lists, such as days of the week or months of the year, it automatically increments those. For example, if the selected cell contains August, AutoFill places September in the next adjacent cell.

- ✔ When AutoFill doesn't recognize the selected text, it fills the chosen cell with a duplicate of the selected text.

- ✔ When AutoFill is used on a single cell containing a number, it fills with a duplicate of the number.

- ✔ When AutoFill is used on a range of two or more cells containing numbers, AutoFill attempts to determine the interval between them and continues filling using that same pattern. For example, if the two selected cells contain 2 and 4, the next adjacent cell would be filled with 6.

In the following exercise, you AutoFill cell content using two methods.

Files needed: Lesson 5 Mortgage.xlsx

1. **In the Lesson 5 Mortgage file from the preceding exercise, select cell A8 and type** Amortization Table**.**

2. **Type the following:**

   a. *In cell A10, type* **Date**.

   b. *In cell B10, type* **Pmt#**.

   c. *In cell A11, type* **January 2015**. *(Note that Excel automatically changes it to Jan-15.)*

   d. *In cell B11, type* **1**.

3. **Click cell A11 and move the mouse pointer over the fill handle.**

   The mouse pointer becomes a black crosshair, as shown in Figure 5-16.

Crosshair mouse pointer hovering over the fill handle

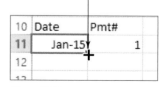

Figure 5-16

4. **Drag the fill handle down to cell A22.**

   The first year of dates fill in the cells, as shown in Figure 5-17.

5. **Click cell B11 and drag the fill handle down to C22. The same number fills all the cells. That's not what you want for this exercise, so press Ctrl+Z to undo the fill.**

6. **Click cell B12, and type 2. Select B11:B12 and then drag the fill handle down to cell B22.**

   Figure 5-18 shows the completed series.

7. **Select A22:B22 and drag the fill handle down to B190.**

   Both series are filled in, down to row 190, where the date is December 2029 and the payment number is 180.

   Here you do Step 7 because the number of periods for this loan is 180 (see cell C5), so the number of payments should be 180 in the amortization table.

8. **Press Ctrl+Home to return to the top of the worksheet.**

9. **Click the Save button on the Quick Access toolbar to save the changes to the workbook.**

10. **Choose File⇨Close to close the workbook.**

Leave Excel open for the next exercise.

Using Flash Fill to extract content

New in Excel 2013, the Flash Fill feature enables you to extract data from adjacent columns intelligently by analyzing the patterns in that data. For example, suppose you have a list of e-mail addresses in one column, and you would like the usernames (that is, the text before the @ sign) from each e-mail address to appear in an adjacent column. You would extract the first few yourself by manually typing the entries into the adjacent column, and then you would use Flash Fill to follow your example to extract the others.

	A	B	C
9			
10	Date	Pmt#	
11	Jan-15		1
12	Feb-15		
13	Mar-15		
14	Apr-15		
15	May-15		
16	Jun-15		
17	Jul-15		
18	Aug-15		
19	Sep-15		
20	Oct-15		
21	Nov-15		
22	Dec-15		
23			
24			

Fill handle dragged down to cell A22.

Figure 5-17

	A	B	C
9			
10	Date	Pmt#	
11	Jan-15	1	
12	Feb-15	2	
13	Mar-15	3	
14	Apr-15	4	
15	May-15	5	
16	Jun-15	6	
17	Jul-15	7	
18	Aug-15	8	
19	Sep-15	9	
20	Oct-15	10	
21	Nov-15	11	
22	Dec-15	12	
23			
24			

Fill handle dragged down to cell B22.

Figure 5-18

In the following exercise, you use Flash Fill to extract first and last names into separate columns. This exercise also demonstrates how to open files in Excel and save them with different names, a skill you use throughout this book.

Files needed: `Lesson 5 Names.xlsx`

1. **Open the** `Lesson 5 Names.xlsx` **file and save it as** `Lesson 5 Roster.xlsx`.

2. **In cell B3, type** Tom, **and in cell C3, type** Bailey.

3. **In cell B4, type** Latasha, **and in cell C4, type** Newland.

   See Figure 5-19 for the result.

4. **Click cell B5.**

   For Flash Fill to work, the active cell must be in the column that you want to fill.

5. **On the Home tab, in the Editing group, click the Fill button to open a menu.**

6. **Choose Flash Fill, as shown in Figure 5-20.**

   The first names fill into column B for the remaining entries on the list.

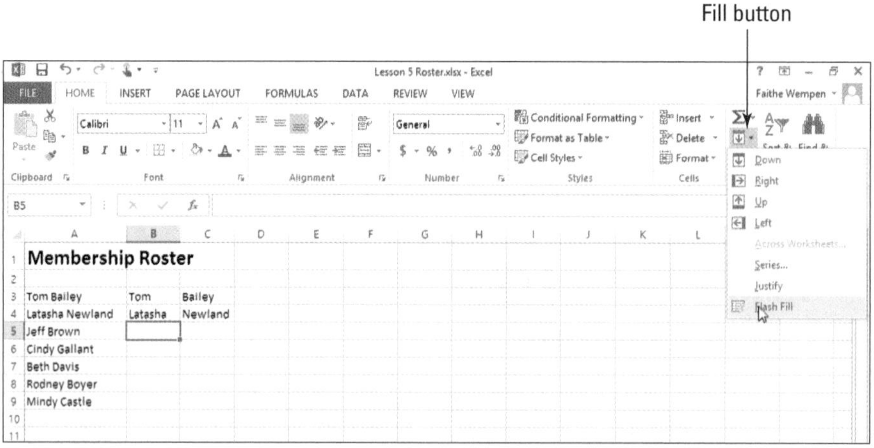

Figure 5-19

Fill button

Figure 5-20

7. **Click cell C5.**

8. **On the Home tab, in the Editing group, click the Fill button again, and then choose Flash Fill again.**

The last names fill into column C for the remaining entries on the list, as shown in Figure 5-21.

9. **Choose File⇨Close to close the workbook. When prompted to save your changes, click Save.**

Leave Excel open for the next exercise.

Figure 5-21

Changing the Worksheet Structure

Even if you're a careful planner, you'll likely decide that you want to change your worksheet's structure. Maybe you want data in a different column, or certain rows turn out to be unnecessary. Excel makes it easy to insert and delete rows and columns to deal with these kinds of changes.

Inserting and deleting rows and columns

When you insert a new row or column, the existing ones move to make room for it. You can insert multiple rows or columns at once by selecting multiple ones before issuing the Insert command. (There's no limit on the number you can insert at once!) Similarly, you can delete multiple rows or columns by selecting them before using the Delete command.

In the following exercise, you insert and delete rows and columns.

Files needed: `Lesson 5 Mortgage.xlsx`

1. **Reopen the Lesson 5 Mortgage file you created earlier in the chapter and click anywhere in column A.**

2. **On the Home tab, click the down arrow on the Insert button and choose Insert Sheet Columns, as shown in Figure 5-22.**

   A new column is placed to the left of the selected column.

Figure 5-22

3. **Click the column header for column A to select the entire column and then choose Home⇨Delete.**

The entire column is deleted.

4. **Select rows 7 and 8 by dragging across their row headers and then choose Home⇨Insert.**

Two new rows are inserted.

5. **Click any cell in row 7; then, from the Home tab, click the down arrow on the Delete button and choose Delete Sheet Rows.**

Figure 5-23 shows the worksheet after the insertions and deletions.

Save the changes and leave the workbook open for the next exercise.

	A	B	C	D	E
1		Mortgage Calculator			
2					
3		Amount	30000		
4		Interest	0.0635		
5		Periods	180		
6		Payment			
7					
8					
9	Amortization Table				
10					
11	Date	Pmt#			
12	Jan-15	1			
13	Feb-15	2			
14	Mar-15	3			
15	Apr-15	4			
16	May-15	5			
17	Jun-15	6			
18	Jul-15	7			
19	Aug-15	8			
20	Sep-15	9			
21	Oct-15	10			
22	Nov-15	11			
23	Dec-15	12			
24					

Sheet1 ⊕

Figure 5-23

Inserting and deleting cells and ranges

You can also insert and delete individual cells or even ranges that don't neatly correspond to entire rows or columns. When you do so, the surrounding cells shift. In the case of an insertion, cells move down or to the right of the area where the new cells are being inserted. In the case of a deletion, cells move up or to the left to fill in the voided space.

Deleting a cell is different from clearing a cell's content, and this becomes apparent when you start working with individual cells and ranges. When you clear the content, the cell itself remains. When you delete the cell itself, the adjacent cells shift.

When shifting cells, Excel is smart enough that it tries to guess which direction you want existing content to move when you insert or delete cells. If you have content immediately to the right of a deleted cell, for example, Excel shifts it left. If you have content immediately below the deleted cell, Excel shifts it up. You can still override that, though, as needed.

In the following exercise, you insert and delete cells.

Files needed: `Lesson 5 Mortgage.xlsx`

1. **In the Lesson 5 Mortgage file from the preceding exercise, select A1:A6 and then choose Home⇨Delete.**

   Excel guesses that you want to move the existing content to the left, and it does so.

2. **Click cell A1, and choose Home⇨Insert.**

   Excel guesses that you want to move the existing content down, which is incorrect. The content in column B is off by one row, as shown in see Figure 5-24.

3. **Press Ctrl+Z to undo the insertion; then from the Home tab, click the down arrow to the right of the Insert button and choose Insert Cells.**

   The Insert dialog box opens, as shown in Figure 5-25.

4. **Select Shift Cells Right and then click OK.**

   A new cell A1 is inserted, and the previous A1 content moves into B1.

5. **Save the changes to the workbook.**

Leave the workbook open for the next exercise.

Column A is off one row in relation to column B.

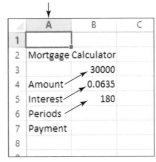

Figure 5-24

Figure 5-25

Working with Worksheets

Each new workbook starts with one sheet — Sheet1. (Not the most interesting name, but you can change it.) You can add or delete worksheets, rearrange the worksheet tabs, and apply different colors to the tabs to help differentiate them from one another, or to create logical groups of tabs.

In the following exercise, you insert, rename, and delete worksheets, and you change a tab's color.

Files needed: `Lesson 5 Mortgage.xlsx`

1. **In the Lesson 5 Mortgage file from the preceding exercise, double-click the Sheet1 worksheet tab to move the insertion point into it.**

2. **Type** Calculator **and press Enter.**

   The new name replaces the old one.

3. Right-click the worksheet tab, choose Tab Color, and click the Red standard color, as shown in Figure 5-26.

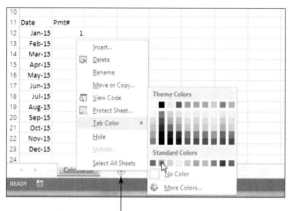

New Sheet button

Figure 5-26

4. Right-click the Calculator tab and choose Insert.

The Insert dialog box opens, as shown in Figure 5-27.

5. Click Worksheet and then click OK.

A new sheet named Sheet1 is inserted.

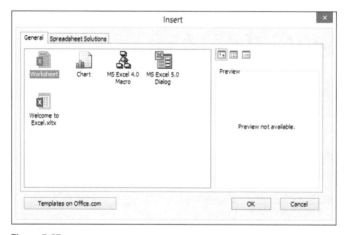

Figure 5-27

6. **Click the New Sheet button to the right of the existing tabs.**

   The New Sheet button looks like a plus sign inside a circle. (Refer to Figure 5-26.) Another new sheet named Sheet2 is inserted.

7. **Click the Sheet1 tab and then right-click it and choose Delete.**

   The sheet is deleted.

8. **Double-click the Sheet2 tab, type** Amortization, **and press Enter.**

9. **Double-click the tab on the Amortization sheet, type** Chart, **and press Enter.**

   The two tabs in the workbook are named and arranged as shown in Figure 5-28.

10. **Save the changes to the workbook.**

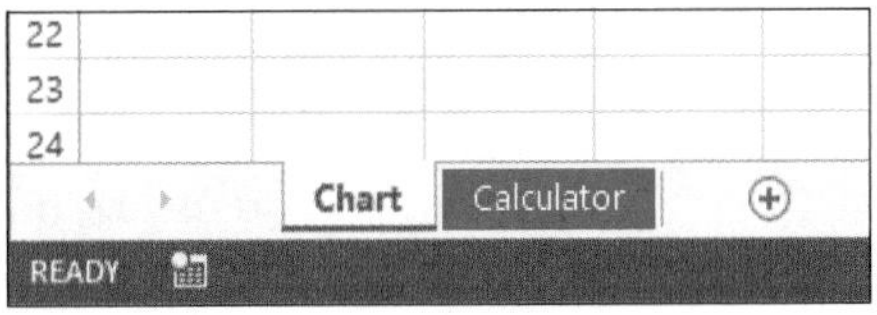

Close the workbook and exit Excel.

Figure 5-28

Summing Up

Excel is an excellent choice for storing data in rows and columns. In this chapter, you learned how to navigate the Excel interface, including entering and editing content in cells, inserting and deleting cells, and selecting ranges. Here's a quick review:

- ✔ Excel data files are called workbooks. Each workbook can hold multiple worksheets. Each worksheet has a tab at the bottom of the Excel window for quick access to it.

- ✔ Each cell has a cell address consisting of the column letter and row number, such as A1.

- ✔ The active cell is indicated by the cell cursor, a thick green outline. You can move the cell cursor with the mouse or the keyboard arrow keys. When you type text, it is entered into the active cell.

- ✔ A range is a selection that consists of one or more cells. (It's usually more than one.) A contiguous range consists of a single rectangular block of cells.

- ✔ To clear cell contents, select the cell and press the Delete key or choose Home⇨Clear⇨Cell Contents.

✔ To move data between cells, select the cells and then drag the outline around them, or use the Cut and Paste commands. To copy data, hold down Ctrl and drag the cells, or you can use the Copy and Paste commands.

✔ To fill data from the selected range to adjacent cells, drag the fill handle, which is the green rectangle in the lower-right corner of the selected range.

✔ To use Flash Fill to intelligently fill columns, complete a few examples and then use the Home⇨Fill⇨Flash Fill command.

✔ To insert a row or column, from the Home tab, open the Insert button's menu and choose either Insert Sheet Rows or Insert Sheet Columns, respectively.

✔ When you insert individual cells, the existing content moves over to make room. You can choose which direction it needs to move.

✔ To insert a new sheet, right-click an existing sheet and choose Insert. To delete a sheet, right-click its tab and choose Delete.

✔ To rename a sheet, double-click its tab name and type a new name.

Try-it-yourself lab

Complete the following exercise for extra practice with Excel:

1. **Start Excel, and start a new blank workbook.**

2. **In cell A1, type** Membership List.

3. **In row 3, enter the column headings you would need to store information about the members of an organization you're part of.**

   For example, you might have **First Name**, **Last Name**, and **Phone**.

4. **Starting in row 4, enter the information about the members of the organization.**

   If the organization has many members, you do not have to enter every member in the list.

5. **Insert a new column between two of the existing columns.**

   For example, you could enter a MI column (for Middle Initial) between First and Last.

6. **Change the name of the worksheet tab to Membership.**

7. **Save your workbook as** Lesson 5 Lab.xlsx.

8. **Close your workbook and then close Excel.**

Know this tech talk

active cell: The cell in which new content that you type will be placed.

cell address: The column letter and row number of a cell, such as A1.

cell cursor: The thick green border surrounding the active cell.

cell: The intersection of a row and column in a spreadsheet.

contiguous: A range in which all the selected cells are adjacent to one another in a rectangular block.

fill handle: The small square handle in the lower-right corner of a selected range.

Flash Fill: A new feature in Excel 2013 that intelligently fills columns with data based on the example of data in adjacent cells.

Formula bar: The bar above the worksheet grid where the formula appears from the selected cell.

Name box: The box to the left of the Formula bar that lists the active cell's cell address.

range: One or more selected cells.

spreadsheet: A grid of rows and columns in which you can store data.

workbook: An Excel data file.

worksheet: The Excel term for a spreadsheet.

worksheet tabs: Tabs at the bottom of a workbook for each worksheet that it contains.

Chapter 6
Creating Formulas and Functions in Excel

✔ Formulas *perform math calculations* on fixed numbers or on cell contents.

✔ The order of precedence *settles any uncertainties* about which math operations execute first.

✔ Cell references that include sheet names can *reference cells on other sheets.*

✔ Relative cell referencing *allows cell references to automatically update when copied.* Absolute cell referencing *keeps a cell reference fixed when copied to other locations.*

✔ Functions perform *complex math operations on cell content.*

✔ Named ranges *substitute friendly, easy-to-understand words* for plain cell and range addresses.

✔ The new Quick Analysis feature *displays formatting, charts, tables, and more that aid analysis.*

1. **What character must all formulas and functions start with?**

Find out on page 205

2. **Which comes first in a formula: exponentiation or division?**

Find out on page 206

3. **How do you reference a cell on a different worksheet?**

Find out on page 209

4. **What does a dollar sign mean in a cell address?**

Find out on page 213

5. **How do you refer to a range in a function?**

Find out on page 215

6. **How can you use a function if you don't know its exact name?**

Find out on page 218

7. **What function inserts today's date?**

Find out on page 221

8. **How do you create a name to refer to a range of cells?**

Find out on page 223

9. **What tool enables you to color cells based on the cells' values?**

Find out on page 226

ath. Excel is really good at it, and it's what makes Excel more than just data storage. Even if you hated math in school, you might still like Excel because it does the math for you.

In Excel, you can write math formulas that perform calculations on the values in various cells, and then, if those values change later, you can see the formula results update automatically. You can also use built-in functions to handle more complex math activities than you might be able to set up yourself with formulas. That capability makes it possible to build complex worksheets that calculate loan rates and payments, keep track of your bank accounts, and much more.

In this chapter, I show you how to construct formulas and functions in Excel, how to move and copy formulas and functions (there's a trick to it), and how to use functions to create handy financial spreadsheets.

Finding Out About Formulas

In Excel, formulas are different from regular text in two ways:

- Formulas begin with an equal sign, like this: =2+2.

- Formulas don't contain text (except for function names and cell references). They contain only symbols that are allowed in math formulas, such as parentheses, commas, and decimal points.

Writing formulas that calculate

Excel formulas can do everything that a basic calculator can do, so if you're in a hurry and don't want to pull up the Windows Calculator application, you can enter a formula in Excel to get a quick result. Experimenting with this type of formula is a great way to get accustomed to formulas in general.

TIP

Excel also has an advantage over some basic calculators (including the one in Windows): It easily does exponentiation. For example, if you want to calculate 5 to the 8th power, you would write it in Excel as $=5\wedge8$.

REMEMBER

Just as in basic math, formulas are calculated by an order of precedence. Table 6-1 lists the order.

Table 6-1	Order of Precedence in a Formula	
Order	*Item*	*Example*
1	Anything in parentheses	$=2*(2+1)$
2	Exponentiation	$=2\wedge3$
3	Multiplication and division	$=1+2*2$
4	Addition and subtraction	$=10-4$

In the following exercise, you enter some formulas that perform simple math calculations.

Files needed: None

1. **Launch Excel if needed and open a new blank workbook. If you already have another workbook open, press Ctrl+N to create a new workbook.**

2. **Click cell A1, type** =2+2, **and press Enter.**

   The result of the formula appears in cell A1.

3. **Click cell A1 again to move the cell cursor back to it; then look in the Formula bar.**

   Notice that the formula you entered appears there, as shown in Figure 6-1.

Formula bar shows the formula.

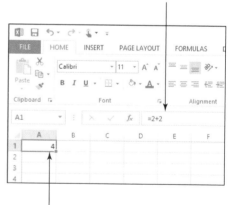

Cell shows the result of the formula.

Figure 6-1

4. **Click cell A2, type** =2+4*3, **and press Enter.**

The result of the formula appears in cell A2.

In this case, because of the order of operations (see Table 6-1), the multiplication was done first (4 times 3 equals 12), and then 2 was added for a total of 14.

5. **Press the up-arrow key once to move the cell cursor back to A2 and examine the formula in the formula bar. (See Figure 6-2.)**

6. **In cell A3, type** =(2+4)*3 **and press Enter.**

In this case, the parentheses forced the addition to occur first (2 plus 4 equals 6), and then 3 was multiplied for a total of 18.

7. **Press the up-arrow key once to move the cell cursor back to A3 and then note the formula shown in Figure 6-3.**

8. **Close the workbook without saving changes to it.**

Leave Excel open for the next exercise.

Writing formulas that reference cells

One of Excel's best features is that it can reference cells in formulas. When a cell is referenced in a formula, whatever value it contains is used in the formula. When the value changes, the result of the formula changes too.

Formula bar shows the formula.

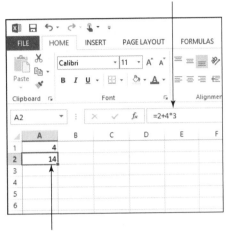

Cell shows the result of the formula.

Figure 6-2

Formula bar shows the formula.

Cell shows the result of the formula.

Figure 6-3

In the following exercise, you enter some formulas that contain cell references.

Files needed: `Lesson 6 Budget.xlsx`

1. **Open** `Lesson 6 Budget.xlsx` **from the data files for this chapter and save it as** `Lesson 6 Budget Calculations.xlsx`.

2. **In cell E6, type** =E4.

   The value shown in E4 is repeated in cell E6.

   In cell E6, you could have just as easily retyped the value from E4, but this way if the value in E4 changes, the value in E6 also changes.

3. **In cell B7, type** =B4+B5+B6 **so that B7 shows $1,425; in cell B15, type** =B10+B11+B12+B13+B14 **so that B15 shows $975.**

   Typing each cell reference is a lot of work. Later in this chapter in the section "Introducing Functions," you see how to use the SUM function to dramatically cut down on the typing required to sum the values in many cells at once.

4. **In cell B17, type** =B7+B15 **so that B17 shows $2,400; in cell E9, type** =E6–B17 **so that E9 shows –$578. (See Figure 6-4.)**

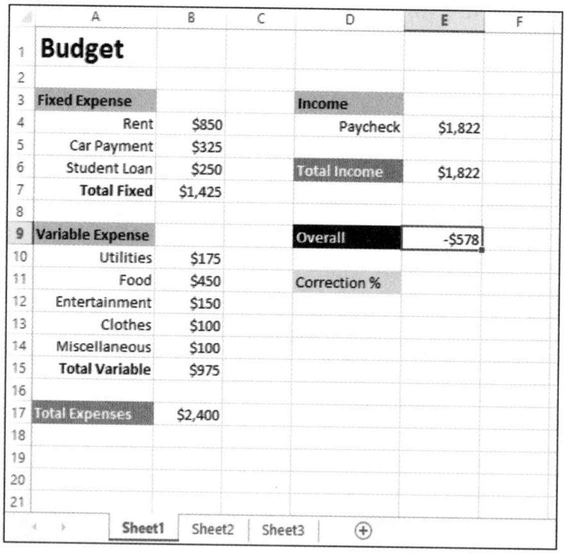

	A	B	C	D	E	F
1	**Budget**					
2						
3	**Fixed Expense**			**Income**		
4	Rent	$850		Paycheck	$1,822	
5	Car Payment	$325				
6	Student Loan	$250		**Total Income**	$1,822	
7	**Total Fixed**	$1,425				
8						
9	**Variable Expense**			**Overall**	-$578	
10	Utilities	$175				
11	Food	$450		**Correction %**		
12	Entertainment	$150				
13	Clothes	$100				
14	Miscellaneous	$100				
15	**Total Variable**	$975				
16						
17	**Total Expenses**	$2,400				
18						
19						
20						
21						

Sheet1 Sheet2 Sheet3 ⊕

Figure 6-4

5. **In cell E11, type** =E9/B17.

The value –24.08% appears in E11.

6. **Save and close the workbook.**

Leave Excel open for the next exercise.

TIP

This worksheet was set up to use the appropriate formatting for each cell so that the formulas make sense. You learn to do this in Chapter 7.

Referencing a cell on another sheet

When referring to a cell on the same sheet, you can simply use its column and row: A1, B1, and so on. However, when referring to a cell on a different sheet, you have to include the sheet name in the formula.

The syntax for doing this is to list the sheet name, followed by an exclamation point, followed by the cell reference, like this:

```
=Sheet1!A2
```

In the following exercise, you practice using this notation by creating some multisheet formulas.

Files needed: Lesson 6 Sheets. xlsx

1. **Open** Lesson 6 Sheets.xlsx **from the data files for this chapter and save it as** Lesson 6 Budget Sheets.xlsx.

TIP

This workbook has the same data that you worked with in the preceding exercise, but the data is split into multiple worksheets.

2. **Click the workbook's Expenses tab and look at the data there.**

When calculating the overall budget amount in Step 4, you will refer to cell B15. (See Figure 6-5.)

	A	B	C	D
1	**Fixed Expense**			
2	Rent	$850		
3	Car Payment	$325		
4	Student Loan	$250		
5	**Total Fixed**	$1,425		
6				
7	**Variable Expense**			
8	Utilities	$175		
9	Food	$450		
10	Entertainment	$150		
11	Clothes	$100		
12	Miscellaneous	$100		
13	**Total Variable**	$975		
14				
15	**Total Expenses**	$2,400		
16				
17				
18				

Figure 6-5

3. **Click the workbook's Income tab and look at the data there.**

   In Step 4, you will refer to cell B4. (See Figure 6-6.)

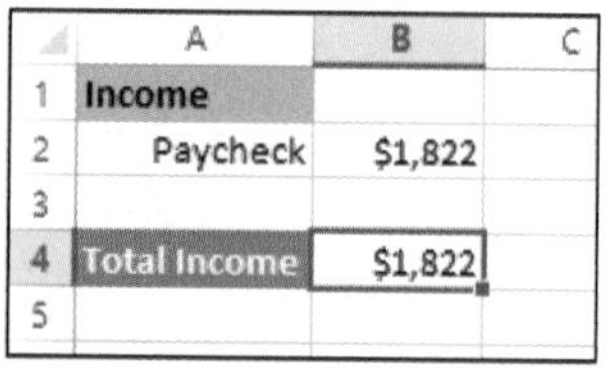

4. **Click the workbook's Overall tab, click in cell B3, and type** =Income!B4-Expenses!B15.

   Cell B3 displays –$578.

   If you hadn't looked at the cells to reference on the other tabs, you might have been at a loss as to what to type when constructing the formula in this step.

   You can use another method to refer to cells when writing a formula. The next steps practice that method.

5. **In cell B5, type** =B3/.

6. **Click the Expenses tab, click cell B15, and press Enter.**

   The display jumps back to the Overall tab and completes the formula, as shown in Figure 6-7.

7. **Save the changes to the workbook and close it.**

Leave Excel open for the next exercise.

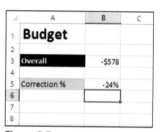

Figure 6-6

Figure 6-7

Moving and Copying Formulas

In Chapter 5, you learn how to move and copy text and numbers between cells, but when it comes to copying formulas, beware of a few gotchas. The following sections explain relative and absolute referencing in formulas and how you can use them to get the results you want when you copy.

Copying formulas with relative referencing

When you move or copy a formula, Excel automatically changes the cell references to work with the new location. That's because, by default, cell references in formulas are *relative references.* For example, in Figure 6-8, suppose you wanted to copy the formula from B5 into C5. The new formula in C5 should refer to values in column C, not to column B; otherwise the formula wouldn't make much sense. So, when B5's formula is copied to C5, it becomes =C3+C4 there.

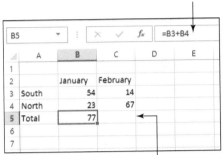

Formula in B5 is relative.

When formula is copied from B5 to C5,
it becomes =C3+C4.

Figure 6-8

LINGO

A **relative reference** is a cell reference that changes if copied to another cell.

In this exercise, you copy formulas using relative referencing (the default) and examine the results.

Files needed: `Lesson 6 Appliance.xlsx`

1. **Open** `Lesson 6 Appliance.xlsx` **from the data files for this chapter and save it as** `Lesson 6 Appliance Sales.xlsx`.

2. **On Sheet1, click cell B13 and examine the formula in the Formula bar, which contains references to values in column B. (See Figure 6-9.)**

B13		fx	=B4+B5+B6+B7+B8+B9+B10+B11					
	A	B	C	D	E	F	G	H
1		**Appliance Sales**						
2								
3	Item	Q1	Q2	Q3	Q4	Total	Bonus	
4	Blenders	90	49	81	76	296		
5	Dishwashers	99	80	38	91			
6	Ranges	66	91	59	42			
7	Refrigerators	95	69	39	60			
8	Mixers	71	42	75	75			
9	Toasters	34	55	44	75			
10	Bread Makers	87	74	73	63			
11	Food Processors	77	86	42	74			
12								
13	Total	619						
14								
15	Sales Bonus Per Item	$10						
16								

Figure 6-9

3. **Press Ctrl+C to copy the formula to the Clipboard (a dotted outline appears around B13) and then select C13:E13 and press Ctrl+V to paste the formula into those cells. Then press Enter.**

4. **Click cell C13 and examine the formula in the Formula bar, which contains references to values in column C. (See Figure 6-10.)**

C13	▾	:	✕	✓	*fx*	=C4+C5+C6+C7+C8+C9+C10+C11			

	A	B	C	D	E	F	G	H
1			**Appliance Sales**					
2								
3	Item	Q1	Q2	Q3	Q4	Total	Bonus	
4	Blenders	90	49	81	76	296		
5	Dishwashers	99	80	38	91			
6	Ranges	66	91	59	42			
7	Refrigerators	95	69	39	60			
8	Mixers	71	42	75	75			
9	Toasters	34	55	44	75			
10	Bread Makers	87	74	73	63			
11	Food Processors	77	86	42	74			
12								
13	Total	619	546	451	556			
14								
15	Sales Bonus Per Item	$10						
16								

Figure 6-10

5. **Click cell F4 and then drag the fill handle down to F11.**

The formula from F4 is copied into that range, and the row numbers change to refer to the new positions, as shown in Figure 6-11.

F4	▾	:	✕	✓	*fx*	=B4+C4+D4+E4	

	A	B	C	D	E	F	G
1			**Appliance Sales**				
2							
3	Item	Q1	Q2	Q3	Q4	Total	Bonus
4	Blenders	90	49	81	76	296	
5	Dishwashers	99	80	38	91	308	
6	Ranges	66	91	59	42	258	
7	Refrigerators	95	69	39	60	263	
8	Mixers	71	42	75	75	263	
9	Toasters	34	55	44	75	208	
10	Bread Makers	87	74	73	63	297	
11	Food Processors	77	86	42	74	279	
12							
13	Total	619	546	451	556		
14							
15	Sales Bonus Per Item	$10					
16							

Figure 6-11

6. **Click each of the cells in the F column and examine their formulas in the Formula bar.**

Note that each one uses the correct row number.

7. **Save the changes to the workbook.**

Leave the workbook open for the next exercise.

Copying formulas with absolute referencing

You might not always want the cell references in a formula to change when you move or copy it. In other words, you want an *absolute reference* to that cell. To make a reference absolute, you add dollar signs before the column letter and before the row number. So, for example, an absolute reference to cell C1 would be =C1.

LINGO

An **absolute reference** is a cell reference that doesn't change when copied to another cell. You can mix relative and absolute references in the same formula. When you do, the result is a **mixed reference**.

If you want to lock down only one dimension of the cell reference, you can place a dollar sign before only the column or only the row. For example, =$C1 would make only the column letter fixed, and =C$1 would make only the row number fixed.

In this exercise, you create absolute references and copy formulas that contain them.

Files needed: Lesson 6 Appliance Sales.xlsx *from the preceding exercise*

1. **In** Lesson 6 Appliance Sales.xlsx, **click cell G4 and type** =F4*B15. **Press Enter.**

The formula multiplies cell F4 by cell B15, referring to F4 with a relative reference and referring to B15 with an absolute reference.

2. **Click cell G4 again and then drag the fill handle down to G11, copying the formula to that range.**

3. **Click cell G11 and examine its formula in the Formula bar, as shown in Figure 6-12.**

G11	▼	:	✕	✓	f_x	=F11*B15		

⊿	A	B	C	D	E	F	G	H
1			Appliance Sales					
2								
3	Item	Q1	Q2	Q3	Q4	Total	Bonus	
4	Blenders	90	49	81	76	296	$2,960	
5	Dishwashers	99	80	38	91	308	$3,080	
6	Ranges	66	91	59	42	258	$2,580	
7	Refrigerators	95	69	39	60	263	$2,630	
8	Mixers	71	42	75	75	263	$2,630	
9	Toasters	34	55	44	75	208	$2,080	
10	Bread Makers	87	74	73	63	297	$2,970	
11	Food Processors	77	86	42	74	279	$2,790	
12								
13	Total	619	546	451	556			
14								
15	Sales Bonus Per Item	$10						

Figure 6-12

Notice that the reference to column F is updated to show cell F11, but the reference to cell B15 has remained fixed.

4. **Select F11:G11 and then press Ctrl+C to copy; select F13:G13 and then press Ctrl+V to paste. Then press Enter.**

5. **Click cell G13 and examine the formula in the Formula bar to confirm it is correct.**

You could have dragged the fill handle all the way down to cell G13 in Step 2 so you wouldn't have to copy and paste the formula into G13 in Step 4. However, there still would have been another step because you would have had an extraneous function in cell G12 that you would've had to delete.

6. **Save the changes to the workbook.**

Leave the workbook open for the next exercise.

Introducing Functions

Sometimes, as you've seen in earlier exercises in this chapter, it's awkward or lengthy to write a formula to perform a calculation. For example, suppose you want to sum the values in cells A1 through A10. To express that as a formula, you'd have to write each cell reference individually, like this:

```
=A1+A2+A3+A4+A5+A6+A7+A8+A9+A10
```

With a function, you can represent a range with the upper-left corner's cell reference, a colon, and the lower-right corner's cell reference. In the case of A1:A10, there is only one column, so the upper-left corner is cell A1, and the lower-right corner is cell A10.

LINGO

In Excel, a **function** refers to a certain math calculation. Functions can greatly reduce the amount of typing you have to do to create a particular result. For example, instead of using the =A1+A2+A3+A4+A5+A6+A7+A8+A9+A10 formula, you could use the SUM function like this: =SUM(A1:A10).

An **argument** is a placeholder for a number, text string, or cell reference. For example, the SUM function requires at least one argument: a range of cells. So, in the preceding example, A1:A10 is the argument. The arguments for a function are enclosed in a set of parentheses.

The **syntax** is the sequence of arguments for a function. When there are multiple arguments in the syntax, they are separated by commas.

REMEMBER

Range references cannot be used in simple formulas — only in functions. For example, =A6:A9 would be invalid as a formula because no math operation is specified in it. You can't insert math operators within a range. To use ranges in a calculation, you must use a function.

Each function has one or more arguments, along with its own rules about how many required and optional arguments there are and what they represent. You don't have to memorize the sequence of arguments (the *syntax*) for each function; Excel asks you for them. Excel can even suggest a function to use for a certain situation if you aren't sure what you need.

Using the SUM function

The SUM function is by far the most popular function; it sums (that is, adds) a data range consisting of one or more cells, like this:

```
=SUM(D12:D15)
```

You don't *have* to use a range in a SUM function; you can specify the individual cell addresses if you want. Separate them by commas, like this:

```
=SUM(D12, D13, D14, D15)
```

If the data range is not a contiguous block, you need to specify the individual cells that are outside the block. The main block is one argument, and each individual other cell is an additional argument, like this:

```
=SUM(D12:D15, E22)
```

In this exercise, you replace some formulas with equivalent functions.

Files needed: `Lesson 6 Appliance Sales.xlsx` *from the preceding exercise*

1. **In `Lesson 6 Appliance Sales.xlsx`, click cell B13 and type =SUM(B4:B11). Then press Enter.**

   This function replaces the formula that was previously there. The value in the cell is 619.

2. **Enter a function using another method:**

   a. *Click cell C13 and type* ***=SUM(***.

   b. *Drag across the range C4:C11 to select it and then press Enter to enter that range into the function in cell C13.*

   The value in the cell is 546.

3. **Use the AutoSum button to enter a function:**

   a. *Click cell D13 and then choose Formulas⇨AutoSum, as shown in Figure 6-13.*

   A dotted outline appears around B13:C13. However, this is not the range you want to sum.

   b. *Drag across D4:D11 to select that range and then press Enter.*

   The value in D13 is 451.

   c. *Click cell D13 and drag the fill handle to cell F13, copying the function to the adjacent cells.*

   Figure 6-14 shows the sheet when finished.

   Note that the sheet doesn't look any different than before; the functions perform the exact same calculations that the formulas did previously.

4. **Save the changes to the workbook.**

Leave the workbook open for the next exercise.

AutoSum

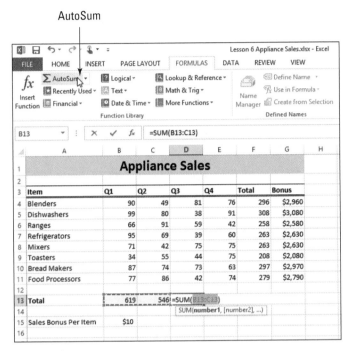

Figure 6-13

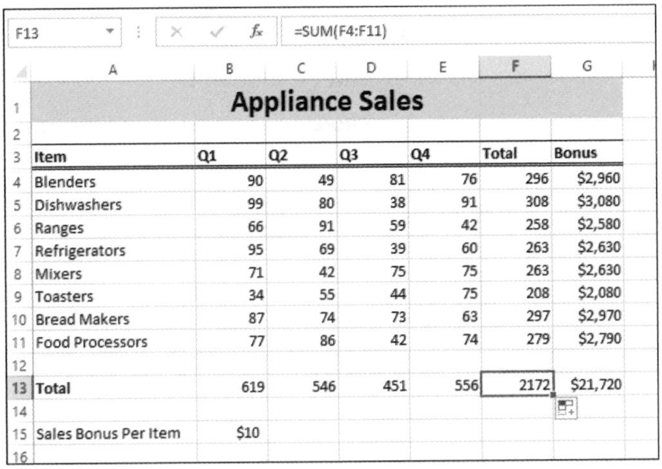

Figure 6-14

Inserting a function

Typing a function and its arguments directly into a cell works fine if you happen to know the function you want and its arguments. Many times, though, you may not know these details. In those cases, the Insert Function feature can help you.

Insert Function enables you to pick a function from a list based on descriptive keywords. After you make your selection, it provides fill-in-the-blank prompts for the arguments.

In this exercise, you find an appropriate function and use Insert Function to create it.

Files needed: Lesson 6 Appliance Sales.xlsx *from the preceding exercise*

1. **In** Lesson 6 Appliance Sales.xlsx, **click cell A16 and type** Average Per Item/Qtr.

2. **Click in cell B16 and then choose Formulas⇨Insert Function.**

   The Insert Function dialog box opens.

3. **In the Search for a Function box, delete the placeholder text, type** average, **and click the Go button.**

   A list of all the functions that have something to do with averages appears, as shown in Figure 6-15.

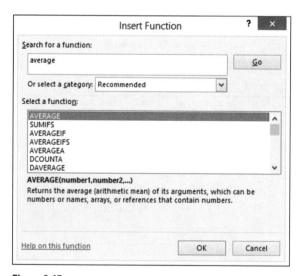

Figure 6-15

4. **From the Select a Function list, select Average and click OK.**

The Function Arguments dialog box opens.

5. **If there is already a cell reference in the Number1 text box, delete it; then click the Collapse Dialog button next to the Number1 text box. (See Figure 6-16.)**

Collapse Dialog button

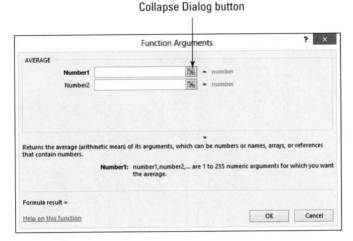

Figure 6-16

6. **Drag across B4:E11 to select that range, as shown in Figure 6-17.**

7. **Press Enter or click the Expand Dialog button to return to the Function Arguments dialog box (shown in Figure 6-18) and then click OK.**

The function enters into cell B16 with the result of 67.875.

8. **Click cell B16 and examine the =AVERAGE (B4:E11) function in the Formula bar.**

9. **Save the changes to the workbook.**

Leave the workbook open for the next exercise.

Range appears here.

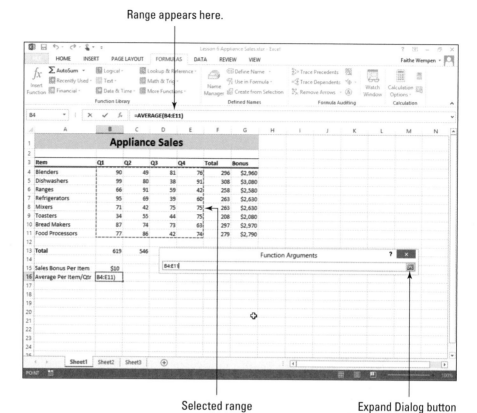

Selected range   Expand Dialog button

Figure 6-17

Preview of the values
in that range

Range appears here.

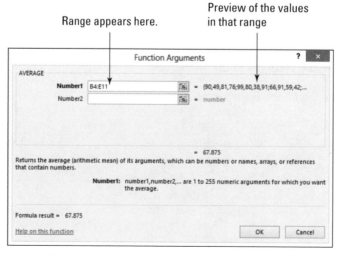

Figure 6-18

Touring some basic functions

Excel has hundreds of functions, but most of them are very specialized. The basic set that the average user works with is much more manageable.

Start with the simplest functions of them all — those without arguments. Two prime examples are

✔ NOW: Reports the current date and time.

✔ TODAY: Reports the current date.

Even though neither uses any arguments, you still have to include the parentheses, so they look like this:

```
=NOW( )

=TODAY( )
```

Another basic kind of function performs a single, simple math operation and has a single argument that specifies what cell or range it operates on. Table 6-2 summarizes some important functions that work this way.

Table 6-2	Simple One-Argument Functions	
Function	**What It Does**	**Example**
SUM	Sums the values in a range of cells	=SUM(A1:A10)
AVERAGE	Averages the values in a range of cells	=AVERAGE(A1:A10)
MIN	Provides the smallest number in a range of cells	=MIN(A1:A10)
MAX	Provides the largest number in a range of cells	=MAX(A1:A10)
COUNT	Counts the number of cells that contain numeric values in the range	=COUNT(A1:A10)
COUNTA	Counts the number of non-empty cells in the range	=COUNTA(A1:A10)
COUNTBLANK	Counts the number of empty cells in the range	=COUNTBLANK(A1:A10)

In this exercise, you add some basic functions to a worksheet.

Files needed: Lesson 6 Appliance Sales.xlsx from the preceding exercise

1. In `Lesson 6 Appliance Sales.xlsx`, in cell A17, type Lowest and in cell A18, type Highest.

2. In cell B17, type =MIN(and then drag across B4:E11 to select the range. Press Enter to complete the function.

   You don't need to type the closing parenthesis; Excel fills it in for you. The result is 34.

3. In cell B18, type =MAX(B4:E11).

   The result is 99.

4. In cell H1, type As of, and in cell I1, type =TODAY( ).

   Today's date appears in cell I1. Figure 6-19 shows the completed worksheet.

	A	B	C	D	E	F	G	H	I	J
1		**Appliance Sales**						As of	3/27/2013	
2										
3	Item	Q1	Q2	Q3	Q4	Total	Bonus			
4	Blenders	90	49	81	76	296	$2,960			
5	Dishwashers	99	80	38	91	308	$3,080			
6	Ranges	66	91	59	42	258	$2,580			
7	Refrigerators	95	69	39	60	263	$2,630			
8	Mixers	71	42	75	75	263	$2,630			
9	Toasters	34	55	44	75	208	$2,080			
10	Bread Makers	87	74	73	63	297	$2,970			
11	Food Processors	77	86	42	74	279	$2,790			
12										
13	Total	619	546	451	556	2172	$21,720			
14										
15	Sales Bonus Per Item	$10								
16	Average Per Item/Qtr	67.875								
17	Lowest	34								
18	Highest	99								
19										

Figure 6-19

5. Save the changes to the workbook.

Leave the workbook open for the next exercise.

Working with Named Ranges

When constructing formulas and functions, naming a range can be helpful because you can refer to that name rather than the cell addresses. Therefore you don't have to remember the exact cell addresses, and you can construct formulas based on meaning.

For example, instead of remembering that the number of employees is stored in cell B3, you could name cell B3 *Employees*. Then in a formula that used B3's value, such as =B3*2, you could use the name instead: =Employees*2.

Naming a range

You can name a range in three ways, and each has its pros and cons:

- ✔ **If the default names are okay to use, you may find choosing Formulas⇨Create from Selection useful.** With this method, Excel chooses the name for you based on text labels it finds in adjacent cells (above or to the left of the current cells). This method is fast and easy, and it works well when you have to create a lot of names at once and when the cells are well-labeled with adjacent text.

- ✔ **You can select the range and then type a name in the Name text box (the area immediately above the column A heading, to the left of the Formula bar).** With this fast and easy method, you get to choose the name yourself. However, you have to do each range separately; you can't do a big batch at a time like you can with Formulas⇨Create from Selection.

- ✔ **If you want to more precisely control the options for the name, you can choose Formulas⇨Define Name.** This method opens a dialog box from which you can specify the name, the scope, and any comments you might want to include.

In this exercise, you name several ranges using three methods.

Files needed: Lesson 6 Appliance Sales.xlsx from the preceding exercise

1. **Select cells B3:G11 and then choose Formulas⇨Create from Selection.**

   The Create Names from Selection dialog box opens.

2. **Select the Top Row check box (see Figure 6-20) if it isn't already selected and then click OK.**

   The ranges are assigned names based on the labels in row 3. For example, cells G4:G11 now form a Bonus range because that's the label in G3.

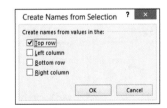

Figure 6-20

3. **Choose Formulas⇨Name Manager.**

   The Name Manager dialog box opens. The names appear on the list that you just created, as shown in Figure 6-21.

4. **Click Close to close the Name Manager dialog box.**

5. **Click cell B15 and, in the Name text box above column A, type BonusPer and press Enter. (See Figure 6-22.)**

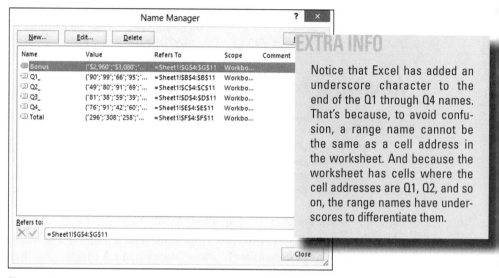

Figure 6-21

Range name

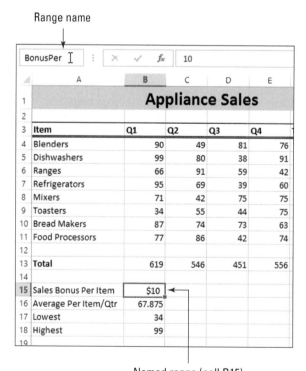

Named range (cell B15)

Figure 6-22

6. **Click cell B13 and then choose Formulas⇨Define Name.**

   The New Name dialog box opens.

7. **In the Name text box, type Q1Total, and from the Scope drop-down list, select Sheet1.**

   Q1Total applies only to this worksheet, as shown in Figure 6-23.

8. **Click OK to create the name.**

   The dialog box closes.

9. **Choose Formulas⇨Name Manager.**

   The Name Manager dialog box reopens.

10. **Examine the list of all the named ranges you've created and then click Close to close the dialog box.**

11. **Save the workbook.**

Figure 6-23

Leave the workbook open for the next exercise.

Using a named range in a formula

The main reason for naming a range is to refer to it in a formula. You can substitute the range name for the cell addresses in any situation where using a range would be appropriate.

When a range contains multiple cells and you use the name in a formula, Excel treats it as if you had specified the range with the starting and ending cell addresses.

In this exercise, you use range names in formulas.

Files needed: Lesson 6 Appliance Sales.xlsx *from the preceding exercise*

1. **In cells B13, C13, D13, and E13 respectively, enter the following formulas that sum based on the range names (see Figure 6-24):**
   ```
   =SUM(Q1_)
   =SUM(Q2_)
   =SUM(Q3_)
   =SUM(Q4_)
   ```

E13		▼	:	×	✓	*fx*	=SUM(Q4_)		

	A	B	C	D	E	F	G	H	I
1			**Appliance Sales**					As of	3/27/2013
2									
3	Item	Q1	Q2	Q3	Q4	Total	Bonus		
4	Blenders	90	49	81	76	296	$2,960		
5	Dishwashers	99	80	38	91	308	$3,080		
6	Ranges	66	91	59	42	258	$2,580		
7	Refrigerators	95	69	39	60	263	$2,630		
8	Mixers	71	42	75	75	263	$2,630		
9	Toasters	34	55	44	75	208	$2,080		
10	Bread Makers	87	74	73	63	297	$2,970		
11	Food Processors	77	86	42	74	279	$2,790		
12									
13	Total	619	546	451	556	2172	$21,720		
14									
15	Sales Bonus Per Item	$10							
16	Average Per Item/Qtr	67.875							
17	Lowest	34							
18	Highest	99							
19									

Figure 6-24

2. **In cell G4, edit the formula in the Formula bar as follows:** =F4*BonusPer.

3. **Select cell G4 and drag the fill handle down to G11, copying the revised formula there.**

TIP

The reference to BonusPer is an absolute reference (as are all named range references), so it copies correctly.

4. **Save the workbook and close it.**

EXTRA INFO

Range names that refer to multiple cells may produce an error in a formula where a multicell range would not be an appropriate argument. For example, if a Sales range referred to B4:B8, the formula =Sales would result in an error because no math operation is specified. However, =SUM(Sales) would work just fine, as would =SUM(B4:B8).

Using Quick Analysis

New in Excel 2013, you can use Quick Analysis to perform common data analysis actions on a range of cells. Choose from five categories of actions. You'll try out each of these categories in the exercise that follows:

✔ **Formatting:** Adding data bars, a color scale, icon sets, and other formatting to cells to compare their values to others at a glance. For example, you could make the cells containing the best numbers in the range green and the worst ones red.

✔ **Charts:** Generating charts based on the data in the range.

✔ **Totals:** Adding functions that summarize the data in the range, such as SUM, AVERAGE, or COUNT.

✔ **Tables:** Converting the range to a table for greater ease of data analysis.

✔ **Sparklines:** Sparklines are mini-charts placed in single cells. They can summarize the trend of the data in adjacent cells.

In this exercise, you use Quick Analysis.

Files needed: Lesson 6 Quick.xlsx

1. **Open** Lesson 6 Quick.xlsx **from the data files for this chapter and save it as** Lesson 6 Sales Analysis.xlsx.

2. **Select the range B3:E11.**

   A Quick Analysis icon appears in the lower-right corner of the selected range.

3. **Click the Quick Analysis icon.**

   A panel of the available actions appears, as shown in Figure 6-25. The five categories of actions appear in all-caps across the top. The first one, FORMATTING, is selected by default, and the available formatting-related actions appear below it.

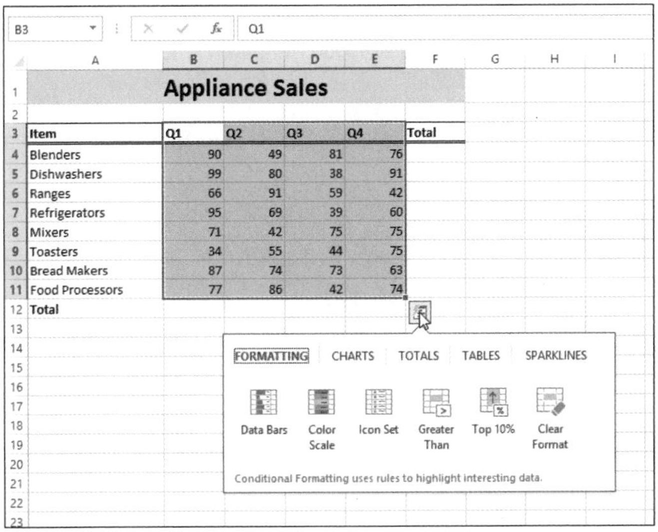

LINGO

A **table** is different in Excel than in other programs. In Excel, it refers to a range of cells that have been specially designated as being part of a related data set. You can perform data analysis functions on a table that you can't easily perform on non-tabular ranges.

Figure 6-25

4. Click Color Scale.

Colors are applied to the cells in the range according to their value, with lower numbers in red and higher numbers in green.

5. Click away from the selection to clear the selection so you can see the formatting more clearly. (See Figure 6-26.)

	A	B	C	D	E	F
1			**Appliance Sales**			
2						
3	Item	Q1	Q2	Q3	Q4	Total
4	Blenders	90	49	81	76	
5	Dishwashers	99	80	38	91	
6	Ranges	66	91	59	42	
7	Refrigerators	95	69	39	60	
8	Mixers	71	42	75	75	
9	Toasters	34	55	44	75	
10	Bread Makers	87	74	73	63	
11	Food Processors	77	86	42	74	
12	Total					
13						

Figure 6-26

PRACTICE

You can access all the formatting in the FORMATTING category via the Home⇨Conditional Formatting command, and that's where you would go to fine-tune the effect. For example, you could change the values or colors used in the color scale by choosing Home⇨Conditional Formatting⇨Manage Rules. You could then select the Graded Color Scale rule and click Edit Rule to change its properties.

6. Press Ctrl+Z to undo the last action, removing the color-scale formatting from the range.

7. Select the range A3:E11.

8. Click the Quick Analysis icon again and then click the Charts tab.

9. Point your cursor at the Stacked Column icon.

A preview appears of a stacked column chart that would be created from the selected data if you chose that action, as shown in Figure 6-27.

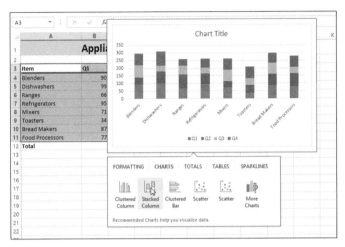

Figure 6-27

10. **Click the Totals tab.**

    Actions appear for various types of summaries involving functions.

11. **Point your cursor at the Sum icon.**

    A boldface Sum row appears below the data in the worksheet, simulating what would appear if you chose this action, as shown in Figure 6-28.

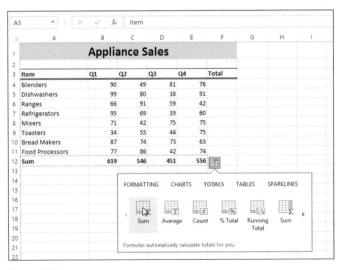

Figure 6-28

12. **Click the Tables tab.**

   Actions appear for creating a table from the range.

13. **Point your cursor at the Table icon.**

   An example appears above the panel, showing what the range would look like if you chose this action to convert it into a table, as shown in Figure 6-29.

Figure 6-29

14. **Click the Sparklines tab.**

   Actions appear for adding sparklines for the range.

15. **Point your cursor at the Line icon.**

   An example appears in column F of sparklines that summarize the data in columns B through E, as shown in Figure 6-30.

16. **Click away from the panel without making a selection.**

   The panel closes.

17. **Close the workbook, saving your changes if prompted, and exit Excel.**

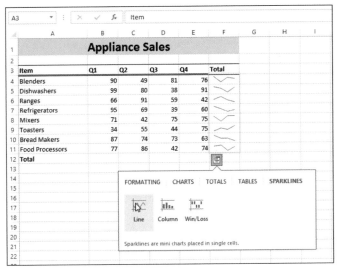

Figure 6-30

Summing Up

Here are the key points you learned in this chapter:

- ✔ A formula is a math calculation. Every formula begins with an equal sign.

- ✔ The order of precedence determines the order in which math is processed in a formula: first parentheses, then exponentiation, then multiplication and division, and finally addition and subtraction.

- ✔ Formulas can contain cell references that substitute the cell's value for the reference when the formula is calculated.

- ✔ When you copy a formula, by default, the cell references in it are relative, so they change based on the new position.

- ✔ Placing dollar signs in a cell reference, such as A1, makes it an absolute reference so it doesn't change when the formula is copied.

- ✔ A function is a word or string of letters that refers to a certain math calculation. A function starts with an equal sign, followed by the function name and a set of parentheses. Arguments for the function go in the parentheses.

- ✔ In functions, you can refer to ranges of cells, such as =SUM(A1:A4).

- ✔ If you don't know which function you want, choose Formulas⇨Insert Function.

- ✔ The NOW function shows the current date and time; the TODAY function shows the current date.

- ✔ SUM sums a range of cells. AVERAGE averages a range of cells.

- ✔ MIN shows the smallest number in a range, and MAX shows the largest number in a range.

- ✔ COUNT counts the number of cells in a range that contains numeric values. Two related functions are COUNTA, which counts the number of non-empty cells, and COUNTBLANK, which counts the number of empty cells.

- ✔ Naming a range enables you to refer to it by a friendly name. Use the commands in the Defined Names group on the Formulas tab.

- ✔ Quick Analysis provides quick access to common tools for analyzing data, including formatting, charting, adding totals, creating tables, and adding sparklines.

Try-it-yourself lab

Complete these steps for more practice using Excel:

1. **Start Excel and enter at least six numeric values along with text labels that explain what each value represents.**

   For example, you might enter the calorie counts of the last six food items you ate or the prices you paid for the last six books you purchased.

2. **Analyze the data you entered using at least four functions.**

   For example, you could sum, average, and count the data. You could find the minimum and maximum values. You could add text labels that clearly identify what each function's result represents.

3. **Save your work as** Lesson 6 Try It Formulas.xlsx.

Know this tech talk

absolute reference: A cell reference that doesn't change if copied to another cell.

argument: A placeholder for a number, text string, or cell reference in a function.

AVERAGE: A function that averages a range of values.

COUNT: A function that counts the number of cells that contain numeric values in a range.

COUNTA: A function that counts the number of non-empty cells in the range.

COUNTBLANK: A function that counts the number of empty cells in the range.

formula: A math calculation performed in a cell.

function: A text name that represents a math calculation, such as SUM or AVERAGE.

MAX: A function that provides the largest number in a range of cells.

MIN: A function that provides the smallest number in a range of cells.

mixed reference: A cell reference in which either the row is absolute and the column is relative, or vice versa.

NOW: A function that reports the current date and time.

relative reference: A cell reference that changes if copied to another cell.

sparklines: Mini-charts placed in single cells. They can summarize the trend of the data in adjacent cells.

SUM: A function that sums a range of values.

syntax: The rules that govern how arguments are written in a function.

table: A range of cells that have been specially designated as being part of a related data set. You can perform data-analysis functions on a table that you can't easily perform on non-tabular ranges.

TODAY: A function that reports the current date.

Chapter 7

Formatting and Printing Excel Worksheets

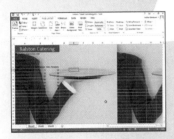

✔ Resizing rows and columns *prevents content from being truncated* when an entry is larger than the cell.

✔ A worksheet background *allows a graphic to be used as a backdrop* to the worksheet content.

✔ Headers and footers *place repeated information on each page of a printout.*

✔ Customizing a theme enables you to *reuse custom font, color, and effect settings easily.*

✔ Formatting a range as a table enables you to *apply table styles for quick formatting.*

✔ Creating a new table style enables you to *reuse custom table formatting easily.*

✔ Printing a worksheet enables you to *share it with others* who may not have computer access.

1. How do you adjust row height?

Find out on page 238

2. How do you create a colored background in a worksheet?

Find out on page 242

3. How do you insert codes into the header and footer?

Find out on page 245

4. How do you apply workbook themes?

Find out on page 248

5. How can you create your own themes?

Find out on page 249

6. How do you format a range as a table?

Find out on page 252

7. Can you customize a table style?

Find out on page 254

8. How do you print only selected cells in a worksheet?

Find out on page 258

*F*ace it: Plain worksheets aren't that much fun to look at. A worksheet packed full of rows and columns of numbers is enough to make anyone's eyes glaze over. However, formatting can dramatically improve a worksheet's readability, which in turn enables the reader to understand its meaning much more easily.

You can apply formatting at the whole-worksheet level or at the individual-cell level. This chapter focuses on formatting entire worksheets — or at least big chunks of them. You learn how to adjust rows and columns, apply worksheet backgrounds, create headers and footers, and format ranges as tables, complete with preset table formatting. You also learn how to print your work in Excel.

Adjusting Rows and Columns

Each column in a worksheet starts with the same width, which is 8.43 characters (based on the default font and font size) unless you've changed the default setting. That's approximately seven digits and either one large symbol (such as $) or two small ones (such as decimal points and commas).

> **TIP**
> You can define the default width setting for new worksheets: Choose Home➪Format➪Default Width and then fill in the desired default width.

As you enter data into cells, those column widths may no longer be optimal. Data may overflow out of a cell if the width is too narrow, or there may be excess blank space in a column if its width is too wide. (Blank space is not always a bad thing, but if you're trying to fit all the data on one page, for example, it can be a hindrance.)

In some cases, Excel makes an adjustment for you automatically, as follows:

- **For column widths:** When you enter numbers in a cell, Excel widens a column as needed to accommodate the longest number in that column, provided you haven't manually set a column width for it.

- **For row heights:** Generally, a row adjusts automatically to fit the largest font used in it. You don't have to adjust row heights manually to allow text to fit. You can change the row height if you want, though, to create special effects, such as extra blank space in the layout.

After you manually resize a row's height or a column's width, it won't change its size automatically for you anymore. That's because manual settings override automatic ones.

The units of measurement are different for rows versus columns, by the way. Column width is measured in characters of the default font size. Row height is measured in points. A point is $1/72$ of an inch.

Changing a row's height

You can resize rows and columns in several ways. You can auto-fit the cells' sizes to their content, manually drag the widths and heights, or enter a precise value for the widths and heights.

In the following exercise, you adjust row heights in a variety of ways.

Files needed: `Lesson 7 Catering.xlsx`

1. **Start Excel if needed, open** `Lesson 7 Catering.xlsx`, **and save it as** `Lesson 7 Catering Format.xlsx`.

2. **Click the header for row 4 to select the entire row; then choose Home➪Format➪Row Height.**

   The Row Height dialog box opens. Note that the row height is currently set to around 18.75. (Yours may be slightly off from that. See Figure 7-1.)

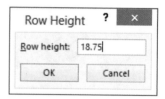

   Figure 7-1

   The largest font in this row is 14-point, and the additional 4.75 points of height are used for padding. What would happen if you didn't have that extra for padding? The next few steps show you how to remove extra space.

3. **Type** 14 **in the Row Height box and click OK.**

   Notice how the top of the capital letters in row 4 is too close to the cell's upper border now.

4. **Position the mouse pointer between the 4 and 5 row headers so the pointer turns into a double-headed arrow. Then click and hold the mouse pointer over the divider.**

   A ScreenTip appears, showing the current height.

5. **Drag downward until the ScreenTip reads 20.25 points, as shown in Figure 7-2, and then release the mouse button.**

Drag here.   See height setting here.

	A	B	C	D	
1	Ralston Catering				
2	No job is too large or too small				
3	Height: 20.25 (27 pixels)				
4	Price List				
5					
6	Item	Per Perso	Min. Persons		
7	Barbecue	9	12		
8	Lemon Ch	8	12		
9	Grilled Ha	12	12		
10	Beef Well	16	12		
11	Ribeye Ste	16	12		
12	Prime Rib	20	24		
13	Surf and T	35	12		

Figure 7-2

EXTRA INFO

You might not be able to drag to an exact amount because the amount has to match with a whole number of pixels. Depending on your screen resolution, the number of pixels that corresponds to a certain number of points may vary. In Figure 7-2, 27 pixels equal 20.25 points, but that might not be so for you. The same goes in Steps 5 and 7: The amounts may be slightly off, depending on your screen resolution.

6. **Position the mouse pointer again over the divider between the row 4 and 5 headers and then double-click.**

   The row height auto-resizes to fit.

7. **Click the row 4 header to select the row; then right-click anywhere in the row and choose Row Height.**

   The Row Height dialog box opens again. Notice that its setting is back to somewhere around 18.75.

8. **Click Cancel to close the dialog box.**

Leave the workbook open for the next exercise.

Changing a column's width

When content overruns a cell's width, different results occur depending on the type of data and whether the cell's column width has been adjusted manually.

In the following exercise, you adjust row heights in a variety of ways.

Files needed: `Lesson 7 Catering Format.xlsx` *from the preceding exercise*

1. **In** `Lesson 7 Catering Format.xlsx`, **double-click the divider between the headers for columns A and B.**

   Column A widens enough that the title in cell A1 fits in the cell, as shown in Figure 7-3. Although that looks okay, it's not optimal, because column A appears too wide for the other data in the column.

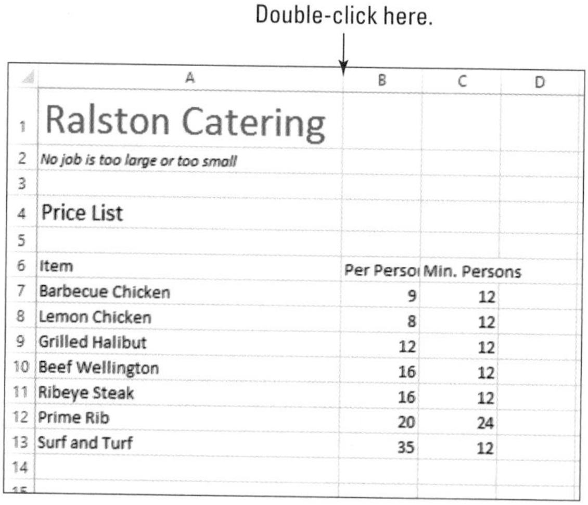

Double-click here.

	A	B	C	D
1	Ralston Catering			
2	No job is too large or too small			
3				
4	Price List			
5				
6	Item	Per Perso Min. Persons		
7	Barbecue Chicken	9	12	
8	Lemon Chicken	8	12	
9	Grilled Halibut	12	12	
10	Beef Wellington	16	12	
11	Ribeye Steak	16	12	
12	Prime Rib	20	24	
13	Surf and Turf	35	12	
14				

Figure 7-3

2. **Click and drag the divider between columns A and B headers to the left so that the content of cell A7 fits in the cell with a few characters of space to spare.**

   The content of cell A1 hangs off into cells B1 and C1, but that's okay because they're empty.

3. **Click the column header for column B to select that column and then choose Home⇨Format⇨AutoFit Column Width.**

   Column B's width increases to accommodate the longest entry (in cell B6).

4. **Click the column header for column C to select it and then choose Home⇨Format⇨Column Width.**

   The Column Width dialog box opens.

5. **Type 12 in the dialog box, as shown in Figure 7-4, and then click OK.**

   The column width changes to exactly 12 characters.

   Figure 7-5 shows the worksheet after the column-width adjustments.

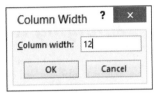

Figure 7-4

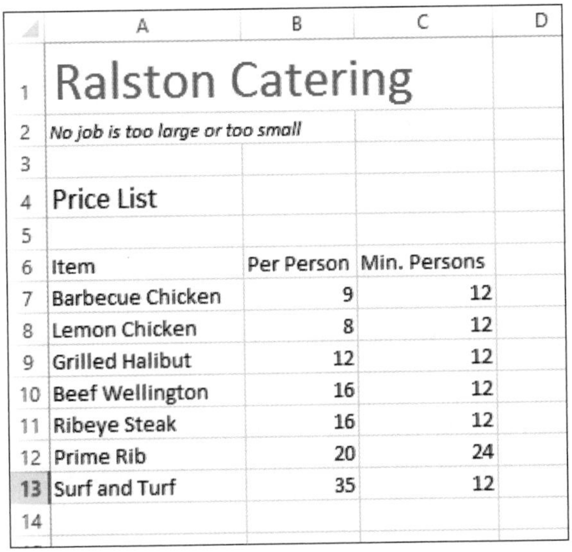

◢	A	B	C	D
1	Ralston Catering			
2	No job is too large or too small			
3				
4	Price List			
5				
6	Item	Per Person	Min. Persons	
7	Barbecue Chicken	9	12	
8	Lemon Chicken	8	12	
9	Grilled Halibut	12	12	
10	Beef Wellington	16	12	
11	Ribeye Steak	16	12	
12	Prime Rib	20	24	
13	Surf and Turf	35	12	
14				

Figure 7-5

6. **Save the changes to the workbook and close it.**

Leave Excel open for the next exercise.

Formatting an Entire Worksheet

In addition to formatting individual cells, you can apply some types of formatting to the entire sheet. For example, you can apply a worksheet background that appears onscreen and can optionally be set to print, and you can control what text appears in a printout's header and footer areas.

Applying a worksheet background

You can't set a worksheet background to be a solid color with the Background command. However, you can select the entire worksheet by pressing Ctrl+A and then apply a solid color fill to every cell on that worksheet, creating essentially the same effect as applying a solid-color background.

In the following exercise, you apply a worksheet background.

Files needed: Lesson 7 Sheet.xlsx

> **LINGO**
>
> A **worksheet background** is a picture that appears behind the cells. If a cell has no background fill assigned to it, the worksheet background image or color appears as its fill. If the cell already has its own fill, that fill obscures the worksheet background.

1. **Open** Lesson 7 Sheet.xlsx **and then save it as** Lesson 7 Sheet Formatting.xlsx.

2. **Choose Page Layout⇨Background.**

   The Insert Pictures dialog box opens.

3. **In the From a File section, click the Browse button.**

4. **Navigate to the folder containing the data files for this chapter and click** Lesson 7 Image.jpg.

   See Figure 7-6.

5. **Click the Insert button.**

   The image appears as the worksheet background, as shown in Figure 7-7.

   Notice that cells A1:C1 appear with their original background colors, but everything else takes on the background image because they had no fill of their own. This makes the text in them next to impossible to read. Notice also that the image repeats. This image is not the best one for this worksheet, so try a different one — this time an image that is designed to be tiled (or repeated) as a texture.

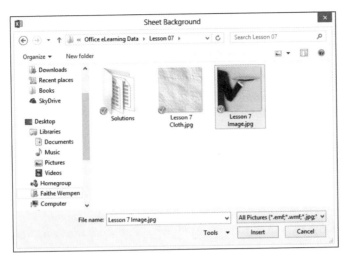

Figure 7-6

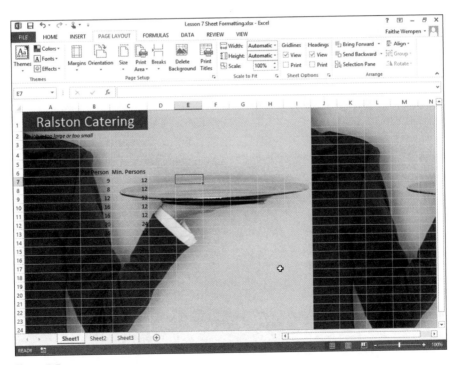

Figure 7-7

6. **Choose Page Layout⇨Delete Background and then choose Page Layout⇨Background.**

The Insert Pictures dialog box opens.

7. **In the From a File section, click the Browse button.**

8. **In the folder containing the data files for this chapter, click** `Lesson 7 Cloth.jpg` **and then click the Insert button.**

This image is more suitable for a background because it tiles attractively. See Figure 7-8.

9. **Choose File⇨Print and examine the print preview.**

Notice that the background doesn't print. Backgrounds do not print by default, to save printer ink or toner.

10. **Press Esc to return to normal viewing and save the workbook.**

Leave the workbook open for the next exercise.

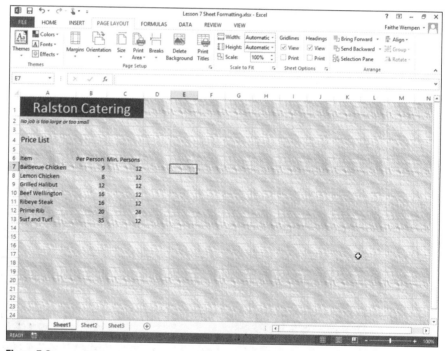

Figure 7-8

Creating a header or footer

If you plan to print your worksheet, you might want to set up a header and/or footer.

In the following exercise, you create a header and footer that print the company name and a page number.

Files needed: `Lesson 7 Sheet Formatting.xlsx` *from the preceding exercise*

LINGO

Headers and **footers** are lines of information that repeat at the top and bottom of each page. These lines can contain any text you want plus codes that print page numbers, the current date and time, or other information.

1. **In** `Lesson 7 Sheet Formatting.xlsx`, **choose Insert⇨Header & Footer.**

   The view changes to Page Layout view so you can see the Header and Footer sections.

   The insertion point moves to the center section of the header.

   If your Excel window isn't very wide, you might need to click the Text button to open the options in the Text group and, from there, click Header & Footer in Step 1.

2. **Type** Ralston Catering Price List **in the center section of the header, as shown in Figure 7-9.**

3. **Choose Header & Footer Tools Design⇨Go to Footer.**

   The display jumps down to the footer.

4. **Click in the right section of the footer to move the insertion point there.**

5. **Choose Header & Footer Tools Design⇨Page Number.**

   The `&[Page]` code appears.

6. **Click to place the insertion point to the right of the** `&[Page]` **code, press the spacebar, type** of, **and press the spacebar again.**

7. **Choose Header & Footer Tools Design⇨Number of Pages.**

   The `&[Pages]` code appears, as shown in Figure 7-10.

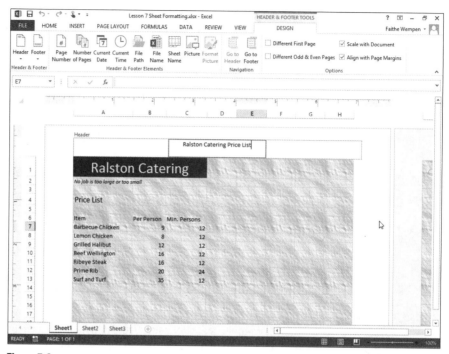

Figure 7-9

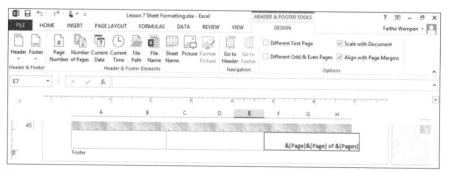

Figure 7-10

8. **Click in the middle section of the footer to move the insertion point away from the page number codes.**

They change to appear as the actual page numbers: 1 of 1.

9. **Choose Header & Footer Tools Design⇨Go to Header to return to the top of the page and then click in the left section of the header to move the insertion point there.**

10. **Choose Header & Footer Tools Design⇨File Name.**

    The `&[File]` code appears, as shown in Figure 7-11.

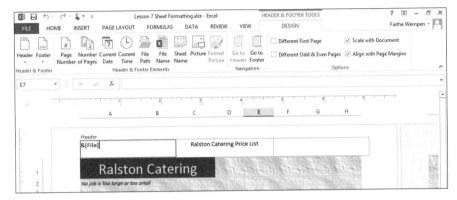

Figure 7-11

11. **Click in the right section of the header to move the insertion point away from the filename code.**

    The actual filename appears in the header.

For more practice, examine the rest of the tools on the Header & Footer Tools Design tab on the Ribbon and see whether you can determine how each tool might be used. Consult the Help system as needed.

12. **Choose File⇨Print and examine the print preview. Notice that the header and footer appear on the page. Press Esc to leave Backstage view without printing.**

13. **Save your changes and close the workbook.**

Leave Excel open for the next exercise.

Using Theme Formatting

Themes and table styles are two ways of applying formatting to an entire worksheet or data range at once. Each one can be used with preset settings or customized for an individual look. For each one, you can then save your custom formatting to reuse in other workbooks and tables.

Applying a workbook theme

Themes are standard across most Office applications (including Word, Excel, and PowerPoint), so you can standardize your formatting across all the documents you create.

LINGO

Themes are formatting presets that you can apply to entire worksheets.

In the following exercise, you apply a theme and a color theme.

Files needed: Lesson 7 Theme.xlsx

1. **Open** Lesson 7 Theme.xlsx **and save it as** Lesson 7 Theme Formatting.xlsx.

2. **Choose Page Layout⇨Themes.**

   A list of themes appears, as shown in Figure 7-12.

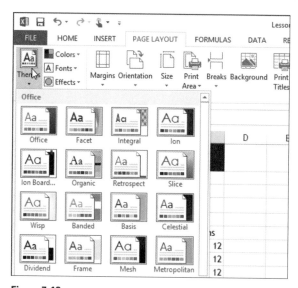

Figure 7-12

3. **Choose the Slice theme to apply it.**

   Notice that the color of the fill behind cells A1:C1 changes, as do the fonts, as shown in Figure 7-13.

4. **Choose Page Layout⇨Colors.**

   A list of color themes appears, as shown in Figure 7-14.

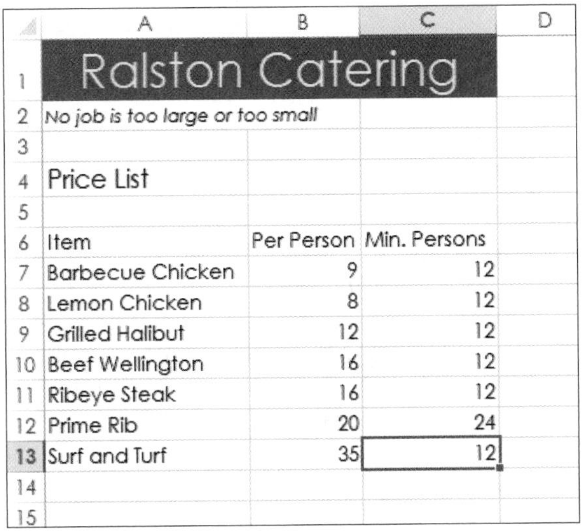

	A	B	C	D
1	Ralston Catering			
2	No job is too large or too small			
3				
4	Price List			
5				
6	Item	Per Person	Min. Persons	
7	Barbecue Chicken	9	12	
8	Lemon Chicken	8	12	
9	Grilled Halibut	12	12	
10	Beef Wellington	16	12	
11	Ribeye Steak	16	12	
12	Prime Rib	20	24	
13	Surf and Turf	35	12	
14				
15				

Figure 7-13

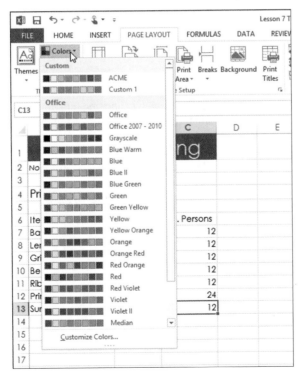

Figure 7-14

5. **Select Red.**

The colors change to a black background and yellow letters in cells A1:C1.

6. **Save the workbook.**

Leave the workbook open for the next exercise.

Customizing a theme

If none of the themes suit your needs, you may want to create your own theme. You can do this by choosing the colors, fonts, and effects that you want (from the Page Layout tab) and then saving the unique combination you chose as a
new theme.

In this exercise, you create a custom theme.

Files needed: `Lesson 7 Theme Formatting.xlsx` *from preceding exercise*

1. **If you didn't already**
   change the Color theme to Red in the previous exercise, choose Page Layout➪Colors and then select Red from the list of color themes that appears.

   Refer to Figure 7-14.

You can also create a custom theme by choosing one of the existing themes from the Theme button and then customizing it by selecting a different set of colors, fonts, or effects.

2. **Choose Page Layout➪Fonts and then choose Trebuchet MS from the list of font themes that appears, as shown in Figure 7-15.**

3. **Choose Page Layout➪Effects and then choose Glow Edge from the list of effect themes that appears.**

4. **Choose Page Layout➪Themes➪Save Current Theme.**

   The Save Current Theme dialog box opens.

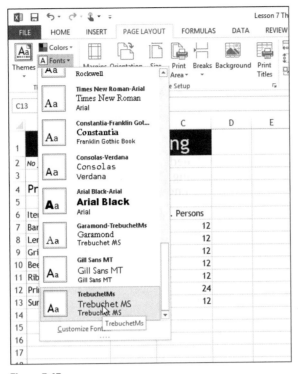

Figure 7-15

5. **In the File Name box, type** Intensity, **as shown in Figure 7-16, and then click Save to save the new theme.**

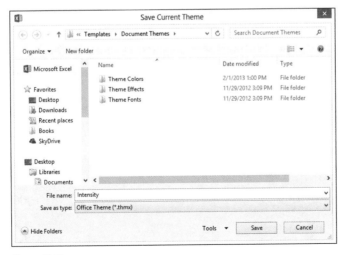

Figure 7-16

Themes are stored in a common location for all Office applications, so you can reuse your custom themes in Word and PowerPoint.

6. **Choose Page Layout⇨Themes.**

   Notice that your new theme appears at the top of the list.

7. **Click away from the menu to close it without making a selection.**

8. **Save the workbook.**

Leave the workbook open for the next exercise.

Formatting a range as a table

You can format certain ranges as tables in Excel, which not only enables you to apply formatting presets more easily but also gives the range special properties that make it easier to search and sort them. There are many data management benefits to converting a range to a table, but this chapter looks at creating a table primarily for formatting purposes.

LINGO

A **table,** in the context of an Excel worksheet, is a range that has been marked as a single logical unit for data storage and retrieval.

In this exercise, you convert a range to a table and apply table style formatting.

Files needed: `Lesson 7 Theme Formatting.xlsx` *from the preceding exercise*

1. **In** `Lesson 7 Theme Formatting.xlsx`, **select cells A6:C13 and then choose Home⇨Format as Table.**

   A gallery of formatting styles appears, as shown in Figure 7-17.

2. **Select the Table Style Medium 9 style. It's the ninth style in the Medium section.**

   The Format as Table dialog box opens with the range already filled in from the selection you made in Step 1. See Figure 7-18.

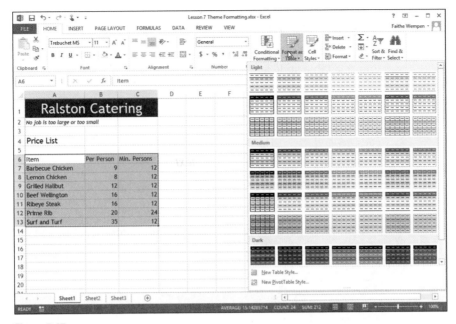

Figure 7-17

3. **Click OK.**

   The range is converted to a table, and the style is applied. The Table Tools Design tab becomes active. On this tab are commands for formatting that you can use only on ranges that are defined as tables.

4. **Deselect the Banded Rows check box to see how the alternate-row color banding is removed. Select the check box to restore the banding.**

5. **Save the workbook.**

Leave the workbook open for the next exercise.

Figure 7-18

Creating a custom table style

You can rely on the standard table styles that Excel provides, or you can customize a table style and then save it as a new style that you can then apply to other ranges.

In this exercise, you create a custom table style.

Files needed: `Lesson 7 Theme Formatting.xlsx` *from the preceding exercise*

1. **Choose Home⇨Format as Table⇨New Table Style.**

    The New Table Quick Style dialog box opens.

2. **In the Name box, replace the default name with** Custom Table 1.

3. **In the Table Element list, select Header Row, as shown in Figure 7-19.**

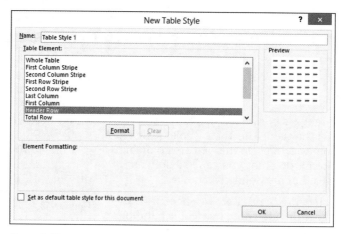

Figure 7-19

4. **Click the Format button to open the Format Cells dialog box.**

5. **Click the Fill tab and then select the fifth square in the next-to-the-last row of colors, as shown in Figure 7-20.**

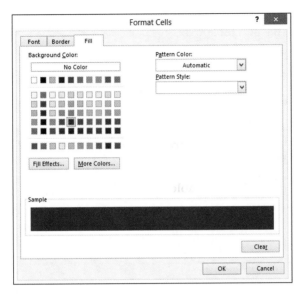

Figure 7-20

6. Click the Font tab; then open the Color drop-down list and select the white square in the Theme Colors section, as shown in Figure 7-21.

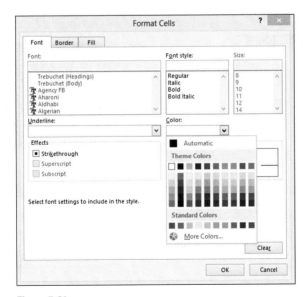

Figure 7-21

7. **Click OK to return to the New Table Quick Style dialog box and then click OK to create the new table style.**

REMEMBER

Creating a new table style doesn't automatically apply it to the selected range, so you must apply the style.

8. **Select cells A6:C13 and then choose Home⇨Format as Table. In the Custom section at the top of the menu, select the new style you just created, as shown in Figure 7-22.**

9. **Save the workbook.**

Leave the workbook open for the next exercise.

Custom style

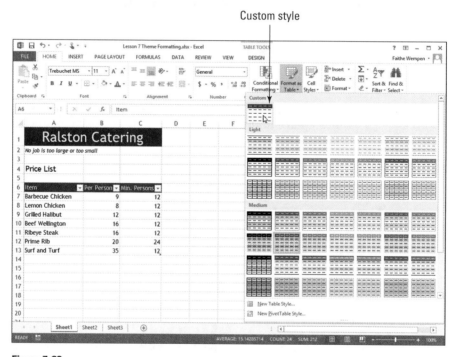

Figure 7-22

Printing Worksheets

You can print your work in Excel on paper to share with people who may not have computer access or to pass out as handouts at meetings and events. You can print the quick-and-easy way with the default settings or customize the settings to fit your needs.

Previewing and print the active worksheet

By default, when you print, Excel prints the entire active worksheet — that is, whichever worksheet is displayed or selected at the moment. But Excel also gives you other printing options:

✔ **Print multiple worksheets:** If more than one worksheet is selected (for example, if you have more than one worksheet tab selected at the bottom of the Excel window), all selected worksheets are included in the printed version. As an alternative, you can print all the worksheets in the workbook. To select more than one worksheet, hold down the Ctrl key as you click the tabs of the sheets you want.

✔ **Print selected cells or ranges:** You can choose to print only selected cells, or you can define a print range and print only that range (regardless of what cells happen to be selected).

In Excel 2013, Print Preview is built into Backstage view, so you see a preview of the printout at the same place where you change the print settings.

In this exercise, you preview and print a worksheet.

Files needed: `Lesson 7 Theme Formatting.xlsx` *from the preceding exercise*

1. **Choose File⇨Print.**

   The Print settings appear, along with a preview of the printout. (See Figure 7-23.)

2. **In the Copies box, click the up-increment arrow to change the value to 2.**

3. **Click the Print button to send the job to the printer.**

Leave the workbook open for the next exercise.

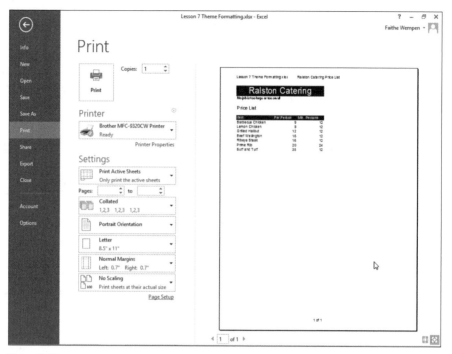

Figure 7-23

Setting and using a print range

You have two ways to print only a certain range of cells on the active worksheet. If you want to select a range for a one-time print job, you can just select the range and then choose to print only the selection. If you want the same cells (only) to print each time you print this worksheet in the future too, you can select them as a print range, and Excel remembers them.

In this exercise, you print only a selected range of cells by using two methods.

Files needed: Lesson 7 Theme Formatting.xlsx *from the preceding exercise*

1. **Select the range A6:C13 and then choose File⇨Print.**

2. **Click the Print Active Sheets button and then choose Print Selection from the menu that appears, as shown in Figure 7-24.**

Figure 7-24

3. **Click Print.**

   The copy that prints contains only the range you specified.

4. **Choose Page Layout⇨Print Area⇨Set Print Area, as shown in Figure 7-25.**

5. **Click away from the selected range to deselect it and then choose File⇨Print.**

Figure 7-25

6. **Click the Print Selection button and select the Print Active Sheets option.**

7. **Examine the preview of the print job, as shown in Figure 7-26. Notice that even though Print Active Sheets is selected, only the print area you specified appears.**

8. **Press Esc to close Backstage view.**

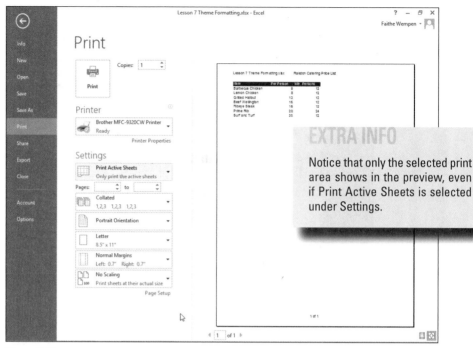

EXTRA INFO

Notice that only the selected print area shows in the preview, even if Print Active Sheets is selected under Settings.

Figure 7-26

    9. **Choose Page Layout⇨Print Area⇨Clear Print Area.**

  10. **Save the workbook.**

Leave the workbook open for the next exercise.

Adjusting the page size, orientation, and margins while printing

You can set the page size, orientation, and margins at any time from the Page Layout tab. Doing so permanently changes those settings. If you want to change any of those settings for only one particular print job, though, you can change them from Backstage view as part of the printing options. When you change the settings in Backstage view, they don't stick. The next time you open and work with the workbook, the settings go back to what they were before.

In this exercise, you change the page size, orientation, and margins for a one-time print job.

Files needed: `Lesson 7 Theme Formatting.xlsx` *from the preceding exercise*

1. **Choose Page Layout⇨Print Area⇨Clear Print Area to make sure there is no print area set from a previous exercise.**

2. **Choose File⇨Print.**

3. **Click the Portrait Orientation button to open a menu and choose Landscape Orientation.**

   As in Figure 7-27, the print preview changes to show the new orientation.

4. **Click the Letter 8.5" x 11" button to open a menu and choose B6 4.92" x 6.93".**

   Figure 7-28 shows the menu.

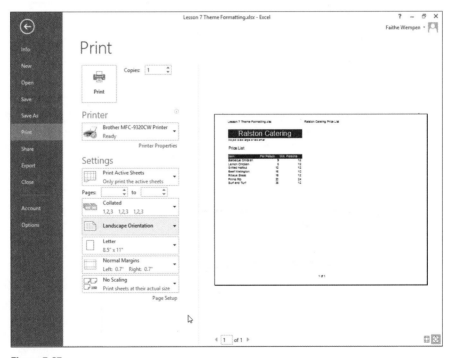

Figure 7-27

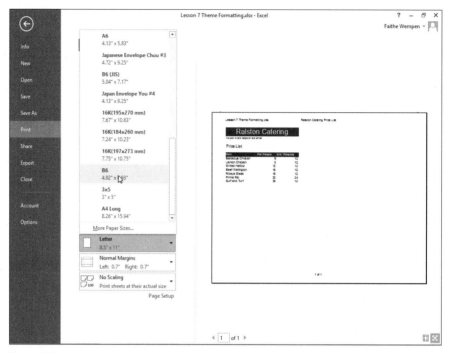

Figure 7-28

The paper size changes in the preview to the smaller size. This change, shown in Figure 7-29, bunches up the text in the header so that the text overlaps unattractively.

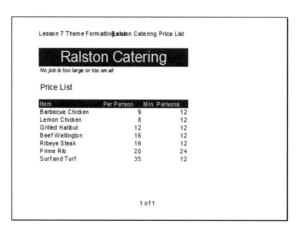

Figure 7-29

5. **Click the Page Setup hyperlink.**

   The Page Setup dialog box opens.

6. **Click the Header/Footer tab and then click the Custom Header button.**

   The Header dialog box opens, as shown in Figure 7-30.

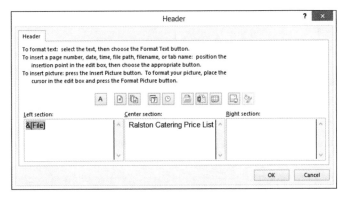

Figure 7-30

7. **Delete the code in the Left Section box to remove that element from the header, click OK to close the Header dialog box, and then click OK to close the Page Setup dialog box.**

8. **Click the Normal Margins button and choose Narrow.**

9. **Click the No Scaling button and choose Fit Sheet on One Page.**

   Steps 8 and 9 aren't necessary for this worksheet because it all fit on one page already, but you might have a worksheet in the future that won't fit on one page unless you use these options.

10. **Click Print to print the worksheet.**

11. **Save the workbook and close it.**

Exit Excel.

Summing Up

Here are the key points you learned about in this chapter:

- ✔ You can adjust the sizes of rows and columns by dragging the dividers between row or column headers or by double-clicking the dividers to auto-size.

- ✔ To add a background to a worksheet, choose Page Layout⇨Background.

- ✔ Choose Insert⇨Header & Footer to create headers and footers that repeat on each page of a printout.

- ✔ Themes standardize the fonts, colors, and effects across multiple workbooks. To apply a theme, choose Page Layout⇨Theme.

- ✔ Formatting a range as a table enables you to apply the table-formatting presets from the Home tab.

- ✔ You can format the text in a cell in much the same way as in Word: Use the controls in the Font group on the Home tab or on the Mini toolbar.

- ✔ When you print from Excel, you can print the active worksheet or select only a range of cells to print by setting the print area.

Try-it-yourself lab

For more practice with the features covered in this chapter, try the following exercise on your own:

1. **Start Excel, open the file** `Lesson 7 Try It Table.xlsx,` **and save it as** `Try It Table Final.xlsx.`

2. **Adjust the column widths so that no text is truncated.**

3. **Format cells A10:F12 as a table, using your choice of table styles.**

4. **In the center of the worksheet's footer, place the text** Thank You for Your Business. **Then return to Normal view.**

5. **Apply the Organic theme or another theme of your choice.**

6. **Print one copy of the worksheet in Landscape orientation.**

7. **Save the workbook and close Excel.**

Know this tech talk

footer: Repeated text at the bottom of each page of a printout.

header: Repeated text at the top of each page of a printout.

print range: A defined range of cells that prints whenever the active worksheet is printed, rather than the entire worksheet printing.

table: In Excel, a range that has been marked as a single logical unit for data storage and retrieval.

theme: A formatting preset that you can apply to an entire worksheet, consisting of fonts, colors, and effects.

worksheet background: A picture that appears behind the cells of a worksheet.

Chapter 8
Managing E-Mail with Outlook

✔ Outlook allows you to *send and receive e-mail* from your e-mail accounts at specified intervals.

✔ You can *compose an e-mail message in Outlook* to anyone whose e-mail address you have.

✔ You can *include file attachments* along with text-based e-mail messages.

✔ The Reading pane, which you can set to appear either at the bottom or right of the message list, enables you to *preview message content.*

✔ When you *reply to a message,* the subject and recipient are filled into the message composition window.

✔ You can *manage incoming messages efficiently* by organizing them into folders.

✔ Create message handling rules to *automatically sort messages* into the folders you specify.

1. How do you set up an e-mail account in Outlook?

Find out on page 275

2. Can you use Outlook to get mail from web accounts such as Gmail?

Find out on page 280

3. How do you compose an e-mail message?

Find out on page 284

4. How do you attach a file to a message?

Find out on page 292

5. Can you change the interval at which Outlook checks for new mail?

Find out on page 287

6. How do you save a received e-mail attachment to your hard drive?

Find out on page 294

7. How do you configure the Junk Mail filter in Outlook?

Find out on page 306

Outlook is a multipurpose program. It's an address book, a calendar, a to-do list, and an e-mail handling program, all in one. The most popular Outlook feature, though, is the e-mail handling. Millions of people use Outlook as their primary e-mail program, and for good reason! It's fast, full-featured, and easy to use and customize.

In this chapter, I show you how to set up an e-mail account in Outlook and then how to use it to send and receive e-mail messages.

Touring the Microsoft Outlook Interface

Outlook 2013 is like other Office 2013 applications in many ways. For example, it has a Ribbon, a File tab that opens Backstage view, and a status bar that shows status messages and provides a Zoom slider for changing the magnification of the application's content.

The unique thing about Outlook is that it has several diverse areas, and each area has a different interface. These areas are Mail, Calendar, People, Tasks, and Notes. (Two other items that are also listed aren't really separate areas: Folders and Shortcuts.) You click a button in the lower-left corner of the Outlook application window to switch to the area you want to work with, as shown in Figure 8-1.

Even though this chapter covers only the e-mail component of Outlook, it's a good idea to familiarize yourself with the entire application so you can get an idea of how the areas fit together.

In the following exercise, you switch among the different areas of Outlook to see what they have to offer.

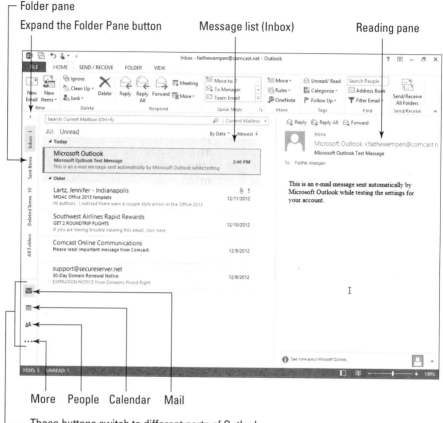

Figure 8-1

Files needed: None

1. Start Outlook from the Start screen.

If Outlook hasn't been used previously on this PC, a dialog box prompts you to set up an e-mail account. Skip to the "Setting Up Outlook for E-Mail" section, later in this chapter; then come back here to finish the tour after you've set up your e-mail.

If anyone has used Outlook previously on this PC, you see the area of the program that was displayed the last time the program was closed.

2. In the lower-left part of the Outlook window, click Mail.

The Mail interface appears. (Refer to Figure 8-1.) Your messages will be different, obviously, and you'll probably have different folders than those shown in the figure.

3. **If the mail folder names appear vertically, as on the left in Figure 8-1, click the Expand the Folder Pane button at the top of the Folder pane.**

The mail folders appear, as shown in Figure 8-2. By default, the Inbox folder appears. You can switch to viewing a different folder, such as Sent Items, by clicking the folder name in the Folder pane. If you want to widen the Folder pane, drag the divider between the Folder pane and the adjacent pane.

When you're viewing Mail, the message list appears in the center, and the selected message appears in the Reading pane, which can be either to the right of (as in Figure 8-2) or below the message list. You can switch the orientation of the Reading pane by clicking the View tab and then the Reading Pane button. (Choose Right, Bottom, or None.)

The Folder pane shows all the available mail folders; the Favorites list shows a subset of folders that you (or some other users on this PC) have hand-picked to be placed there. Your Favorites list may not have any folders in it yet. You can drag and drop a folder from the Folder pane to the Favorites list to place it there.

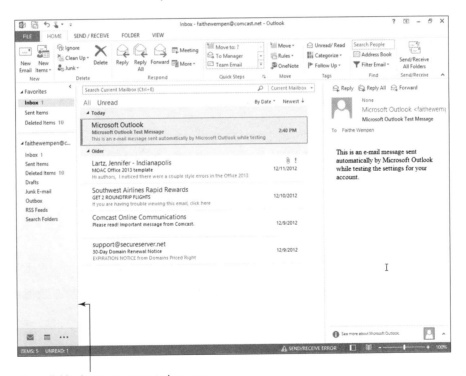

Drag divider between panes to increase
width of Folder pane.

Figure 8-2

4. **Click one of the messages in the message list.**

   A preview of that message appears in the Reading pane, as shown in Figure 8-2.

5. **Click the Calendar button in the lower-left corner of the Outlook window.**

   If you don't see a Calendar button, click the More button (. . .) to see a list of other services and then select Calendar from there.

   A calendar appears, as shown in Figure 8-3. Figure 8-3 shows a dentist appointment on May 1st. This is how appointments appear on the monthly calendar.

6. **Choose Home⇨Day.**

   The calendar changes to Day view, as shown in Figure 8-4. Each calendar has a number of views available.

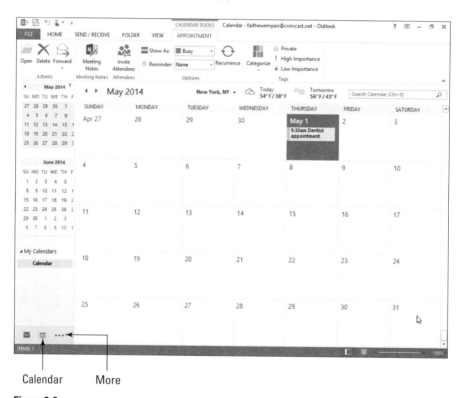

Calendar   More

Figure 8-3

Calendar views

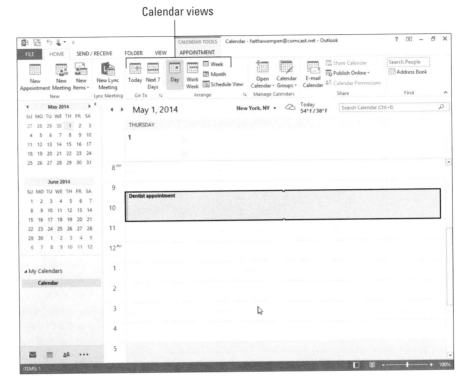

Figure 8-4

PRACTICE For more practice, click each of the other views in the Arrange group on the View tab to see how they display a calendar.

7. **Click the People button in the lower-left corner of the Outlook window.**

   If you don't see a People button, click the More button (. . .) to see a list of other services and select People from there.

   A list of any contacts you've already set up in Outlook appears. Contact listings provide names, addresses, e-mail addresses, phone numbers, and so on for people you want to keep in touch with. Notice the letters along the side of the listing, as in Figure 8-5:

   • You can click a letter to jump quickly to the people with last names starting with that letter.

   • You can double-click any listing to see its full record in a separate window.

Contacts list

Details of selected contact

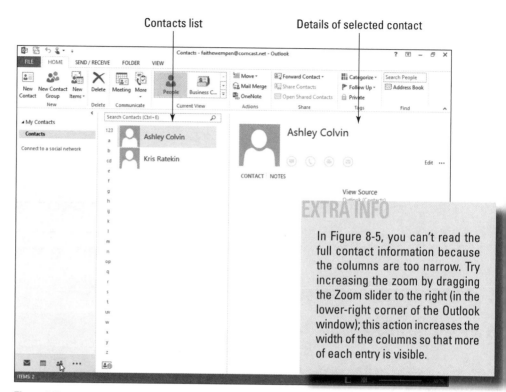

Figure 8-5

EXTRA INFO

In Figure 8-5, you can't read the full contact information because the columns are too narrow. Try increasing the zoom by dragging the Zoom slider to the right (in the lower-right corner of the Outlook window); this action increases the width of the columns so that more of each entry is visible.

PRACTICE

For more practice, double-click one of the contacts to browse its full information. Then close its window.

8. **Choose Home⇨Business Card. (It's in the Current View group.)**

The contacts appear as business cards rather than in a list.

9. **In the lower-left corner, click the More button (. . .) to see a list of other services and then select Tasks.**

A list of any to-do items you have already set up in Outlook appears.

10. **Click the More button (. . .) to see a list of other services and then select Notes.**

A list of any notes you have already set up in Outlook appears.

11. **Click the Mail button to return to the Mail folders.**

Leave Outlook open for the next exercise.

Setting Up Outlook for E-Mail

The first time you start Outlook, you're prompted to complete several setup operations. The most important of these is to set up your e-mail account. The following exercise walks you through the process.

Outlook supports POP3 and IMAP mail accounts. These are different kinds of mail servers. You need to know which type you have before you start setting up your e-mail account in Outlook. Ask your Internet service provider if needed. If that information is not available, try POP3 first; it's by far the more common type.

LINGO

Your **e-mail account** is the unique e-mail address that you use to send and receive messages. Your **Internet service provider (ISP)** probably provided you with at least one e-mail account, and you may have other accounts too.

A third kind of e-mail account is available: a web-based account, such as Yahoo! Mail, Gmail, and so on. These are also known as HTTP accounts (HyperText Transfer Protocol). Outlook doesn't support this type of e-mail account. Some workarounds can force Outlook to recognize certain HTTP mail accounts, but they aren't covered in this chapter.

LINGO

POP3 (Post Office Protocol 3) is the most common for home use and for most offices. With a POP3 account, mail is stored on the server until you retrieve it, and then it's downloaded to your PC (and deleted from the server). This is called a store-and-forward system.

With an **IMAP** (Internet Mail Access Protocol) account, the mail stays on the server at all times. This is convenient because you can get your e-mail from anywhere (and review old messages from anywhere), but it's slower than POP3 to access and more labor-intensive for the company managing the server. Some companies provide IMAP to their employees who travel a lot so they can get their e-mail from different PCs.

Most of the exercises in this book use fictional information and scenarios, but in this case, I ask you to use your own e-mail information. After all, it's *your* e-mail that you want to send and receive and not some fictional person's, right?

In this exercise, you configure Outlook to send and receive e-mail from your primary e-mail address.

Files needed: None

1. **Start Outlook if it isn't already open.**

2. **If this is the first time you've started Outlook, a Welcome to Microsoft Outlook 2013 dialog box opens. Click Next.**

> If you don't see that dialog box, someone might have already started Outlook on this PC before. Choose File⇨Account Settings⇨Account Settings to open a list of the accounts that are already set up. If your e-mail account is listed, you're done; close the dialog box. If not, click New and then pick up at Step 4.

3. **When asked whether you want to create a new e-mail account, click Yes and click Next.**

4. **In the Add Account dialog box, shown in Figure 8-6, fill in your name, e-mail address, and password and then click Next.**

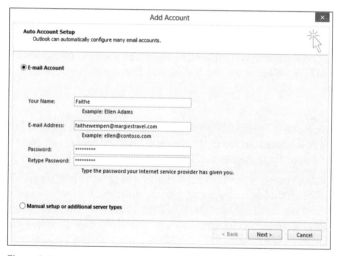

Figure 8-6

Outlook attempts to determine the name of your mail server and then contact it to set up your accounts, using an encrypted connection.

5. **If the encrypted connection works, a message appears, telling you so; in that case, proceed to the next step. If the encrypted connection doesn't work, a message to that effect appears. Click Next, and it tries to connect unencrypted.**

   If Outlook can determine the right settings (and it does in most cases), it logs in to the mail server and sends a test message to you. Wait while all this goes on.

   If, after trying an unencrypted connection, you still see a `Problem Connecting to Server` message, start at Step 3 of "Troubleshooting mail setup problems," later in this chapter.

6. **Check to make sure Outlook correctly detected the account type (probably POP3).**

   You should see a message that says `Your POP3 account has been successfully configured`. If it says IMAP but you don't actually have an IMAP mail account, skip ahead to the next section, "Changing account settings during setup."

7. **Only if the mail server type was correctly identified, click Finish; otherwise, see the next section.**

Leave Outlook open for the next exercise.

TIP

If the test message fails, see the later section "Troubleshooting mail setup problems."

LINGO

Encryption is a security measure that encodes the message content so that it can't be read if intercepted on its way to its destination. Outlook supports both encrypted and unencrypted e-mail connections.

Changing account settings during setup

If Outlook can't successfully detect your mail settings after you follow the steps in the preceding section, you may have to change the settings manually.

If you're configuring a POP3 e-mail account and you see a message saying `Your IMAP account has been successfully configured`, you need to change the account type, which is part of the manual settings you can adjust. You also need to specify a data file in which to store the messages. (IMAP accounts don't require a data file because they store messages only on the server.)

WARNING!

You must change the mail server type *before* clicking Finish as you're configuring the new account. Outlook won't let you change the server type afterwards.

Picking up from Step 6 in the previous section, follow these steps to manually configure settings:

1. **In the Add Account dialog box, select the Change Account Settings check box (if it isn't already selected) and click Next.**

   The Choose Service screen of the Add Account dialog box appears.

2. **Select POP or IMAP and click Next.**

   The POP and IMAP Account Settings screen of the Add Account dialog box appears, as shown in Figure 8-7.

Account type

Add Account	×

POP and IMAP Account Settings
Enter the mail server settings for your account.

User Information

Your Name:	Faithe
Email Address:	faithewempen@comcast.net

Server Information

Account Type:	POP3
Incoming mail server:	mail.comcast.net
Outgoing mail server (SMTP):	smtp.comcast.net

Logon Information

User Name:	faithewempen
Password:	********
	☑ Remember password

☐ Require logon using Secure Password Authentication (SPA)

Test Account Settings

We recommend that you test your account to ensure that the entries are correct.

Test Account Settings ...

☑ Automatically test account settings when Next is clicked

Deliver new messages to:

○ New Outlook Data File
● Existing Outlook Data File

C:\Users\Faithe\Documents\Outlook   Browse

Data file selection

More Settings ...

< Back   Next >   Cancel

Figure 8-7

3. **Open the Account Type drop-down list and select POP3 if it isn't already selected.**

4. **In the Deliver New Messages To area, specify a data file in which to store your messages. Select one of these two options:**

   • *Existing Outlook Data File:* Select this option and then click Browse and locate the existing data file to save to.

     If Outlook 2013 was installed from scratch on this PC, or if it replaced Outlook 2010 as an upgrade, the path to your existing data file is probably C:\Users*username*\Documents\ Outlook Files\Outlook.pst or C:\Users*username*\

`AppData\Local\Microsoft\Outlook\`*e-mail-address*`.ost`
(where *username* is your login name in Windows and *e-mail-address* is an e-mail address you have already set up).

If you upgraded to Outlook 2013 from Outlook 2007 or earlier, the path probably is `C:\users\`*username*`\AppData\Local\ Microsoft\Outlook` (where *username* is your login name in Windows).

If the AppData folder doesn't appear, you have to enable the display of hidden files and folders in Windows. To do so in Windows 8, open any File Explorer window and, on the View tab, select the Hidden Items check box. In Windows 7, open a Computer window (Start⇨Computer) and choose Organize⇨Folder and Search Options. The Folder Options dialog box appears. On the View tab, select the option labeled Show Hidden Files, Folders, and Drives and then click OK.

- *New Outlook Data File:* Select this option if you want to allow Outlook to create a data file just for the messages you receive from this account.

5. **Complete the setup by using the correct server type and settings, click Next, and then click Finish**

Leave Outlook open for the next exercise.

Should you create a new Outlook data file or use an existing one? That's up to you. Some people prefer to have a separate Outlook file for each e-mail address they have; others like all their POP3 accounts to be stored in a single file.

Setting up additional mail accounts

If you have other e-mail accounts, you can set them up in Outlook. If you have a separate account for a home-based business or hobby, for example, you might want to be able to get the mail for that address at the same time you retrieve the mail for your main account.

In this exercise, you set up an additional e-mail account in Outlook. You need an additional account of your own for this exercise because it doesn't provide a sample account.

Files needed: None

1. **Choose File⇨Info⇨Account Settings⇨Account Settings.**

The Account Settings dialog box opens.

2. **On the E-Mail tab, click New.**

The Auto Account Setup screen appears. (Refer to Figure 8-6.)

3. **To complete the setup process, follow Steps 4–7 in the earlier section "Setting Up Outlook for E-Mail."**

4. **When you finish setting up the account, click Close to close the Account Settings dialog box.**

Leave Outlook open for the next exercise.

Troubleshooting mail setup problems

Each e-mail service has its own quirks for setting up the account in Outlook (or any mail program) to properly send and receive messages. Outlook can automatically detect the settings in many cases, but it can't always detect every service correctly.

If Outlook wasn't able to successfully send a test message (see the earlier section, "Setting Up Outlook for E-Mail"), you need to do some troubleshooting. Don't panic, though. It's not that difficult. If you get stuck, you can always call your ISP's tech support line and get help.

If you're using a web-based e-mail provider such as Yahoo! Mail or Gmail, it might not work with Outlook. This is a known issue. Some services have workarounds that you can follow to make them work in Outlook; check the tech support section at the website where you get your web-based mail to see whether there is anything you can do.

To troubleshoot mail problems, make sure you have the following information handy. If you don't have it, contact your ISP. It may also be available on the ISP's website.

✔ **Your e-mail address and password:** You probably have this already from your earlier attempt.

✔ **The incoming and outgoing mail server addresses:** They might be the same.

The *server address* is usually whatever comes after the @ sign in your e-mail address, preceded by the word *mail*. For example, if your e-mail address is `tom@myprovider.com,` the mail server might be `mail.myprovider.com`. If there are separate servers for incoming and outgoing mail, the incoming one might be `pop.myprovider.com`, and the outgoing one might be `smtp.myprovider.com`. Those are just guesses, though; you need to get that information from your ISP.

✔ **Information about whether an encrypted connection should be used.**

✔ **Information about whether your outgoing mail server requires authentication:** If it requires authentication, you also need to know whether the outgoing server requires a different username and password than your regular one.

Armed with all that information, follow these steps to troubleshoot:

1. **Choose File⇨Account Settings⇨Account Settings.**

   The Account Settings dialog box opens.

2. **Double-click the e-mail account you want to troubleshoot.**

   The Change Account dialog box opens, as shown in Figure 8-8.

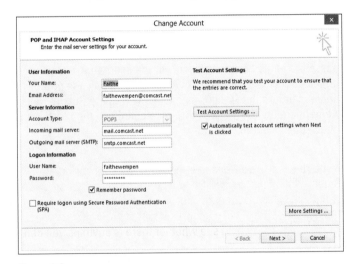

Figure 8-8

3. **Check all the information in the dialog box to make sure it matches the information you have about your account.**

   In particular, check the Account Type, Incoming Mail Server, and Outgoing Mail Server (SMTP).

You may not be able to change the account type. If you can't, and it's wrong, you need to delete that account from Outlook and set it up again as if it were a new account.

4. **Select or deselect the Require Login Using Secure Password Authentication (SPA) check box, whichever is different from the current setting.**

5. **Click the Test Account Settings button to see whether that fixed the problem. If it did, skip the rest of the steps. If it didn't, go back to the original setting and go on to the next step.**

6. **Click the More Settings button.**

   The Internet E-Mail Settings dialog box opens.

7. **Click the Outgoing Server tab and then select the My Outgoing Server (SMTP) Requires Authentication check box, as shown in Figure 8-9.**

8. **Try each of the three options. After each one, click OK and then click the Test Account Settings button to check whether it helped. If one of the options works, skip the rest of the steps.**

If you select the Log On Using radio button, fill in your username and password in the boxes provided. For the username, use your complete e-mail address. If that doesn't work, try using only the part of your e-mail address before the @ sign. Try it with the Require Secure Password Authentication (SPA) check box deselected and then try it with that check box selected.

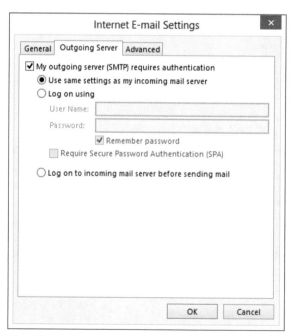

Figure 8-9

9. **If you closed the Internet E-mail Settings dialog box, click the More Settings button again to reopen it. Then on the Advanced tab (see Figure 8-10), drag the Server Timeouts slider closer to the word *Long* (that is, farther to the right).**

This change can help give more time to a mail server that is slow to respond. A timeout delay of more than two minutes isn't usually needed.

Some mail servers use different port numbers for incoming and/or outgoing mail. Check with your service provider to make sure that it uses the defaults of 110 for incoming and 25 for outgoing, and make changes on the Advanced tab if needed. If you use an encrypted connection, the incoming server's default is 995. Check with your provider to find out for sure.

10. **Click OK and click the Test Account Settings button.**

11. **If you got Outlook to successfully complete a test message, great. Close all dialog boxes. If not, contact your e-mail service provider's tech support and find out what setting you need to change to make it work.**

Leave Outlook open for the next exercise.

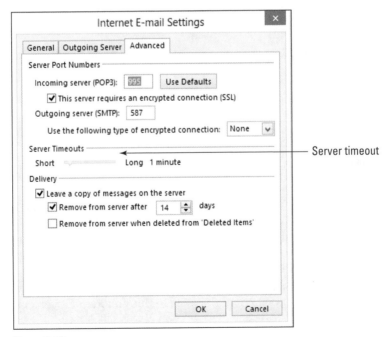

Figure 8-10

Composing a New Message

You can send a new e-mail message to anyone for whom you have an e-mail address. Just fill in the recipient, subject, and message and then send it off.

In the following exercise, you send yourself an e-mail message. By doing so, you'll then have a received message later so you can practice reading and replying to it.

Needed: An e-mail account set up in Outlook

1. **With the Inbox displayed onscreen, click the Home tab and then click the New E-Mail button.**

   A new Untitled – Message window appears, as shown in Figure 8-11.

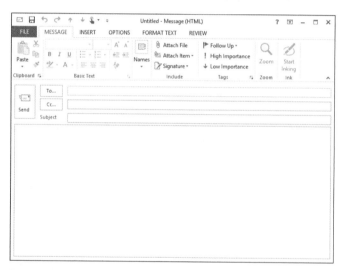

Figure 8-11

2. **In the To text box, type your own e-mail address.**

   If you want to send mail to multiple recipients, separate their e-mail addresses with commas in the To box. You can use the Cc box for additional recipients who should get a courtesy copy. (Both To and Cc recipients get identical messages.)

   You can choose a recipient from Outlook's Address Book by clicking the To button. I don't cover that skill in this chapter, but you can experiment with it on your own.

3. **In the Subject text box, type** Reminder.

> Including an appropriate subject line is important to alert the recipient about the topic you're writing about.

4. **In the body area, type the following:**

Make sure you remember to order the tickets to the graduation ceremony tonight.

> If you want to, you can format the body text in your message. Use the formatting buttons in the message composition window, such as Bold, Italic, Font, Font Size, and so on, just as you do in Word and other Office applications.

5. **Check the message to make sure it looks like Figure 8-12 (except with your own e-mail address in the To box rather than the dummy one shown in the figure).**

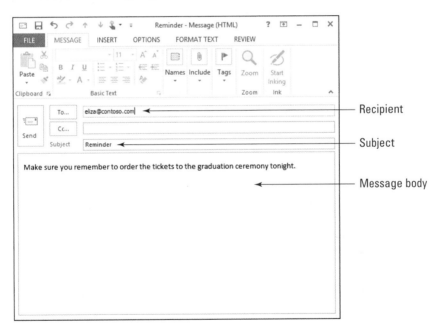

Figure 8-12

6. **Click the Send button.**

The message is sent. Depending on your Outlook settings, it may go out immediately, or it may wait until the next scheduled send/receive operation.

7. **To make sure that the message goes out, click the Send/Receive tab and then click the Send/Receive All Folders button.**

The message should appear in your Inbox as a new message. If the message doesn't appear, repeat the Send/Receive operation after a few minutes.

Leave Outlook open for the next exercise.

The Three Rs of Mail: Receiving, Reading, and Replying

After you configure your e-mail account(s) in Outlook, receiving mail is an automatic process. Outlook automatically sends and receives mail when you start it and also at 30-minute intervals (by default) whenever Outlook is running. Your incoming mail comes automatically into the Inbox folder. You can also initiate a manual send/receive operation at any time.

Sending and receiving e-mail manually

When you manually send and receive mail, Outlook connects to the mail server(s), sends any mail you have waiting to be sent, and downloads any waiting mail for you.

Here are the three ways you can manually send and receive e-mail in Outlook:

Send/Recieve All Folders

- Click the Send/Receive All Folders button on the Quick Access toolbar, as shown in Figure 8-13.

- Click the Send/Receive tab and then click the Send/Receive All Folders button.

- Press F9.

Figure 8-13

Leave Outlook open for the next exercise.

If the Send/Receive All Folders button doesn't appear on the Quick Access toolbar, click the Send/Receive tab, right-click the Send/Receive All Folders button, and choose Add to Quick Access Toolbar.

Setting the send/receive interval

By default, the automatic send/receive interval is 30 minutes. You might prefer a different interval. For example, because I need to respond quickly to business requests via e-mail, I have mine set to check every 5 minutes.

In the following exercise, you change the interval at which Outlook automatically sends and receives mail.

1. **Click the Send/Receive tab, click the Send/Receive Groups button, and then choose Define Send/Receive Groups.**

Alternatively, you can press Ctrl+Alt+S.

The Send/Receive Groups dialog box opens.

2. **In the Setting for Group "All Accounts" section, make sure that the Schedule an Automatic Send/Receive Every *X* Minutes check box is selected.**

3. **Click the down increment arrow on the text box to change the number of minutes to 5, as shown in Figure 8-14.**

4. **Click the Close button.**

Leave Outlook open for the next exercise.

Set the send/receive
interval here.

Figure 8-14

Reading an e-mail message

You can read messages in the Reading pane, or you can open each message in its own separate window.

In the following exercise, you read an e-mail message.

Needed: An e-mail account set up in Outlook and the Reminder e-mail message that you sent yourself in the preceding exercise

1. **Click the View tab, click the Reading Pane button, and choose Right to turn on the Reading pane at the right if it isn't already there.**

2. **Click the Reading Pane button again and choose Bottom to move the Reading pane below the Inbox.**

3. **Click the Reminder message in the Inbox pane.**

   This is the message you sent to yourself in the preceding section.

   The message appears in the Reading pane, as shown in Figure 8-15.

4. **Double-click the message in the Inbox pane to display the message in a separate window, as shown in Figure 8-16.**

TIP

Click the Close (X) button in the message window to close it.

Leave Outlook open for the next exercise.

Message content in
Reading pane   Selected message

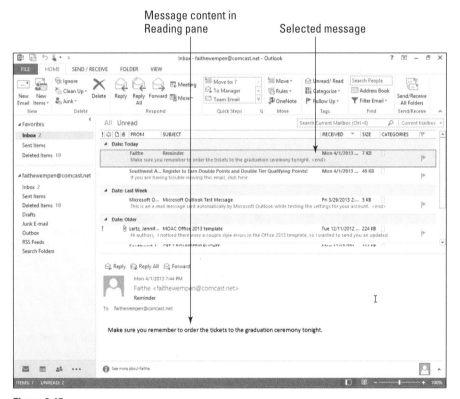

Figure 8-15

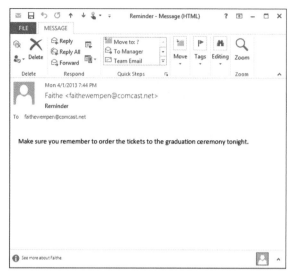

Figure 8-16

Replying to a message

Replying to a message is quick and easy because you don't have to look up the recipient's e-mail address. It's already filled in for you.

In the following exercise, you reply to an e-mail message.

Needed: An e-mail account set up in Outlook and the Reminder e-mail that you sent yourself earlier in this chapter

1. **In the Inbox pane, click the Reminder e-mail message.**

2. **On the Home tab, click the Reply button.**

If multiple people had received the e-mail and you wanted to reply to them all, you could click the Reply All button in Step 2. In this exercise, you were the only recipient, so it's a moot point.

In place of the Reading pane, a reply pane appears with the original message quoted in the body area, your e-mail address filled in on the From text box, and the original sender (also you) filled in on the To line. In the Subject text box, the original subject appears with *RE:* in front of it.

3. **At the top of the message body area, type your reply:** Thank you, I will.

   See Figure 8-17.

4. **Click the Send button.**

   The reply is sent.

Leave Outlook open for the next exercise.

Draft indicator appears when reply is being composed (below).

Click here to send reply.

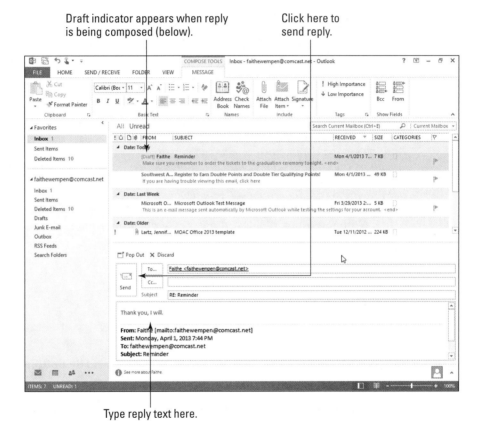

Type reply text here.

Figure 8-17

Working with Attachments

You can attach a file to an e-mail so that the file travels along with the message to the recipient. The recipient can then open the attachment directly from the Inbox or save it to her hard drive for later use. In the following exercises, you send and receive attachments.

Attaching a file to a message

Attach a file to a message when you want the recipient to have a copy of the file. Sending a file does not delete that file from your local PC; it sends a copy.

In the following exercise, you send yourself an e-mail message that contains an attachment. By doing so, you'll then have a received message with an attachment later to practice reading.

Needed: An e-mail account set up in Outlook

LINGO

Some e-mail messages have attachments, which are additional files that travel along with the e-mail message as it is sent and received.

1. **With the Inbox displayed onscreen, click the Home tab and then click the New Email button.**

   A new Untitled – Message window appears.

2. **In the To text box, type your own e-mail address.**

3. **In the Subject text box, type** Map.

4. **In the body area, type the following:** Please refer to the attached map for directions to the party.

5. **Click the Message tab and then click the Attach File button.**

   The Insert File dialog box opens.

6. **Navigate to the folder containing the data files for this chapter and select** Lesson 8 Map.xps.

   See Figure 8-18.

7. **Click the Insert button.**

8. **Check the message to confirm that it looks like Figure 8-19 (except with your own e-mail address in the To box).**

9. **Click the Send button.**

   The message is sent. Depending on your Outlook settings, it may go out immediately, or it may wait until the next scheduled send/receive operation.

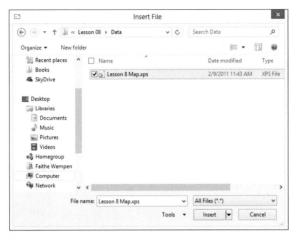

Figure 8-18

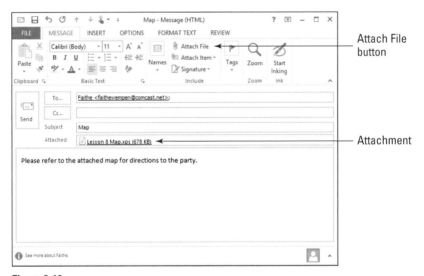

Figure 8-19

10. **To make sure that the message goes out, click the Send/Receive tab and then click the Send/Receive All Folders button.**

The message should appear in your Inbox as a new message. If it doesn't, repeat the Send/Receive operation after a few minutes.

Leave Outlook open for the next exercise.

Viewing and saving an e-mail attachment

Using attachments, people can exchange all types of files with one another, such as files from Word, Excel, and PowerPoint.

WARNING!

Some types of attachments can carry viruses. (Pictures are generally safe, though.) If you have any doubts about the safety of any file you receive, *do not open it.*

In the following exercise, you read an e-mail message that has an attachment, and save the attachment to your hard disk.

Needed: An e-mail account set up in Outlook and the Map e-mail that you sent yourself earlier in the chapter

1. **In the Inbox pane, click the Map message to select it.**

   The paper clip icon, shown in Figure 8-20, indicates that the e-mail has an attachment.

Paper clip icon indicates on attachment.　　　　　　　　Attachment

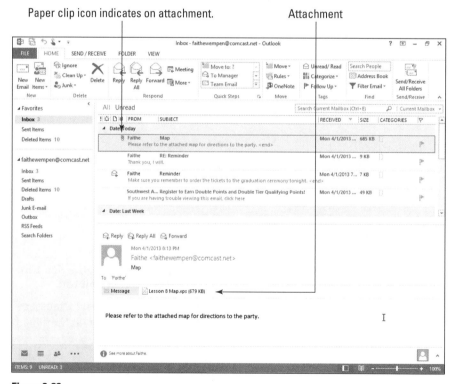

Figure 8-20

In the Reading pane, notice the two files listed above the message. One is called Message, and the other is the attached file's name (`Lesson 8 Map.xps`).

2. **Click `Lesson 8 Map.xps` in the Reading pane.**

A warning appears, stating that you should preview files only if they come from a trustworthy source.

3. **Click the Preview File button.**

A preview of the attachment appears in the Reading pane.

If the file type isn't one that Outlook can preview, a message appears and tells you `This file cannot be previewed because there is no previewer installed for it.`

4. **Click Message to return to seeing the message in the Reading pane.**

5. **Double-click `Lesson 8 Map.xps`.**

An Opening Mail Attachment dialog box appears, as shown in Figure 8-21.

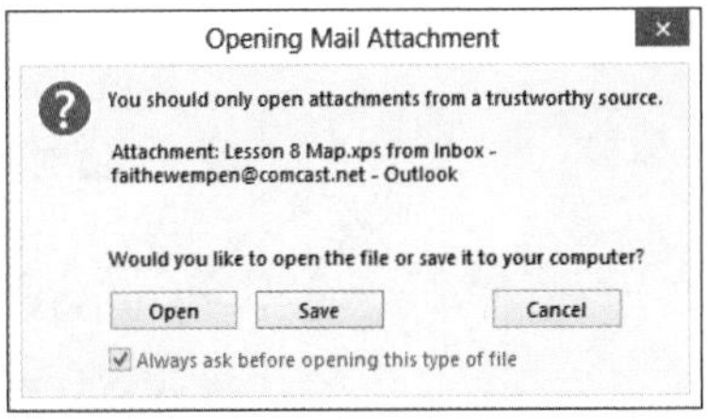

6. **Click the Open button.**

If you're using Windows 8 and haven't set a default for XPS files, a dialog box asks how you want to open this type of file.

7. **Click XPS Viewer.**

Figure 8-21

The map opens in the XPS Viewer application.

The XPS Viewer comes free with Windows.

8. **Click the Close button (X) to close the XPS Viewer application.**

9. **In the Reading pane, right-click the `Lesson 8 Map.xps` file and choose Save As.**

The Save As dialog box opens.

10. **Navigate to the location where you're storing your completed work for this chapter.**

11. **Click Save.**

The attachment is saved.

Leave Outlook open for the next exercise.

Managing Incoming Mail

If you receive a lot of e-mail, you may want to set up some systems for keeping it organized. Your system can include creating folders to store e-mail that you want to keep for later reference, moving messages from one folder to another, deleting e-mail that you no longer need, and flagging an e-mail for later follow-up. You can also configure Outlook's Junk E-Mail filter to be more or less aggressive in trying to filter out unwanted advertisements.

Creating folders for managing mail

Outlook starts with a basic set of folders, which you can see on the Folder pane when viewing the Inbox:

- **Inbox:** Incoming mail
- **Sent Items:** Copies of sent messages
- **Deleted Items:** Messages you have deleted from other folders
- **Junk E-Mail:** Messages that the Junk Mail filter has identified as possible junk
- **Outbox:** Messages waiting to be sent
- **RSS Feeds:** Any RSS feeds you've subscribed to

LINGO

RSS (Really Simple Syndication) feeds enable you to receive updated content from websites automatically in Outlook, without your having to visit those sites.

You can create new folders if you like and then either manually drag and drop messages into them for storage or create mail-handling rules that automatically place messages into those folders upon receipt.

In the following exercise, you create a mail folder.

Needed: An e-mail account set up in Outlook

1. **In the Folder pane to the left of the Inbox pane, right-click Inbox and choose New Folder.**

   A blank text box appears, as shown in Figure 8-22.

2. **Click in the text box and type** Short-Term, **and then press Enter.**

   The new folder is created below the Inbox folder on the Folder pane, as shown in Figure 8-23. There may also be

Figure 8-22

New folder

Figure 8-23

other folders already beneath the Inbox folder, depending on whether anyone has created others on this PC already.

3. **Click the new Short-Term folder to select it.**

Its content appears. It's empty, so both of the panes on the right are blank.

Leave Outlook open for the next exercise.

Moving a message to a folder

One way to move messages to another folder for storage is to drag and drop them there. You can drag individual messages or select multiple messages at once and drag them as a group.

In the following exercise, you move a message into a different folder.

Needed: An e-mail account set up in Outlook, the Short-Term folder created in the previous exercise, and the Reminder e-mail that you sent yourself earlier in this chapter

1. **In the Folder pane to the left of the Inbox pane, click Inbox to return to the Inbox folder.**

2. **If the Short-Term folder isn't visible below the Inbox folder in the Folder pane on the left, click the triangle to the left of Inbox to expand its list of subfolders.**

3. **In the Inbox, click the Reminder e-mail that you sent yourself earlier in the chapter.**

4. **Drag the Reminder e-mail to the Short-Term folder and drop it there.**

   The message is moved into that folder.

5. **Click the Short-Term folder to display its content.**

   It now contains the message you just placed there, as shown in Figure 8-24.

Leave Outlook open for the next exercise.

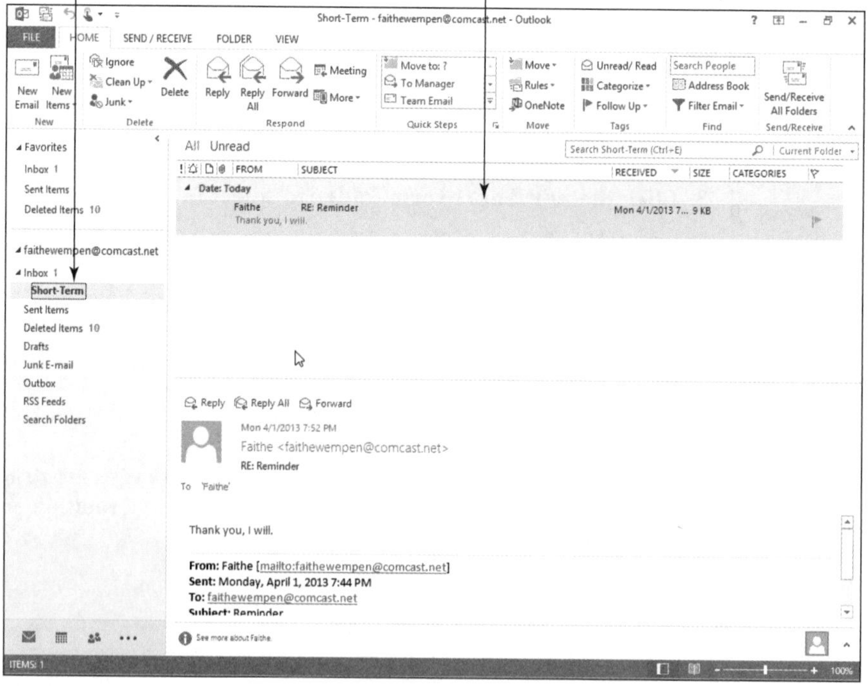

Short-Term folder selected.   Folder contains one message.

Figure 8-24

Creating a rule that moves messages

You can create message-handling *rules,* which are instructions that execute automatically to carry out your wishes for certain situations. For example, a rule can move messages from a certain person or with a certain word in the subject line to a specified folder.

In the following exercise, you create a message-handling rule that moves messages based on a word in the subject line.

Needed: An e-mail account set up in Outlook, the Short-Term folder created in an earlier exercise, and the Map e-mail that you sent yourself earlier in this chapter

1. **Choose File⇨Info⇨Manage Rules & Alerts.**

   The Rules and Alerts dialog box opens.

2. **Click the New Rule button.**

   The Rules Wizard dialog box opens.

3. **In the Stay Organized section of the Step 1 pane, select Move Messages with Specific Words in the Subject to a Folder.**

   See Figure 8-25.

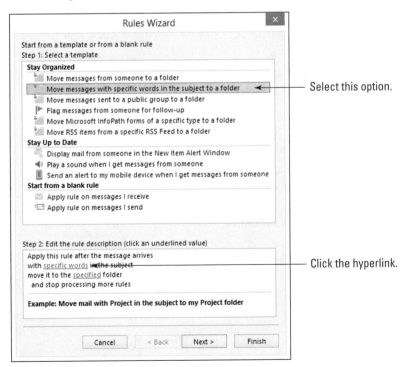

Figure 8-25

4. **In the Step 2 pane, click the underlined phrase** `specific words`.

The Search Text dialog box opens.

5. **In the text box labeled Specify Words or Phrases to Search For in the Subject, type** Map **and then click the Add button to add it to the Search list.**

Figure 8-26 shows the word already added to the search list.

Figure 8-26

6. **Click OK to return to the Rules Wizard dialog box.**

The word *Map* appears underlined in the Step 2 pane.

7. **In the Step 2 pane, click the underlined word** `specified`.

The Rules and Alerts dialog box appears, showing a folder list.

8. **Click the triangle to the left of Inbox to expand the list of subfolders and then click Short-Term.**

See Figure 8-27.

9. **Click OK to return to the Rules Wizard dialog box.**

Now in the Step 2 pane, the rule appears as shown in Figure 8-28.

10. **Click the Finish button.**

The rule is created, and it appears in the Rules and Alerts dialog box.

11. **Click the Run Rules Now button.**

The Run Rules Now dialog box opens.

Figure 8-27

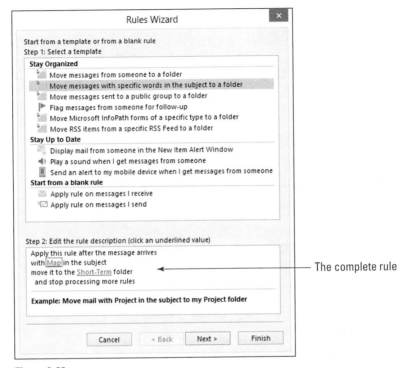

The complete rule

Figure 8-28

12. **Click to mark the Map check box, selecting the Map rule, as shown in Figure 8-29.**

13. **Click the Run Now button.**

    The rule is run, and the message with the Map subject line is moved into the Short-Term folder.

14. **Click Close to close the Run Rules Now dialog box.**

15. **Click OK to close the Rules and Alerts dialog box.**

16. **Press Esc or click the Back arrow to return to the Inbox.**

    Notice that the Map message is no longer in the Inbox.

17. **In the Folder pane at the left, click the Short-Term folder.**

    The Map message appears there.

Leave Outlook open for the next exercise.

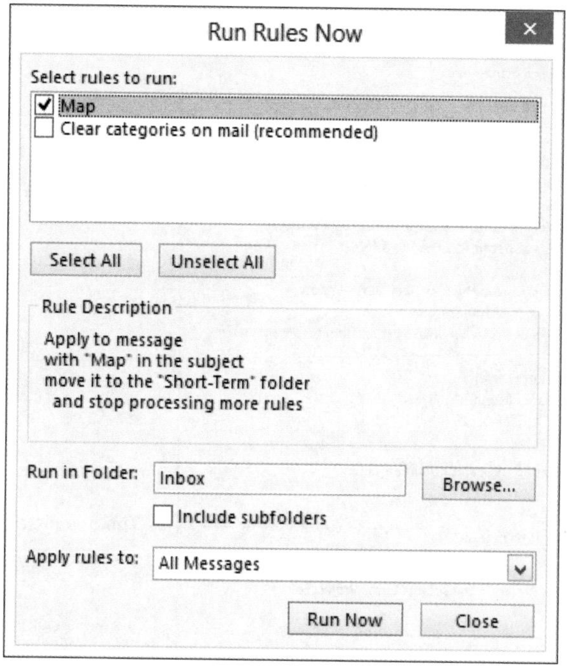

Figure 8-29

Customizing the Favorites list

You can place shortcuts in the Favorites list to the mail folders you use most frequently, so you don't have to wade through a long list of folders every time you want them.

In the following exercise, you add a folder to the Favorites list.

Needed: An e-mail account set up in Outlook and the Short-Term folder created in an earlier exercise

LINGO

The **Favorites list** is a shortcut area that appears at the top of the Folder pane in Outlook when in the Mail area of the application.

1. **In the Folder pane on the left, click the Short-Term folder to select it.**

2. **Drag the Short-Term folder up to the Favorites list and drop it at the top of the list.**

   A shortcut to the Short-Term folder now appears on the Favorites list, as shown in Figure 8-30.

3. **Right-click the Short-Term folder on the Favorites list.**

4. **Choose Remove from Favorites from the shortcut menu.**

   The Short-Term folder no longer appears on the Favorites list. The folder itself still exists.

Leave Outlook open for the next exercise.

Deleting e-mail

Even though so far you've been focusing on how to save e-mail for later reference, there's nothing wrong with deleting e-mail after you read it. In fact, as time goes by, you'll accumulate way too much e-mail if you don't delete most of it.

In the following exercise, you delete an e-mail message and then retrieve it again from the Deleted Items folder.

Needed: An e-mail account set up in Outlook and the Short-Term folder created in an earlier exercise, containing the Map and Reminder e-mails you sent to yourself earlier in the chapter

◢ Favorites	‹
Inbox 1	
Sent Items	
Deleted Items 10	
Short-Term	
◢ faithewempen@comcast.net	
◢ Inbox 1	
Short-Term	
Sent Items	
Deleted Items 10	
Drafts	
Junk E-mail	
Outbox	
RSS Feeds	
Search Folders	

Figure 8-30

1. **In the Folder pane on the left, click Short-Term to display that folder if it isn't already displayed.**

2. **Click the Map e-mail message.**

3. **Press the Delete key to delete it.**

4. **Click the Reminder e-mail message.**

5. **Click the Home tab and click the Delete button to delete it.**

6. **In the Folder pane, click the Deleted Items folder.**

   The display switches to that folder.

7. **Click the Received column heading to sort by that column.**

   A down-pointing triangle should appear on that column heading.

If an up-pointing triangle appears there, click the Received column heading a second time to change the sort order.

Your two deleted messages appear there, as shown in Figure 8-31.

Deleted items folder   Deleted messages

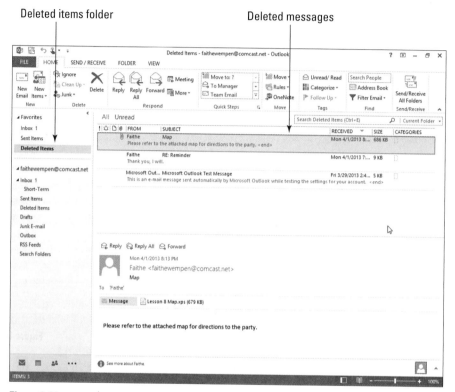

Figure 8-31

8. **Click the Reminder e-mail to select it.**

9. **Hold down the Ctrl key and click the Map e-mail to select it.**

10. **Drag the selected e-mail messages to the Short-Term folder in the Folder pane on the left.**

 The messages are moved back into the Short-Term folder.

11. **Click the Short-Term folder to display its content and confirm that the two messages now appear there.**

Leave Outlook open for the next exercise.

Flagging an e-mail

You can assign different flags to a message depending on when follow-up is due. When a flagged message is overdue, the entire message appears in red text on the message list. After you've done whatever it was you needed to do, you can mark the message as completed.

In the following exercise, you flag an e-mail and then mark it as completed.

Needed: An e-mail account set up in Outlook and the Short-Term folder containing the Map and Reminder e-mails sent to yourself earlier in the chapter

1. **In the Short-Term folder, click the Map message to select it.**

2. **Click the flag outline in the Flag column (on the far right edge of the message list).**

   The flag changes from transparent to bright red. Figure 8-32 shows a flagged message. The default flag is a Today flag, indicating you should follow up on it today.

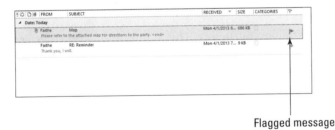

Flagged message

Figure 8-32

3. **Click the red flag.**

   It changes to a check mark, indicating the action has been completed on the message.

4. **Right-click the check mark and, from the shortcut menu that appears, choose Next Week.**

   The flag reappears and changes to a pink flag, indicating a lower priority.

For more practice, try selecting each of the other flags on the shortcut menu to assign them to the message.

5. Right-click the flag choose Clear Flag from the shortcut menu.

The flag goes back to being transparent, as it was when you began.

Leave Outlook open for the next exercise.

Configuring the Junk Mail filter

You can adjust the sensitivity of the Junk Mail filter in the Outlook options. If you set it to be very aggressive, fewer junk messages will get through, but it might sometimes mark legitimate messages as junk. If you set it to be less aggressive, you'll get more junk in your Inbox.

In the following exercise, you configure the Junk Mail filter in Outlook.

Needed: An e-mail account set up in Outlook

1. **Click the Home tab, click the Junk button, and choose Junk E-Mail Options.**

   The Junk E-Mail Options dialog box appears.

2. **On the Options tab, click the option button that best represents the level of filtering you want. See Figure 8-33.**

   - *No Automatic Filtering:* Turns off the filter.

   - *Low:* Moves most obvious junk e-mail.

   - *High:* Catches almost all junk e-mail but also may catch some regular mail.

   - *Safe Lists Only:* Allows only e-mail on your Safe Senders List. (If you choose this option, you must then configure the lists on the Safe Senders and Safe Recipients tabs.)

3. **Click OK to accept the new setting.**

4. **Exit Outlook.**

LINGO

Outlook comes with a **Junk Mail filter** that removes some of the more obvious junk messages from your Inbox before they have a chance to annoy you. The Junk Mail filter relies on internal rules that Outlook receives from Microsoft. Occasionally Microsoft sends out updates for it, which you receive as Windows Updates. The Junk Mail filter is far from perfect, but it does catch some items.

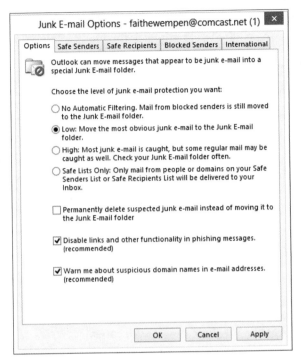

Figure 8-33

 Summing Up

Here are the key points you learned about in this chapter:

✔ Sending and receiving e-mail in Outlook requires a valid e-mail account.

✔ Most e-mail accounts are of the POP3 type; IMAP is a less-common but also supported type.

✔ Outlook doesn't work with most web mail accounts.

✔ To compose a new e-mail message, choose Home➪New E-Mail.

✔ To attach a file, from the e-mail composition window, choose Message➪ Attach File.

✔ To manually send and receive, click the Send/Receive All Folders button on the Quick Access toolbar or on the Send/Receive tab, or press F9.

✔ You can set the Reading pane to appear below or to the right of the message list. Click View and then Reading Pane to change its position.

- ✔ To save an e-mail attachment, right-click it and choose Save As.
- ✔ To create new e-mail folders, right-click the Inbox folder and choose New Folder.
- ✔ To move a message to a folder, drag it there.
- ✔ To add a folder to the Favorites list, drag it there.
- ✔ To create message handling rules, choose File➪Info➪Manage Rules & Alerts.
- ✔ To delete an e-mail, press the Delete key or choose Home➪Delete.
- ✔ To flag an e-mail, click the flag symbol to its right on the message list.
- ✔ To configure the junk mail filter, choose Home➪Junk➪Junk E-Mail Options.

Try-it-yourself lab

For more practice with the features covered in this chapter, try the following exercise on your own:

1. **Ask several friends for their e-mail addresses.**
2. **In Outlook, compose a new e-mail message and address it to at least three people. Separate the addresses with commas in the To box.**
3. **In the Subject text box, type** Best Joke Ever.
4. **In the message body, type your favorite joke. End the message by asking your friends to send a joke back to you using Reply All. Ask them to put the word** *Joke* **in the subject line.**
5. **Click Send.**
6. **Create a new folder called Jokes.**
7. **Create a message-handling rule that sends any incoming jokes to that folder. (Hint: Use the word** *Joke* **in the subject line as the criterion.)**
8. **Sit back and enjoy the jokes that your friends send back to you.**

Know this tech talk

attachment: A file that travels along with an e-mail message.

e-mail account: The unique e-mail address that you use to send and receive messages.

encryption: A security measure that encodes the message content so that it can't be read if intercepted.

Favorites list: A shortcut area that appears at the top of the Folder pane in Outlook when in the Mail area of the application.

flag: To mark an item to remind yourself to take action on it later.

HTTP: HyperText Transfer Protocol, a web-based Internet protocol. This is the protocol that most web-based mail services use, such as Hotmail and Gmail.

IMAP: Internet Mail Access Protocol, an alternative to POP3 where the messages remain on the server.

Internet service provider (ISP): The company that provides your Internet service.

Junk Mail filter: A feature in Outlook that removes some of the more obvious junk messages from your Inbox.

POP3: Post Office Protocol 3, the most common type of e-mail account. This type works on a store-and-forward basis, with messages transferred from the server to your local PC and then deleted from the server.

rule: A message-handling instruction that executes to carry out your wishes for sorting and managing e-mail.

Chapter 9

Using Outlook Contacts and Tasks

✔ Contacts *store information you need to keep in touch* with people.

✔ The File As property for a contact *controls how it is alphabetized* in the Contacts list.

✔ E-mailing contact information to others can *save them time in data entry*.

✔ Creating tasks for the things you need to accomplish helps you *prioritize tasks and track your progress* toward their completion.

✔ You can *set a reminder so that a pop-up box opens* and lets you know when it's time to work on a task.

1. How do you add a person's contact information to Outlook?

Find out on page 313

2. Can you alphabetize a contact by the company name rather than the person?

Find out on page 319

3. How do you get a contact back after accidentally deleting it?

Find out on page 320

4. How do you e-mail contact information to someone who doesn't have Outlook?

Find out on page 324

5. How do you create a Tasks list that includes multiple priorities?

Find out on page 327

6. How do you set a reminder to complete a task?

Find out on page 331

*O*utlook is much more than just an e-mail program. It excels at storing information that you need for your daily business and personal dealings, such as contact information and to-do lists. If you can't keep yourself organized with all these tools available to you, don't blame Outlook!

In this chapter, I show you how to enter and use contact information in the People area of Outlook. I also show how to create and manage tasks and to-do items in the Tasks area.

Storing Contact Information

Outlook stores complete contact information about the people you want to keep in touch with. You can store not only mailing addresses but also phone numbers, e-mail addresses, pager numbers, and personal information such as birthdays, spouse names, departments, and professions.

LINGO

The People area of Outlook stores a **contact** (also called a **record**) for each person or business that you want to save for later use. In earlier versions of Outlook, this area was called Contacts.

Adding and editing a contact

You may not have any contacts yet in the People area of Outlook. Don't worry about that, though, because it's easy to add one.

In the following exercise, you create a contact in Outlook.

Files needed: None

1. **In Outlook, click the People icon in the lower-left corner of the application window.**

   The Contacts pane appears. You may or may not have any contacts in it.

2. **Choose Home⇨New Contact.**

   The Untitled – Contact window opens.

3. Enter the information shown in Figure 9-1.

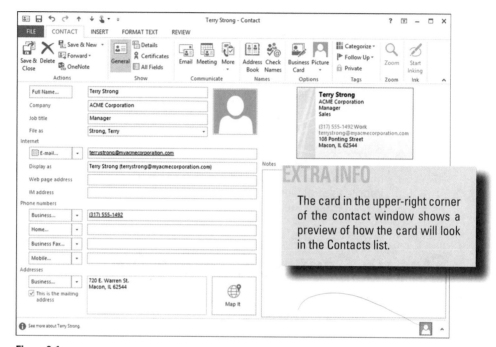

Figure 9-1

4. Choose Contact⇨Details.

Additional fields appear.

Depending on the window width, you might need to click a Show button to open the collapsed group to find the Details button.

5. Enter the additional information shown in Figure 9-2.

6. Click the Save & Close button on the Ribbon.

The contact closes, and a card for it appears on the Contacts list, as shown in Figure 9-3. If you've already entered other contacts, they appear there also.

7. Double-click the contact you just created.

It reopens.

8. Change the job title to Vice President for the contact.

9. Click the Save & Close button.

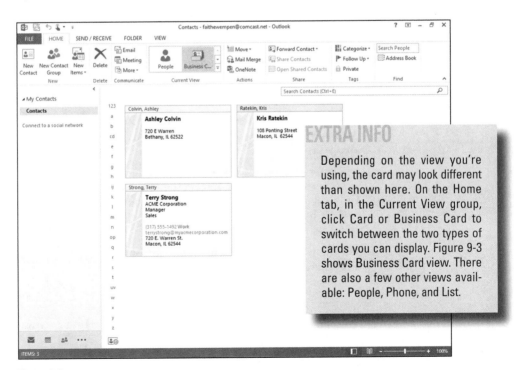

Figure 9-2

Figure 9-3

EXTRA INFO

Depending on the view you're using, the card may look different than shown here. On the Home tab, in the Current View group, click Card or Business Card to switch between the two types of cards you can display. Figure 9-3 shows Business Card view. There are also a few other views available: People, Phone, and List.

10. **If you don't already have other contacts entered, enter the two contacts shown in Figure 9-4.**

    Later exercises assume you have multiple contacts entered.

Leave Outlook open for the next exercise.

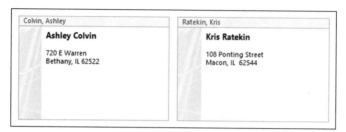

Figure 9-4

Navigating the Contacts list

Depending on the view you're using at the moment, each contact may be displayed as a card, a business card, or an item in a list. You can change the view of the Contacts list in several ways. You can jump to a particular letter of the alphabet by clicking a letter along the left side of the display. You can set viewing options on the View tab, and you can display or hide the Folder pane. The following exercise practices all those skills.

In the following exercise, you change the way contacts are displayed in Outlook.

Files needed: None

1. **Choose View➪Folder Pane and then choose Minimized from the Folder Pane button's drop-down list.**

   This step minimizes the Folder pane so that it appears only as a thin bar on the left side of the screen. You can expand it any time you need it by clicking the arrow at the top of the bar, as shown in Figure 9-5.

2. **On the Home tab, click the More button in the Current View group.**

You can click this arrow to expand or minimize the Folder pane.

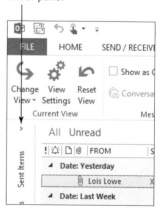

Figure 9-5

The Communicate group also has a More button, but that's not the button you want for this step. The More button for the Current View group is the down-pointing arrow with the horizontal line over it.

The gallery that appears contains five options: People, Business Card, Card, Phone, and List.

3. **Click each of the views to try them out. Apply the Card view last so that you end up in Card view.**

Notice the gray vertical bar that's separating the columns in Card view. You can drag this bar to increase or decrease the width of the column so that each card's details show fully or partially.

4. **Drag the vertical bar to the right until all the text in each card is fully displayed, as shown in Figure 9-6.**

5. **Choose View⇨Reading Pane⇨Right to turn on the Reading pane.**

The selected contact's full information appears in the Reading pane to the right of the list, as shown in Figure 9-7.

Drag vertical bar.

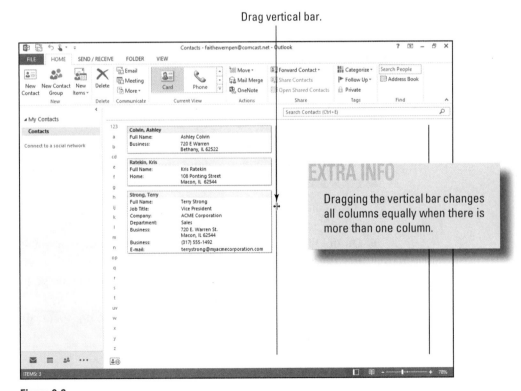

EXTRA INFO

Dragging the vertical bar changes all columns equally when there is more than one column.

Figure 9-6

Reading Pane button   Reading pane

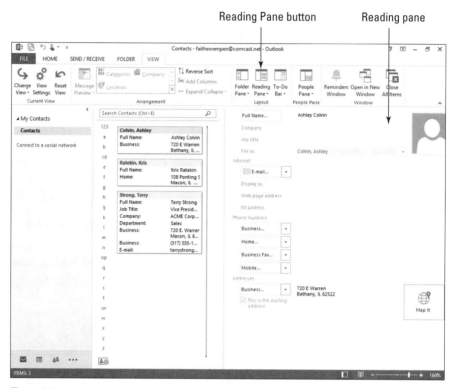

Figure 9-7

6. **Choose View➪Reading Pane➪Off to turn off the Reading pane again.**

7. **Choose View➪To-Do Bar➪Calendar.**

   A monthly calendar appears.

8. **Choose View➪To-Do Bar➪Tasks.**

   Any items you have set up in your To-Do list (covered later in this chapter) appear. See Figure 9-8.

9. **On the View tab, click the To-Do Bar button and choose Off to close the To-Do Bar.**

10. **On the View tab, click the Reverse Sort button to change the sort order of the contacts to Z to A.**

11. **Click the Reverse Sort button again to change the sort order back to the default (A to Z).**

Leave Outlook open for the next exercise.

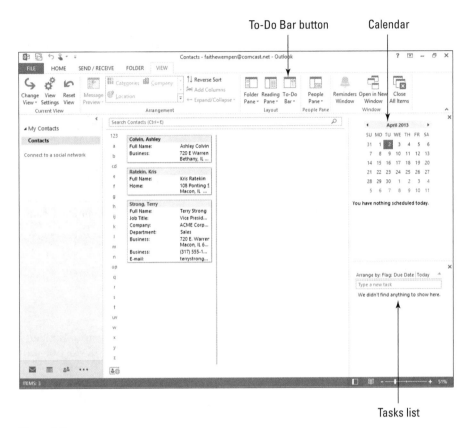

Figure 9-8

Changing how a contact is filed

If someone asked you how contacts were alphabetized in Outlook, you would probably say that they're done by last name, right? And you'd be absolutely . . . *wrong*.

Yes, so far the contacts you've worked with have been alphabetized by last name, but that's just a coincidence. They've been done that way because that's how they're set to be filed. The **File As** setting determines the sort order in the Contacts list. By default, when you create a new contact, the File As setting for it is set to *Last Name, First Name.* But you can change that to some other setting if you prefer, such as the company name or the first name. Set it to whatever way you think you will search for that contact in the future.

In this exercise, you change a contact's File As setting to the business name.

Files needed: Terry Strong contact created earlier in the chapter

1. **Double-click the Strong, Terry contact to reopen it.**

2. **Open the File As drop-down list and select ACME Corporation, as shown in Figure 9-9.**

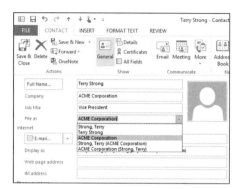

EXTRA INFO

If you want both the company name and the person's name to show, choose one of the File As options that includes both. The one that appears first will be how it is alphabetized. For example, Strong, Terry (ACME Corporation) alphabetizes by Strong but also includes ACME Corporation in the title.

Figure 9-9

3. **Click the Save & Close button.**

The contact closes. Notice that it now appears alphabetized in the A section, at the top of the contact list, and that ACME Corporation appears as the top line.

Leave Outlook open for the next exercise.

Deleting and restoring a contact

With Outlook, you don't have to tear pages out of a paper address book to get rid of a person's information; just delete the contact.

Deleted contacts go to the Deleted Items folder in Outlook until the next time you empty the Deleted Items folder, so you can retrieve them from there if you make a mistake.

In this exercise, you delete a contact and then retrieve it from the Deleted Items folder.

Files needed: ACME Corporation contact created earlier in the chapter

1. **Click the ACME Corporation contact to select it.**

2. **Press the Delete key or click the Home tab and then the Delete button.**

3. **If the Folder pane is minimized, click the arrow at the top of the minimized pane to expand it to normal size.**

4. **At the bottom of the Navigation pane, click the More button (. . .) and click Folders.**

   The Navigation pane changes to show the Folder pane.

5. **In the Folder pane, click Deleted Items, as shown in Figure 9-10.**

   If you see the deleted ACME contact on the list, skip to Step 7. Otherwise, continue to Step 6 to find it.

6. **Click in the Search text box and type** ACME. **Press Enter.**

   The list of deleted items is filtered to show items containing that word. The deleted contact is included on that list.

Deleted Items folder

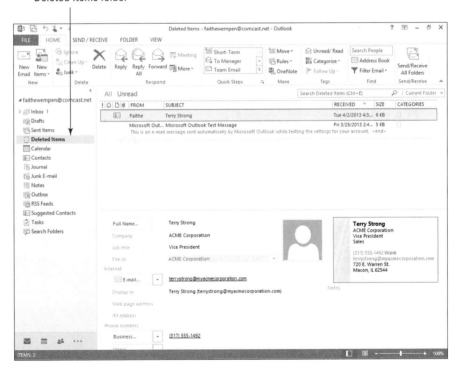

Figure 9-10

7. **Drag the contact to the Contacts folder in the Navigation pane and drop it there.**

   It is moved from the Deleted Items folder back to the Contacts folder.

8. **Click the Contacts folder in the Navigation pane to display its contents.**

   Note that the ACME contact is restored.

Leave Outlook open for the next exercise.

Using Contact Information

Storing contact information is all well and good, but you'll probably want to do something useful with it.

If you need the information for some offline task, such as addressing an envelope by hand or looking up a phone number to dial, you can just browse the Contacts list and double-click the desired contact to open all its details.

You can also perform some actions on the PC with the stored contact information. For example, you can use contact information to address e-mail messages, and you can send contact information to other people.

Sending an e-mail message to a contact

You can easily address an e-mail message to a contact in your Contacts list. You can initiate this process either from the Contacts area of the program or from the Mail area.

In this exercise, you start an e-mail message to a contact using two different methods.

Files needed: ACME Corporation and Terry Strong contacts created earlier in the chapter

1. **In the Folder pane, click Contacts.**

2. **Click the ACME contact to select it.**

3. **On the Home tab, click the E-Mail button.**

   A new e-mail message opens with the ACME contact's e-mail address filled in.

4. **Click the Close (X) button on the new e-mail message's window to close it without sending it.**

5. **When prompted to save changes, click No.**

6. **At the bottom of the Folder pane, click the Mail icon, switching to the Mail section of Outlook.**

7. **Click the New Email button.**

A new e-mail message window opens.

8. **Click the To button.**

The Select Names: Contacts window opens, as shown in Figure 9-11.

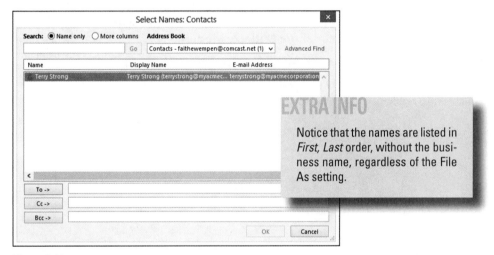

Figure 9-11

9. **Double-click the listing for Terry Strong.**

The address is added to the To line.

10. **Click OK.**

The address is added to the To line in the new message window.

11. **Click the Close (X) button on the new e-mail message's window to close it without sending it.**

When prompted to save changes, click No.

Leave Outlook open for the next exercise.

Attaching contact info to an e-mail

You can share a contact with another e-mail user by attaching the contact record to an e-mail.

In this exercise, you attach a vCard to an e-mail you're composing.

Files needed: ACME Corporation contact created earlier in the chapter

1. **Redisplay the Contacts list, if needed, by clicking the People icon in the bottom-left corner of the Outlook window.**

2. **Click the ACME Corporation contact.**

3. **Choose Home⇨Forward Contact⇨As a Business Card.**

   A vCard version of the contact is inserted in the message, as shown in Figure 9-12.

LINGO

Business card: The attachment is in **vCard** format (`.vcf`), a standard format for personal data that many programs can accept.

Outlook contact: The attachment is an Outlook contact, which only Outlook can accept.

Text message: The contact information appears in the body of the message as plain text, so any recipient can read it.

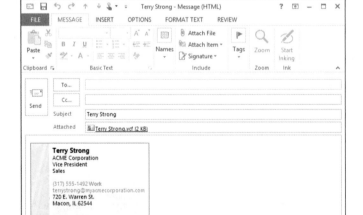

Figure 9-12

4. **Type your own e-mail address in the To text box.**

5. **Click the Send button.**

   The contact is sent via e-mail (to you).

6. **On the Quick Access toolbar, click the Send/Receive All Folders button.**

   The e-mail containing the attached contact should arrive within a few minutes. Repeat the Send/Receive operation if needed.

7. **When you receive the e-mail containing the contact, double-click the message to open it.**

8. **Double-click the `Terry Strong.vcf` attachment to view it.**

9. **Click the Save & Close button.**

   If a Duplicate Contact Detected dialog box opens, click Cancel.

PRACTICE

For more practice, send yourself a copy of the contact by using the As an Outlook Contact option on the Forward Contact button's menu.

Leave Outlook open for the next exercise.

Using Tasks and the To-Do List

The Tasks area in Outlook helps you create and manage action items for yourself and others. Not only can Outlook keep track of what you need to do, but it can also remind you of upcoming deadlines, record what percentage of a large job you've completed, and even send out e-mails that assign certain tasks to other people.

Displaying the Tasks list

To view the Tasks area of Outlook, click More (. . .) in the lower-left part of the Folders pane and then click Tasks. Any tasks or to-do items that you may have already created appear there.

In the upper part of the Folder pane, in the My Tasks section, you can click either To-Do List or Tasks to specify which set of activities you want to look at. For the purposes of this book, I assume that you choose Tasks.

LINGO

It's important to understand the difference in Outlook between Tasks and the To-Do list.

Tasks are specific items you created in the Tasks area of Outlook. Something isn't technically a *task* unless it was created in the Tasks section.

The **To-Do list** contains everything from the Tasks list as well as other items you have marked for action, such as e-mail messages you flag for follow-up.

In the following exercise, you display Tasks items in the Tasks area of Outlook.

Files needed: None

1. **In the lower-left corner of the Outlook window, click More (. . .) and then click Tasks.**

2. **Under My Tasks in the upper-left corner, click Tasks.**

   The list changes to show only tasks, not other to-do items.

3. **Choose View⇨Reading Pane⇨Right to open a reading pane on the right side of the screen.**

   If you already have some tasks created, they appear; if not, both panes appear blank, as shown in Figure 9-13.

Leave Outlook open for the next exercise.

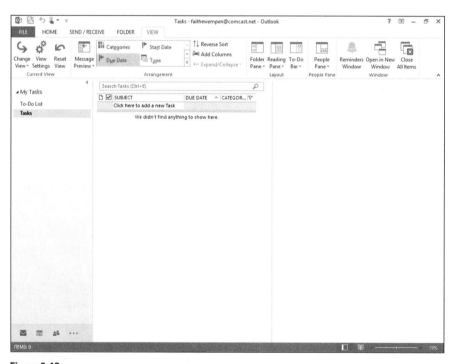

Figure 9-13

Creating a task

As with Contacts, you can enter as much or as little information as you like about each task, depending on what you want to track and how closely you want to monitor it.

In this exercise, you create a task.

Files needed: None

1. **With the Tasks area of Outlook displayed, choose Home⇨New Task.**

   An Untitled – Task window opens.

2. **In the Subject text box, type** Data Conversion Project.

3. **Click the down arrow in the Start Date box and click today's date on the calendar.**

4. **Click the down arrow on the Due Date box and select a date two weeks from today.**

5. **Open the Status drop-down list and select In Progress.**

6. **In the Body area of the task window, type** Data conversion between the UNIVAC system and Windows Server.

7. **Open the Priority drop-down list and select High.**

   Higher-priority tasks appear at the top of the list in certain views or if you sort by priority.

   Figure 9-14 shows the completed task window.

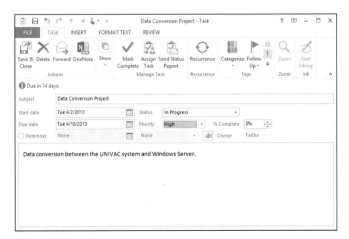

Figure 9-14

8. **Click the Save & Close button.**

   The task appears in the Tasks list.

9. **Click the new task.**

   Its details appear in the Reading pane, as shown in Figure 9-15.

10. **Choose View⇨Change View button and choose Detailed to switch to Detailed view.**

    This action enables you to see the task's priority in the Priority column.

    High-priority tasks appear with a red exclamation point in that column; low-priority tasks show a blue down-pointing arrow there. See Figure 9-16. Notice that in Detailed view, the Reading pane no longer appears. The setting doesn't carry over when you switch views.

Selected task   Task details

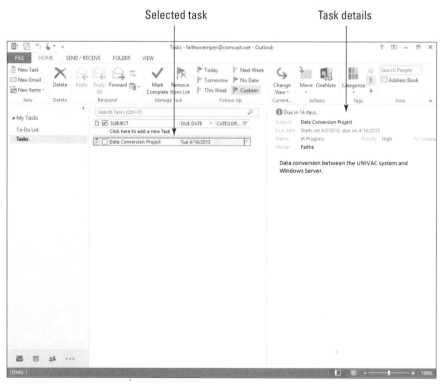

Figure 9-15

Change View   High-priority task

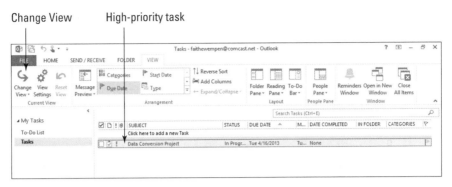

Figure 9-16

Leave Outlook open for the next exercise.

Updating a task

As your work on a task progresses, you may want to update its status in Outlook. You might also want to flag it for follow-up, change its due date, or mark it as completed.

In this exercise, you change a task's settings, including updating its progress and changing its due date.

Files needed: Data conversion task created in previous exercise

1. **In the Tasks area of Outlook, click the task you created in the previous exercise if it isn't already selected.**

2. **Select the check box to the left of the task.**

   It's marked as completed. It turns gray, and a strikethrough line is drawn through it, as shown in Figure 9-17.

Mark the check box.   Task is marked as completed.

Figure 9-17

TIP

Completing a task does *not* automatically delete it. Depending on the view, a completed task might disappear from the Tasks list, but it's not gone.

3. **Click the View tab, click the Change View button, and choose Active.**

   This view displays only active tasks, and the completed task is no longer active, so it doesn't appear.

4. **Click the Change View button again and choose Detailed.**

   This view returns to showing detailed information about each task. The completed task appears here.

5. **Click the task's check box again to toggle the task's status back to being incomplete.**

6. **Double-click the task to reopen its window.**

7. **Open the Status drop-down list and select In Progress.**

8. **Click the up increment arrow on the % Complete box to set the percent to 25%.**

   Figure 9-18 shows the task at this point.

9. **Click the Save & Close button.**

   The task closes.

Set completion percentage.

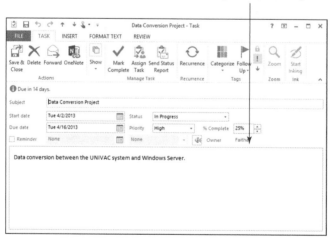

Figure 9-18

10. **On the Tasks list, click the task's status (In Progress). A menu opens. From the menu, choose Deferred, as shown in Figure 9-19.**

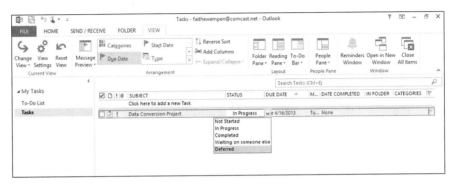

Figure 9-19

11. **Choose Home⇨This Week.**

    This step changes the follow-up flag on the task to this week. It also changes the Due Date field.

12. **On the Home tab, click the No Date button.**

    This step sets the task to have no due date at all. (That's appropriate because its status is now Deferred.)

You can also right-click the flag in the Flag column on the task list and choose a different follow-up flag if you prefer that method.

Leave Outlook open for the next exercise.

Setting a task reminder

You may want to set a reminder to help you stay on top of your task assignments. Reminders pop up at the time you specify to let you know it's time to pay attention to a task. You can also enter your own custom reminder text.

Set your reminder to occur before the task's actual due date to give yourself some time to work on it. For example, set a budget's reminder for two weeks prior to the date.

In this exercise, you set a reminder for a task.

Files needed: Data conversion task created earlier in this chapter

1. **In the Tasks area of Outlook, double-click the task you created earlier.**

   It opens in its own window.

2. **Select the Reminder check box under the due date.**

3. **Today's date may already appear in the Date box. If it doesn't, open the Date drop-down list and select today's date.**

4. **Open the Time drop-down list and select a time that is 3 minutes from now. If the exact time isn't one of the choices, close the drop-down list, click in the Time box, and manually type the time.**

   See Figure 9-20.

Type or select the reminder date.   Type or select the reminder time.

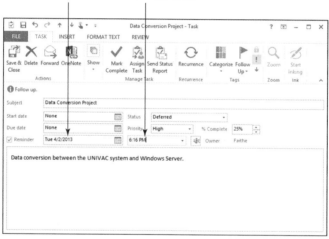

Figure 9-20

A default-assigned sound plays when the reminder occurs. To change the sound, you can click the Sound button (it looks like a speaker) and browse for a different sound file.

5. **Click the Save & Close button.**

6. **Wait 3 minutes for the reminder box to pop up.**

   See Figure 9-21.

7. Click the Dismiss button.

The reminder is dismissed.

TIP

You could have clicked Snooze instead to make it disappear temporarily but pop up again later.

Leave Outlook open for the next exercise.

Figure 9-21

Deleting a task

As I mention earlier, completing a task doesn't delete it. You might want to keep completed tasks around for later reference. If you don't want to see them, switch to a view that doesn't include completed tasks, such as the Active view. If you're sure you want to delete a task, though, it's easy enough to delete it.

In the following exercise, you delete a task in three different ways.

Files needed: Data conversion task created earlier in this chapter

1. In the Tasks area of Outlook, select the task you created earlier.

2. Choose Home⇨Delete.

The task is deleted.

3. Click the Undo button on the Quick Access toolbar to undo the deletion.

4. Select the task and then press the Delete key.

The task is deleted.

5. Click the Undo button on the Quick Access toolbar to undo the deletion.

6. Right-click the task and choose Delete.

The task is deleted.

Close Outlook when you're finished with this exercise.

Summing Up

Here are the key points you learned about in this chapter:

- ✔ A contact (or record) is the information about a single person, business, or family that you store in the Contacts area of Outlook.

- ✔ To add a contact, view the People section of Outlook and then choose Home⇨New Contact.

- ✔ To change the view of the Contacts list, you can choose Home⇨Current View⇨More and then click the desired view.

- ✔ To turn the Reading pane on or off, click View, Reading Pane and then click the position you want (Right, Bottom, or Off).

- ✔ To change how a contact is filed alphabetically, set its File As setting.

- ✔ To delete a contact, select it and press Delete. You can restore it from the Deleted Items folder if you change your mind.

- ✔ To send an e-mail to a contact, select the contact and then choose Home⇨E-Mail.

- ✔ You can attach contact information to an e-mail in any of three formats: Outlook contact, vCard, or text message. Choose Home⇨Forward Contact and choose the desired format.

- ✔ The Tasks area of Outlook can display either Tasks (tasks only) or the To-Do list (tasks plus other items that have due dates or are flagged for follow-up).

- ✔ To create a task, in the Tasks area, choose Home⇨New Task.

- ✔ To update a task, double-click it to reopen its window.

- ✔ To delete a task, select it and press the Delete key.

Try-it-yourself lab

For more practice with the features covered in this chapter, try the following exercise on your own:

1. **In Outlook, use the Tasks section to create a list of all the assignments and readings that are due in your classes in the next two weeks. (If you aren't in any classes, use to-do items for your work or personal commitments instead.) Prioritize them and set appropriate due dates.**

2. **Use the People section to enter contact information for yourself and two other people.**

Know this tech talk

contact: A set of contact data (name, address, phone, and so on) for a person, family, or business. Also called a *record*.

File As: The setting in a contact's properties that controls how it appears in the alphabetical sort of the Contacts list.

record: See *contact*.

reminder: A timed pop-up window that appears at a certain date and time to remind you of a task or other item to deal with.

tasks: Items you create in the Tasks area of Outlook, containing information about a job or responsibility to be accomplished.

To-Do list: A list of things to accomplish in Outlook that includes both tasks and other items that require follow-up, such as e-mail to be answered.

vCard: A standard format for personal data (.vcf).

Chapter 10
Getting Started with PowerPoint

- Presentations *provide visual aids* for live or remotely delivered speeches.

- PowerPoint lets you create presentations you can *print, deliver onscreen, e-mail, or distribute on CD.*

- PowerPoint views enable you to *work with the program in different ways* as needed.

- The File⇨New command enables you to *create a new presentation,* either blank or based on a template or theme.

- Templates *provide a headstart* on both formatting and content.

- Adding new slides to a presentation enables you to *expand its scope and add more content.*

- Duplicating a slide *saves time* by avoiding repetitive data entry.

- Manually created text boxes enable you to *place additional text where no placeholders exist.*

1. **Which view is best for viewing the entire presentation at a glance?**

Find out on page 342

2. **How do you start a new blank presentation?**

Find out on page 346

3. **What's the difference between a template and a theme?**

Find out on page 347

4. **How do you create a new slide with a different layout than the default?**

Find out on page 349

5. **How do you delete a slide?**

Find out on page 354

6. **How do you create extra text boxes on a slide?**

Find out on page 358

7. **How do you move an object on a slide?**

Find out on page 360

8. **How do you resize a text box?**

Find out on page 363

*P*owerPoint is the most popular presentation software in the world. Presentation software creates support materials for people who give speeches. You can project PowerPoint slides on a big screen behind you as you speak, create handouts to distribute to the audience, and print note pages for your own reference. PowerPoint can also create self-running presentations for distribution via CD or online.

This chapter offers you some basics for working with PowerPoint. You learn how to start a new presentation, add slides and text to it, and move and resize the content on a slide. In later chapters, you learn how to add other types of content and special effects to a show.

Exploring the PowerPoint Interface

In PowerPoint, you work with slides and presentations rather than pages and documents (as in Word) or worksheets and workbooks (as in Excel).

At a big-picture level, the PowerPoint interface is very similar to that in Word and Excel: It has a Ribbon, a File tab, and a status bar. The default view of the presentation, called *Normal view,* consists of three panes, as shown in Figure 10-1. (You may or may not see the rulers onscreen, depending on your settings.)

- ✔ **The Slides pane** is the bar along the left side. Thumbnail images of the slides appear here. It is sometimes called the *thumbnails pane.*

- ✔ **The Slide pane** (that's singular, not plural) in the middle shows the active slide in a large, editable pane. Here's where you do most of your work on each slide. It is sometimes called the editing pane.

- ✔ **The Notes pane** runs along the bottom of the screen. Here you can type any notes to yourself about the active slide. These notes don't show onscreen when you display the presentation, and they don't print (unless you explicitly choose to print them).

Slides pane

Slide pane

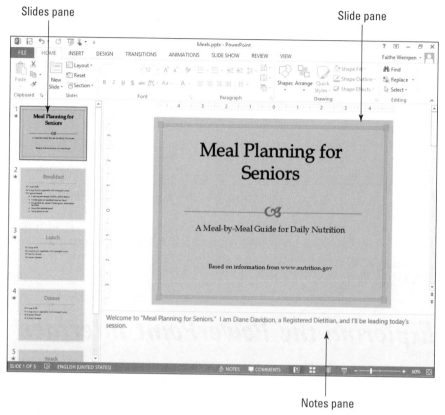

Notes pane

Figure 10-1

Moving around in a presentation

You can navigate a presentation in many of the same ways you moved through other applications' content. The Page Up and Page Down keys scroll one full screen at a time, and you can drag the scroll bars to scroll as well. You can also select slides from the Slides pane.

In this exercise, you open a presentation file and move around in it.

Files needed: Lesson 10 Meals.pptx

1. **Start PowerPoint and open the file** Lesson 10 Meals.pptx. **Save the file as** Lesson 10 Meals Tour.pptx.

   Refer to Chapter 1 if you need help starting Office applications or opening and saving files.

2. **Click the thumbnail image of slide 3.**

That slide becomes active. In other words, it appears in the Slide pane (the large pane on the right), where you can edit it. See Figure 10-2.

3. **Press the Page Down key.**

The next slide (slide 4) becomes active.

4. **In the vertical scroll bar on the Slide pane, click in the blank area above the scroll box.**

The previous slide (slide 3) becomes active.

5. **Press the Home key.**

Slide 1 becomes active.

Click slide 3 to select it.

Selected slide appears here for editing.

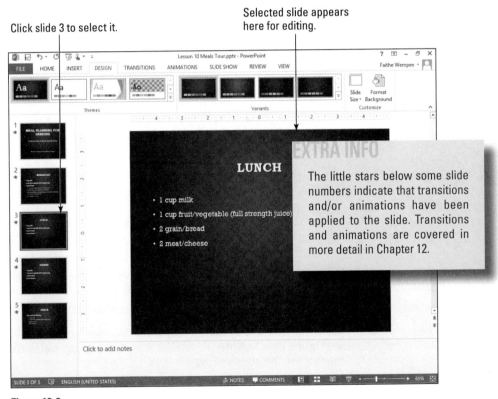

EXTRA INFO

The little stars below some slide numbers indicate that transitions and/or animations have been applied to the slide. Transitions and animations are covered in more detail in Chapter 12.

Figure 10-2

6. **Press the End key.**

Slide 5 (the last slide) becomes active.

7. **Click below slide 5, in the Notes pane, and type** Thank the audience for their attention.

8. **Save the presentation.**

Leave PowerPoint open for the next exercise.

Understanding PowerPoint views

PowerPoint provides several views for you to work with. Each view is useful for a different set of activities. Normal view (refer to Figure 10-1), the default, is the most commonly used view. You can switch to one of the other views in either of these ways:

✔ Click one of the View buttons in the bottom-right corner of the PowerPoint window. (Not all the views are represented there.)

✔ On the View tab, click a button for the view you want.

Figure 10-3 shows Slide Sorter view and also points out the two places where you can switch views: on the View tab and on the status bar. Slide Sorter view is best for rearranging slides and viewing the entire presentation at a glance.

In this exercise, you try several views in PowerPoint.

Files needed: Lesson 10 Meals Tour.pptx, *already open from the previous exercise*

1. **Choose View⇨Slide Sorter.**

The presentation changes to Slide Sorter view, as shown in Figure 10-3.

2. **Choose View⇨Notes Page.**

Notes Page view is available only from the View tab (not the status bar). See Figure 10-4. In Notes Page view, you can see any notes that you've entered for the active slide.

Views

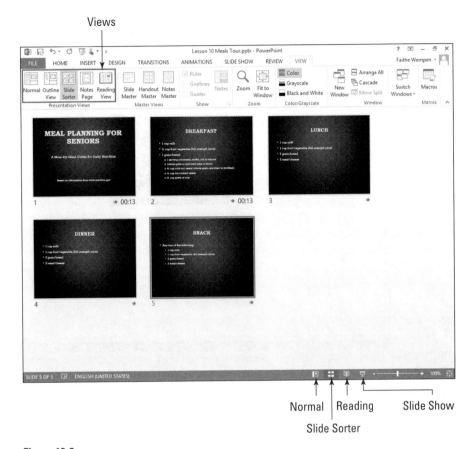

Normal | Reading | Slide Show

Slide Sorter

Figure 10-3

TIP

Use the Zoom slider in the bottom-right corner to zoom in to see the notes more clearly if desired.

3. **Choose View⇨Outline View.**

Outline view (see Figure 10-5) is just like Normal view except the left pane contains a text outline instead of thumbnail images of the slides. Only text in the slides' text placeholders appears on the outline; text from manually placed text boxes does not.

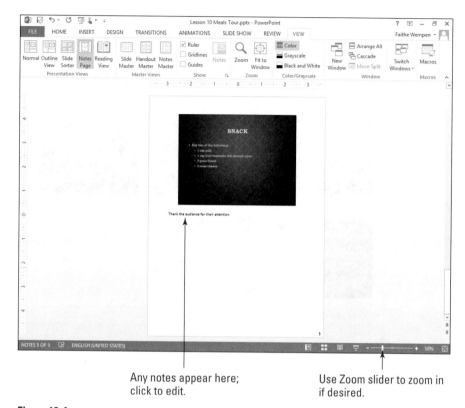

Any notes appear here;
click to edit.

Use Zoom slider to zoom in
if desired.

Figure 10-4

4. **On the status bar, click the Normal button.**

   The presentation switches back to Normal view.

5. **On the status bar, click the Slide Show button.**

   The presentation opens in Slide Show view. The slide fills the entire screen.

6. **Press Esc to leave Slide Show view.**

7. **Look on the View tab and notice that there's no button for Slide Show view there.**

8. **Click the Slide Show tab on the Ribbon.**

   Notice that there are two buttons here for entering Slide Show view: From Beginning and From Current Slide. See Figure 10-6.

Outline pane

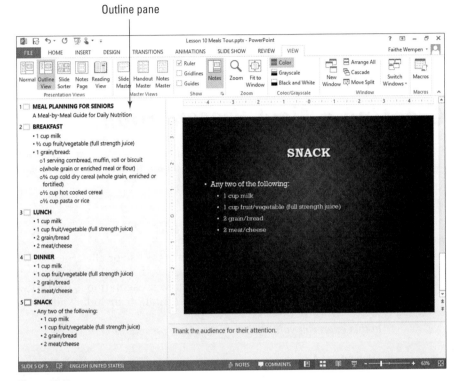

Figure 10-5

These buttons open
Slide Show view.

Figure 10-6

9. **In the Slides pane, click slide 4 to make it active.**

10. **Click the Slide Show tab and then the From Current Slide button.**

    Slide 4 appears in Slide Show view.

11. **Press Esc to return to Normal view.**

12. **Click the Save button on the Quick Access toolbar to save it.**

13. **Choose File⇨Close to close the presentation.**

Leave PowerPoint open for the next exercise.

Creating a New Presentation

You can create a new presentation in several ways. You can create a blank one, or you can base a presentation on a template that contains formatting specs, sample content, or both.

Creating a blank presentation

When you start PowerPoint and then press Esc or click the Blank Presentation template, a new blank presentation appears, containing a single slide. The fastest and simplest way to create a new presentation is to start with a blank one. You can then add text to the presentation, including additional slides.

In this exercise, you create a new blank presentation.

Files needed: None

1. **Choose File⇨New.**

   Backstage view opens, displaying tiles for various types of presentations you can create. See Figure 10-7.

2. **Click the Blank Presentation tile.**

   A new blank presentation opens.

3. **Choose File⇨Close to close the new presentation.**

   Don't save changes if prompted.

4. **Press Ctrl+N.**

   A new blank presentation opens.

This is an alternative method of doing the same thing as in Steps 1 and 2.

5. **Choose File⇨Close to close the new presentation.**

Leave PowerPoint open for the next exercise.

Blank Presentation tile

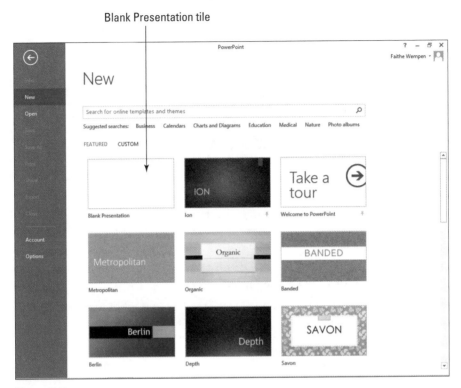

Figure 10-7

Creating a presentation with a template

PowerPoint templates give you a jump start to creating complete presentations. Each template employs one or more themes. A *theme* is a collection of settings including colors, fonts, background graphics, bullet graphics, margins, and placement.

In this exercise, you create a new presentation based on a theme.

Files needed: None

LINGO

A **template** is a reusable sample file that includes a background, layouts, coordinating fonts, and other design elements that work together to create an attractive, finished slide show. Templates may (but are not required to) contain sample content, too.

1. **Choose File➪New. (Refer to Figure 10-7.)**

   Backstage view opens, displaying tiles for various types of presentations you can create.

2. Click the Welcome to PowerPoint tile.

An information box appears for that template, as shown in Figure 10-8.

Figure 10-8

3. Click the Create button.

A new presentation is created based on that template. It includes a theme and five sample slides, as shown in Figure 10-9.

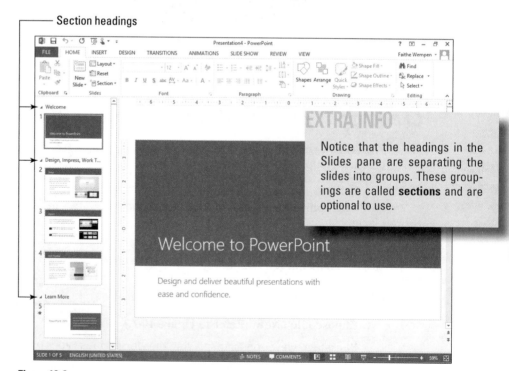

Figure 10-9

4. **Save the presentation as** Lesson 10 Sample.

5. **Close the presentation by choosing File⇨Close.**

Leave PowerPoint open for the next exercise.

Creating New Slides

Each new blank presentation begins with one slide in it: a title slide. You can easily add more slides to the presentation by using the default layout (Title and Content) or any other layout you prefer.

Several methods are available for creating new slides, and each one is best suited for a particular situation. In the following sections, you learn each of the methods.

Creating a new slide with the Ribbon

The most straightforward way to create a new slide is with the New Slide command.

In this exercise, you create three new slides: two using the default layout and one using a different layout.

Files needed: None

1. **In PowerPoint, press Ctrl+N to start a new blank presentation.**

   A single slide appears in it.

2. **Choose Home⇨New Slide.**

   A new slide appears with the Title and Content layout.

3. **Press Ctrl+M.**

   Another new slide appears with the Title and Content layout.

4. **Click the arrow below the New Slide button, opening a menu of other layouts, as shown in Figure 10-10.**

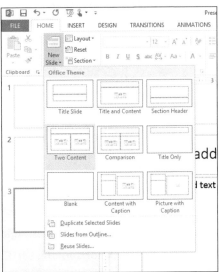

Figure 10-10

5. Click the Two Content layout.

A new slide appears with a title placeholder and two separate content placeholders, as shown in Figure 10-11.

Figure 10-11

6. Close the presentation without saving it.

Leave PowerPoint open for the next exercise.

Creating a new slide in the Slides pane or Outline pane

In the Slides pane in Normal view, you can click to place a horizontal insertion point between two existing slides or at the bottom of the list of slides and then press Enter. In Outline view, you click to place a text insertion point at the beginning of the title of an existing slide in the Outline pane, and then you press Enter to create a new title (and a new slide).

In this exercise, you create new slides using both the Slides pane in Normal view and the Outline pane in Outline view.

Files needed: `Lesson 10 Comstar.pptx`

1. Open the file `Lesson 10 Comstar.pptx` and save it as `Lesson 10 Comstar Practice.pptx`.

2. In Normal view, click between slides 1 and 2 in the Slides pane.

A horizontal insertion point appears there, as shown in Figure 10-12.

Click to place horizontal insertion point line here.

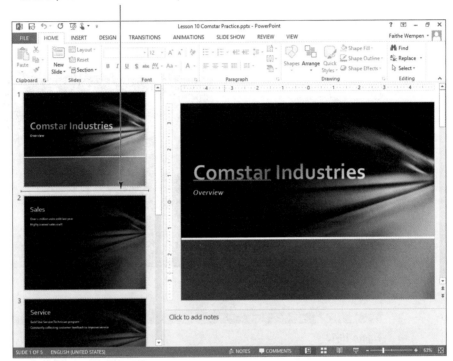

Figure 10-12

You can drag the divider between the two panes to decrease the width of the Slides pane and decrease the size of the thumbnails if desired.

3. **Press Enter.**

   A new slide appears there with the Title and Content layout.

4. **Choose View⇨Outline View.**

   Six small rectangles appear, representing each slide. The text from the slides also appears. The slide titles appear in bold on the first line of each slide, and the slide content appears below it. The line for slide 2 (the newly inserted slide) is blank because there's no content in it yet. See Figure 10-13.

EXTRA INFO

Normally a slide inserted this way uses the same layout as the one above it. However, if the slide above it is a Title Slide, the inserted slide takes on the Title and Content layout. This setup is by design because PowerPoint anticipates that you probably don't want two title slides in a row.

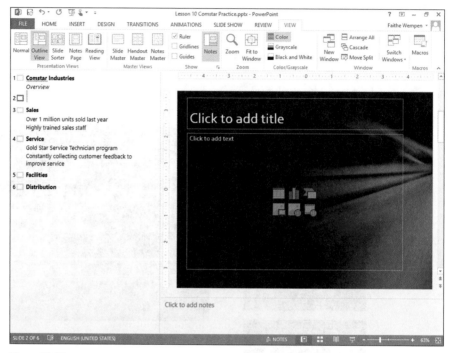

Figure 10-13

5. **In the Outline pane, click to place the insertion point after the word *staff* on slide 3.**

6. **Press Enter.**

   A new line appears in the content for slide 3.

7. **Press Shift+Tab to promote the new line to being a slide title.**

   A slide icon (4) appears next to the new line, as shown in Figure 10-14.

8. **Click to place the insertion point to the left of the slide title (Service) on slide 5.**

Figure 10-14

9. **Press Enter.**

A new slide appears before the Service slide. It's a new slide because it takes its outline level from the line that the insertion point was on when you pressed Enter.

10. **Save the presentation.**

Leave the presentation open for the next exercise.

Duplicating a slide

If you need to create a series of very similar slides, you might find it easier to copy or duplicate a slide and then make the small modifications to each copy.

Copying and duplicating are two separate commands in PowerPoint, but they have essentially the same result.

When you copy a slide (or multiple slides), you place a copy of it on the Clipboard, and then you paste it from the Clipboard into the presentation. You can paste anywhere in the presentation or into a different presentation (or, for that matter, a different document altogether).

When you duplicate a slide (or multiple slides), go to the Home tab, click the New Slide button, and choose Duplicate Selected Slides. You don't have to paste, because that command accomplishes both a copy and a paste operation at the same time. However, you also don't get to choose where they're pasted; they're pasted directly below the original selection.

In this exercise, you copy a slide and duplicate a slide.

Files needed: Lesson 10 Comstar Practice.pptx, *already open from the previous exercise*

1. **Switch to Normal view.**

2. **Click slide 6 to select it.**

3. **Choose Home⇨Copy, or press Ctrl+C.**

4. **Click below slide 8 to place the horizontal insertion point there.**

5. **Choose Home⇨Paste, or press Ctrl+V.**

A copy of slide 6 appears as the new slide 9.

6. **Click slide 1 to select it.**

7. **On the Home tab, click the down arrow under the New Slide button and choose Duplicate Selected Slides.**

A copy of slide 1 appears immediately below the original. You should now have 10 slides in the presentation. On the status bar, the message `Slide 2 of 10` appears, as shown in Figure 10-15.

Original   Copy

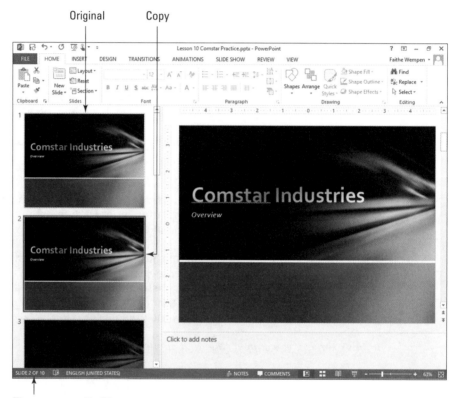

There are now 10 slides.

Figure 10-15

8. **Save the presentation.**

Leave the presentation open for the next exercise.

Deleting a slide

Deleting a slide removes it from the presentation. You can delete a slide either by pressing the Delete key or by right-clicking the slide and choosing Delete Slide from the shortcut menu.

There's no Recycle Bin for slides; you can't get them back after you delete them. However, you can undo your last action(s) with the Undo button on the Quick Access toolbar, and that includes undoing deletions. If you haven't saved your work since you made the deletion, you can also get a deleted slide back by closing the file without saving changes and then reopening it.

In this exercise, you delete some slides.

Files needed: `Lesson 10 Comstar Practice.pptx`, *already open from the previous exercise*

1. **In the Slides/Outline pane, click slide 2 (which is a duplicate of slide 1).**

2. **Press the Delete key.**

   One of the blank slides is now slide 2.

3. **Press the Delete key again.**

   Now slide 2 is the Sales slide.

4. **Click slide 3 (also blank), hold down the Shift key, and click slide 4 (also blank).**

5. **Right-click one of the selected slides (3 or 4) and choose Delete Slide from the shortcut menu.**

   See Figure 10-16.

6. **Click slide 6 (the last slide) to select it.**

7. **Right-click slide 6 and choose Delete Slide from the shortcut menu.**

   The presentation now contains five slides, all of which have a title.

8. **Save the presentation.**

Leave the presentation open for the next exercise.

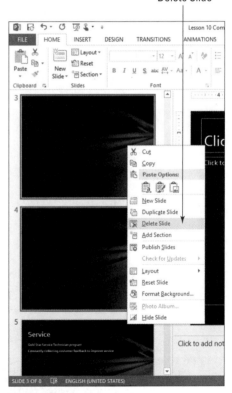

Figure 10-16

Adding Text to a Slide

Adding text to a slide is as easy as clicking in a placeholder box and typing. You can also type text on the Outline pane in Outline view or create your own text boxes in addition to the placeholders.

Typing in a slide placeholder

Some placeholders are specifically for text. For example, the placeholder for each slide's title is text-only. Click in such a placeholder and type the text you want. A content placeholder, such as the large placeholder on the default layout, can hold any *one* type of content: text, table, chart, SmartArt graphic, picture, clip art, or media clip (video or sound). Later chapters explain some of these other types of content in more detail.

You can type either on the slide itself or in the Outline pane in Outline view. Either way, the text is placed in the slide's placeholders. Text you type at the highest outline level on the outline is placed in the slide's Title placeholder, and text you type at subordinate outline levels is placed in the Content placeholder.

LINGO

A **slide layout** is a combination of one or more content placeholders. For example, the default slide layout — Title and Content — has two boxes: a text box at the top for the slide's title, and one multipurpose content placeholder in the middle that can be used for text, a graphic, or any of several other content types.

In this exercise, you type text into slide placeholders.

Files needed: `Lesson 10 Comstar Practice.pptx`, *already open from the previous exercise*

1. **Click slide 5 to select it.**

2. **In the Slide pane, click in the content placeholder (where it says** `Click to add text`**).**

   The insertion point moves into the content placeholder, as shown in Figure 10-17.

3. **Type** Four warehouses totaling over 40,000 square feet.

4. **Choose View➪Outline View.**

5. **In the Outline pane, click to move the insertion point after the last word on slide 5 and then press Enter.**

6. **Type** State-of-the-art environmental controls.

   The typed text appears both on the slide and in the outline, as shown in Figure 10-18.

Insertion point

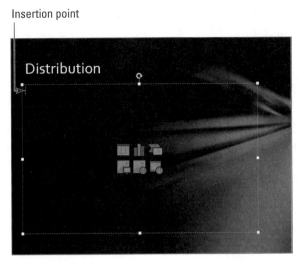

Figure 10-17

Typed text

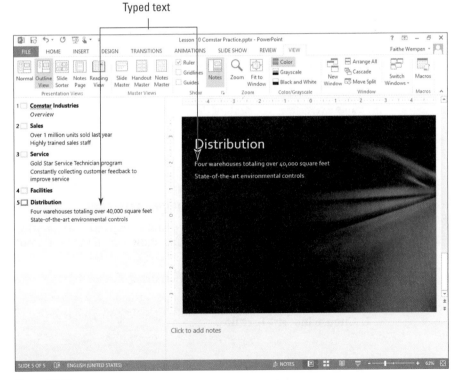

Figure 10-18

7. **Save the presentation.**

Leave the presentation open for the next exercise.

Manually placing text on a slide

Whenever possible, you should use the layout placeholders to insert slide content. However, sometimes you might not be able to find a layout that's exactly what you want. For example, maybe you want to add a caption or note next to a picture, or you want to create a collage of text snippets arranged artistically on a slide.

The text in such a text box doesn't appear in the outline, so use this type of text box sparingly if having a comprehensive outline is important to you.

When you place a text box manually (click the Insert tab and then the Text Box button), you can use two possible techniques: You can drag to draw the width of the box you want, or you can click the slide and start typing. The properties of the resulting text box are different for each method, as you see in the following steps.

In this exercise, you manually place text on a slide.

Files needed: `Lesson 10 Comstar Practice.pptx`, *already open from the previous exercise*

1. **Switch to Normal view.**

2. **Click slide 1 to select it.**

3. **Choose Insert⇨Text Box.**

4. **Click in the gray area at the bottom of the slide.**

   A text box appears there. It starts out collapsed horizontally, with just enough room for one character, as shown in Figure 10-19, but it expands as you type.

5. **Type** Copyright 2014 Comstar Industries.

6. **Click slide 5 to select it.**

7. **Choose Insert⇨Text Box.**

Text box created by
clicking

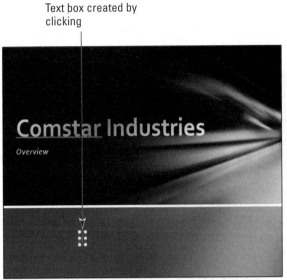

Figure 10-19

EXTRA INFO

This text box doesn't wrap text automatically to additional lines. If you want additional lines, press Enter to create paragraph breaks or press Shift+Enter to create line breaks without paragraph breaks.

8. **Near the bottom of the slide, close to the horizontal center, click and drag to draw a text box that is approximately 2 inches wide.**

See Figure 10-20.

Text box created
by dragging

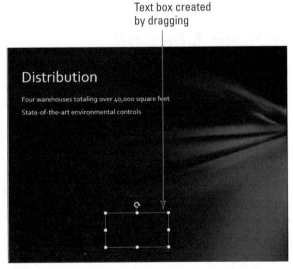

Figure 10-20

9. **Type** Copyright 2014 Comstar Industries.

The text wraps to multiple lines, and the text box increases in height as needed, as shown in Figure 10-21.

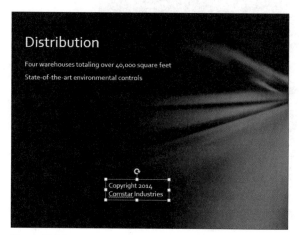

Figure 10-21

10. **Save the presentation.**

Leave the presentation open for the next exercise.

Manipulating Slide Content

Each placeholder box and each manually created text box or other item is a separate object that you can move around and resize freely. In the next several exercises, you learn how to work with the existing content on a slide.

Moving a slide object

To move a text box, position the mouse pointer over the border of the box but not over a selection handle. The mouse pointer changes to a four-headed arrow. Click and drag the box to a new location. It works the same when you're moving nontext objects such as pictures except that you don't have to be so fussy about pointing at the border when you drag a nontext object; you can point anywhere in the center of the object instead if you like.

If you want to move or resize a certain placeholder on every slide in your presentation, do so from Slide Master view. That way, you can make the change to the layout's template, and the change is applied automatically to every slide that uses that layout. To open Slide Master view, choose View⇨Slide Master.

In this exercise, you move some text boxes.

Files needed: `Lesson 10 Comstar Practice.pptx`, *already open from the previous exercise*

1. **Click slide 1 to select it.**

2. **Click in the Overview text box to move the insertion point into it, so you can see its boundaries, and then click the border of the text box to select the box itself.**

When the insertion point is inside the text box, the border of the box appears dashed. When the box itself is selected, the border of the box appears solid.

3. **Position the mouse pointer over the border.**

   The mouse pointer becomes a four-headed arrow.

4. **Drag the text box to the top-left corner of the slide, as shown in Figure 10-22.**

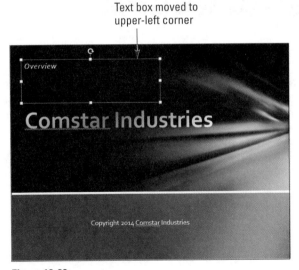

Figure 10-22

5. Click the Comstar Industries text box to select it.

Make sure the border is solid, indicating that the text box itself is selected.

6. Hold down the Shift key and drag the text box downward so that the words appear to float slightly above the white line.

See Figure 10-23.

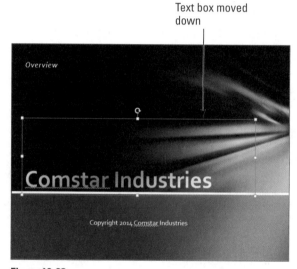

Figure 10-23

Using the Shift key is optional. Holding down the Shift key constrains the movement to one dimension so you don't accidentally change the box's horizontal position as you drag it vertically.

7. Save the presentation.

Leave the presentation open for the next exercise.

Resizing a slide object

To resize an object, select it and then drag a selection handle. To maintain the height-width proportion for the box — its *aspect ratio* — hold down the Shift key while you drag one of the corner selection handles.

In this exercise, you resize some text boxes.

Files needed: Lesson 10 Comstar Practice.pptx, *already open from the previous exercise*

1. **Click slide 5 to select it.**

2. **Click the text box at the bottom of the slide, which you created earlier in this chapter.**

3. **Point to the selection handle in the right side of the text box.**

   The mouse pointer turns into a double-headed arrow, as shown in Figure 10-24.

4. **Drag to the right, widening the text box until all the text fits on one line. Then release the mouse button.**

   Figure 10-25 shows the resized box.

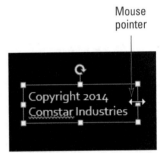

Mouse pointer

Figure 10-24

 TIP

If you don't want a text box to automatically resize to fit the content, change its Autofit setting. You learn about that in Chapter 11.

Figure 10-25

5. **Click slide 3 to select it.**

6. **Click the frame of the text box that contains the body content on the slide.**

EXTRA INFO

Notice that the height of the text box decreased. That's because this particular text box is set to auto-size the height of the box as needed to fit the text, and when you widened it, you caused the text to fit on one fewer lines.

As you can see when the frame is selected, the frame is much larger than it needs to be to contain this content. See Figure 10-26.

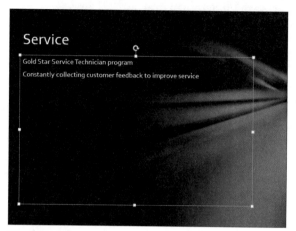

Figure 10-26

There is nothing wrong with leaving the frame at a larger size. Because it has no border, it isn't noticeable to the audience. However, for this exercise, you resize it anyway, just for practice.

7. **If the ruler doesn't appear, select the Ruler check box on the View tab.**

8. **Drag the right side (square) selection handle to the left until it aligns with the 0" mark on the horizontal ruler.**

The text in the placeholder wraps to additional lines as needed, as shown in Figure 10-27.

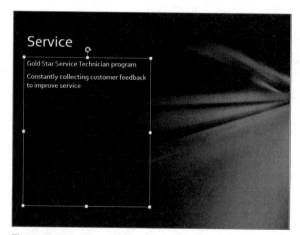

Figure 10-27

TIP

If you resize the placeholder(s) on a slide and then apply a different layout or design to the slide, everything snaps back to the default size and location. So make sure you have the right layout and design chosen before you spend a lot of time resizing or moving placeholders.

9. **Save the presentation.**

Leave the presentation open for the next exercise.

Deleting a slide object

Deleting a slide object is a lot like deleting a slide except that you select the object first rather than selecting an entire slide. The easiest way to get rid of an object is to select it and press the Delete key. You can also right-click the object's border, choose Cut to cut it to the Clipboard, and then just not paste it anywhere.

In this exercise, you delete a text box.

Files needed: `Lesson 10 Comstar Practice.pptx`, *already open from the previous exercise*

1. **Click slide 5 to select it.**

2. **Click inside the Copyright text box at the bottom of the slide.**

   The insertion point moves into the box.

3. **Press the Delete key.**

   Notice that a single character of text was deleted; the entire text box was not.

4. **Click the border of the text box.**

   The border becomes a solid line.

5. **Press the Delete key.**

   The entire text box is deleted.

6. **Save and close the presentation and exit PowerPoint.**

Summing Up

Here are the key points you learned about in this chapter:

- A presentation is a collection of one or more slides in a single data file. A slide is an individual page of a presentation.

- Normal view is the default view for PowerPoint. It consists of three panes: Slides, Slide, and Notes.

- Use the scroll bars to move around in a presentation or use shortcut keys such as Page Up and Page Down.

- Slide Sorter view is handy for browsing all the slides in the presentation at once and rearranging them.

- Notes Page view is good for typing and organizing speaker notes.

- Slide Show view is used to display the presentation onscreen in full-screen mode.

- Reading View is like Slide Show view except it's in a window rather than full-screen.

- To create a new blank presentation, press Ctrl+N.

- To create a presentation based on a template, choose File⇨New and then choose the template you want.

- A template is a reusable sample file that includes both formatting and sample slides. A theme is like a template except that it contains only formatting.

- To create new slides, choose Home⇨New Slide or click where you want the new slide in the Slides or Outline pane and press Enter.

- To delete a slide, select it in the Slides or Outline pane and press Delete.

- A slide layout contains one or more placeholders. To type text in a placeholder, click in it and begin typing.

- To manually create an additional text box on a slide, choose Insert⇨ Text Box.

- To move an object on a slide, drag it by its border (but not by a selection handle).

- To resize an object, drag one of its selection handles.

- To delete an object, select it and press Delete.

Try-it-yourself lab

For more practice with the features covered in this chapter, try the following exercise on your own:

1. **Start PowerPoint and create a new presentation based on a template of your choice.**

2. **Add and edit text in the presentation to deliver information about your favorite hobby or organization.**

   a. Add or delete slides from the presentation as needed to fit the content you want to present.

   b. Add or delete text boxes from slides as needed.

3. **Save the presentation as** `Lesson 10 Hobby.pptx`.

Know this tech talk

aspect ratio: The proportion of height to width.

Normal view: The default view, consisting of the Slide pane, the Slides pane, and the Notes pane.

Outline view: A view similar to Normal view except it contains a text-only Outline pane instead of the Slides pane.

presentation: A collection of one or more slides saved in a single data file.

selection handle: A circle or square on the border of an object's frame that can be dragged to resize the object.

slide: An individual page of a presentation.

slide layout: A slide template that contains one or more content placeholders.

template: A reusable sample file that includes a background, layouts, coordinating fonts, and other design elements. Templates may also include sample content.

theme: A template that includes only formatting and no sample content.

Chapter 11

Formatting a Presentation

➤ You can use themes to *apply consistent formatting* to all the slides in a presentation.

➤ Shape styles provide an *easy shortcut for formatting* an object with a border, a fill, and an effect combination in a single step.

➤ Shape effects *apply special formatting to objects* for a professional look.

➤ Changing the Autofit setting for a text box lets you *determine what happens when text overflows a text box.*

➤ The Insert tab contains commands for *manually inserting graphics,* for situations where content placeholders may not be available.

➤ By using SmartArt, you can *combine the utility of text with the attractiveness of a graphic.*

➤ *SmartArt can easily be converted* between layouts for different looks and meanings.

1. **How can you apply a theme?**

Find out on page 371

2. **How do you add a gradient background fill to a text box?**

Find out on page 380

3. **How do you make the border around a text box dotted or dashed?**

Find out on page 382

4. **What's the advantage of using placeholders to insert graphics?**

Find out on page 390

5. **How do you insert clip art?**

Find out on page 390

6. **How do you use SmartArt to create an organization chart?**

Find out on page 395

7. **How can you make a SmartArt graphic multicolored?**

Find out on page 402

ormatting can dramatically increase a presentation's effectiveness and impact. In PowerPoint, you can use themes to apply preset formatting to the entire presentation at once, or you can format individual elements. You can apply text formatting just as you do in other Office applications, from the Home tab, and you can apply background fills and borders to text boxes as well.

In this chapter, you learn how to apply different themes to a presentation and how to change its color and font theme settings. You also learn how to apply a fill and a border to enhance the impact of a text box, as well as how to insert and format graphics and SmartArt that further enhance a presentation's appearance.

Understanding and Applying Themes

All presentations have a theme, but the default theme — simply named Blank — is so plain that it's almost like it isn't there at all. Blank uses a white background, black Calibri text, and no background or design graphics.

Changing the presentation theme

You can switch to a different theme from the Design tab. Click the More button in the Themes group to open the Themes gallery and make your selection.

LINGO

A **theme** is a design set that you apply to a PowerPoint presentation to change several elements at once, including the background, color scheme, fonts, and the positions of the placeholders on the various layouts. Word and Excel also use themes, but in PowerPoint, the theme feature is exceptionally strong and full featured.

In this exercise, you change a presentation's theme.

Files needed: `Lesson 11 Diner.pptx`

1. **Open the file** `Lesson 11 Diner.pptx` **and save it as** `Lesson 11 Diner Formatting.pptx`.

2. **Click the Design tab.**

3. **Click the More button in the Themes group, opening the Themes gallery.**

   See Figure 11-1.

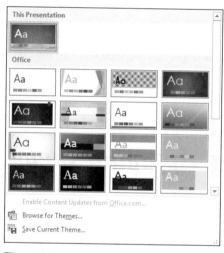

Figure 11-1

4. **Point at several themes with the mouse and check out the previews for them on the slide behind the open gallery.**

5. **Click the Main Event theme.**

Hover the mouse pointer over a theme to see its name pop up in a ScreenTip.

6. **Click each of the slides in the Slides tab to see the effect that the new theme has on each one's content.**

   Figure 11-2 shows slide 1, for example.

7. **Save the presentation.**

Leave the presentation open for the next exercise.

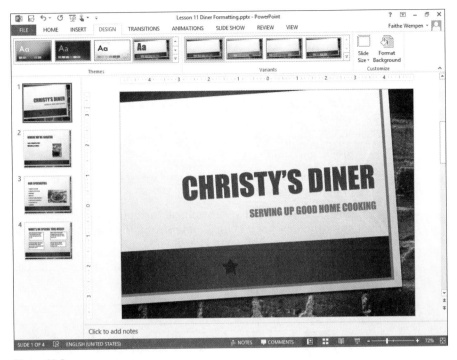

Figure 11-2

Changing the presentation variant and colors

Some themes offer variations on the main design, called variants. Variants may have different colored background images. Themes designed for earlier versions of PowerPoint do not have variants. If available, variants are found in the Variants group on the Design tab.

Besides applying a different variant, you can also change the color theme for a presentation. A color theme redefines the colors used for the color placeholders in the presentation, resulting in a different set of colors being applied to any objects that are formatted with theme colors. Unlike variants, themes are available in all presentations regardless of the design used for them.

LINGO

A **variant** is a variation on a theme, usually involving a different colored background and different font colors.

A **color theme** is a preset combination of colors designed to work well together.

In this exercise, you change a presentation's variant and theme colors and create your own custom color theme.

Files needed: Lesson 11 Diner Formatting.pptx, *already open from the previous exercise*

1. **Click the Design tab and, in the Variants group, click the orange variant.**

   The current design, Main Event, contains four variants: red, orange, green, and blue.

2. **Click the More button on the Variants gallery and, from the menu that appears, choose Colors.**

   The Colors list opens, showing all the colors for each of the available color themes. Each color theme shows the colors it contains and the theme name, as shown in Figure 11-3.

3. **Point to several different color themes and observe the color changes on the slide behind the open gallery.**

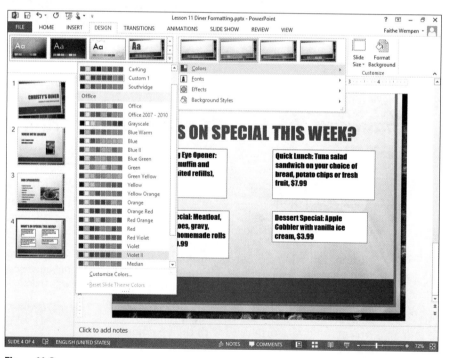

Figure 11-3

4. **Scroll down through the Colors list and select Violet II.**

The accent color on each slide changes to violet. In addition, although it isn't obvious, the other color placeholders change for the presentation. For example, the borders around the text boxes on slide 4 change color.

5. **Click the More button in the Variants group, click Colors, and click Customize Colors.**

The Create New Theme Colors dialog box opens.

6. **Click the Accent 1 color button.**

A menu opens, as shown Figure 11-4.

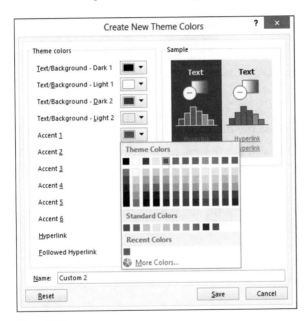

Figure 11-4

7. **Click Plum, Accent 1, Darker 50%.**

The background color on the sample in the dialog box shows a deeper purple as the background.

8. **Click the Accent 3 color button and click More Colors.**

The Colors dialog box opens.

9. **Click the Custom tab in the Colors dialog box if it isn't already displayed.**

10. **In the Color Model drop-down list, make sure RGB is selected.**

11. **Enter the following values: Red:** 78, **Green:** 48, **Blue:** 206.

See Figure 11-5.

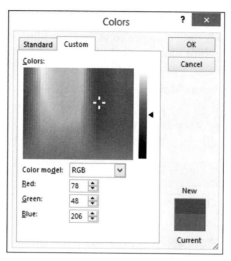

Figure 11-5

12. **Click OK to close the dialog box.**

13. **In the Name box at the bottom of the Create New Theme Colors dialog box, change the name to Violet III.**

14. **Click the Save button.**

    The new color theme is applied to the presentation. Notice that the purple areas are now darker.

15. **Save the presentation.**

Leave the presentation open for the next exercise.

Changing the presentation fonts

Each theme has a set of two fonts that it uses: one designated for headings and one for body text. You can use the fonts from any other theme available if you don't like the ones that your chosen theme provides. You can also create your own custom font theme.

In this exercise, you change a presentation's fonts and create your own custom font theme.

Files needed: `Lesson 11 Diner Formatting.pptx`, *already open from the previous exercise*

LINGO

A **font theme** is a preset combination of two fonts: one for headings and one for body text.

1. **Display slide 4 if it is not already displayed, so you can see examples of both body and heading text.**

   The title of the slide uses the font currently specified for headings (Impact), and the text box content uses the font currently specified for body text (also Impact).

2. **On the Design tab, click the More button in the Variants group and then point to Fonts.**

   The Fonts menu opens, listing many font themes, as shown in Figure 11-6.

3. **Point to several font themes and observe the changes in the slide behind the open menu.**

4. **Click the Calibri-Cambria theme.**

   The fonts from that theme are applied to the presentation. This theme uses Calibri for the headings and Cambria for the body text.

5. **Click the More button in the Variants group again, click Fonts, and choose Customize Fonts.**

   The Create New Theme Fonts dialog box opens.

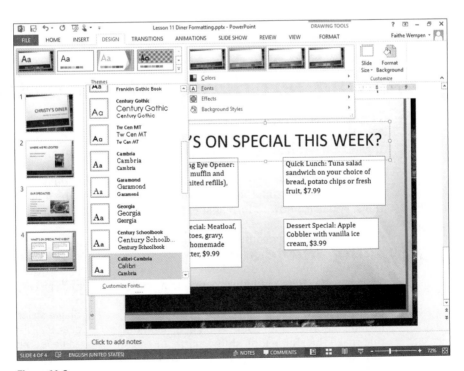

Figure 11-6

6. **Open the Body Font drop-down list and select Calibri Light.**

7. **In the Name text box, type** Calibri Custom, **as shown in Figure 11-7.**

Figure 11-7

8. **Click the Save button.**

   The body text in the presentation changes to reflect the new font chosen for body text.

9. **Save the presentation.**

Leave the presentation open for the next exercise.

Formatting Text Boxes and Placeholders

In most cases, presentations look best when they're consistently formatted. That means that usually your best bet is to apply formatting by changing the theme or the variant.

Sometimes, however, you might want to format an individual text box or object differently from the rest, to make it stand out. In the following sections, you learn how to format specific text boxes in different ways.

Applying shape styles

The easiest way to apply formatting to an object is with the Shape Styles command. Depending on the style you choose, a shape style can include a border, a fill color, and special effects that make the shape look shiny, matte, or raised. Although from the name you might expect shape styles to apply only to graphical shapes, they still work with text boxes because PowerPoint considers a text box to be a shape (a rectangle).

LINGO

Shape styles are formatting presets that use the theme colors and effects in the presentation to format objects in multiple ways at once.

In this exercise, you apply shape styles to two shapes.

Files needed: `Lesson 11 Diner Formatting.pptx`, *already open from the previous exercise*

1. **Display slide 4 if it isn't already displayed.**

2. **Click the border of the Early Morning Eye Opener text box to select it.**

3. **Click the Drawing Tools Format tab.**

4. **In the Shape Styles group, click the More button to open the Shape Styles gallery.**

   See Figure 11-8.

5. **Select Moderate Effect, Plum, Accent 1. The style is applied to the text box.**

   It's the second style in the fifth row.

6. **Click the border of the Dessert Special text box to select it.**

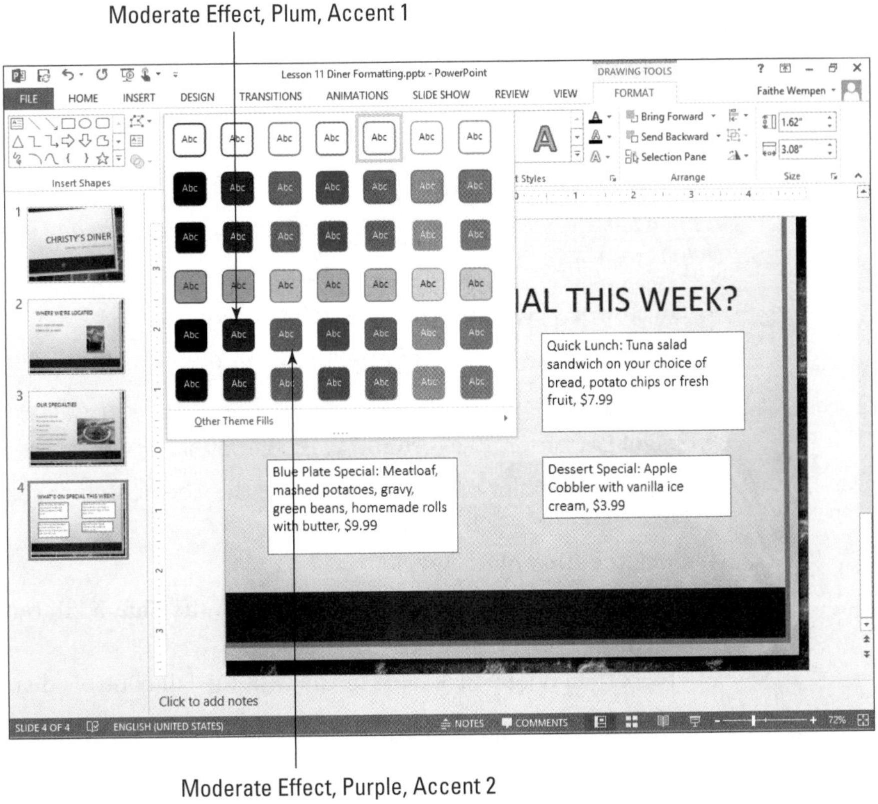

Moderate Effect, Plum, Accent 1

Moderate Effect, Purple, Accent 2

Figure 11-8

7. **Click the More button again to reopen the Shape Styles gallery.**

8. **Select Moderate Effect, Purple, Accent 2.**

   It's the third style in the fifth row.

9. **Save the presentation.**

Leave the presentation open for the next exercise.

Applying a background fill

A text box, by default, has no background fill. Whatever is behind it shows through. You can apply a number of different background fills to a text box to make it opaque. You can choose solid colors, of course, from either the theme colors or the standard colors. You can also choose to apply gradients, textures, patterns, or even pictures as background fills.

This exercise demonstrates text box background fills, but this same skill carries over in other parts of PowerPoint. For example, you can apply a background fill to graphic objects that have transparent backgrounds (such as some clip art images) and to pieces of a chart or a SmartArt graphic.

In this exercise, you apply a background fill to two shapes.

Files needed: `Lesson 11 Diner Formatting.pptx`, *already open from the previous exercise*

1. **On slide 4, select the Quick Lunch text box.**

2. **Click the Drawing Tools Format tab and then the Shape Fill button.**

   A palette of colors appears.

3. **Select Lavender, Background 2, Darker 50%.**

   It's the third color on the fourth row of the Theme Colors section. See Figure 11-9.

4. **Click the Blue Plate Special text box.**

5. **Click the Drawing Tools Format tab, click the Shape Fill button, and choose Gradient⇨More Gradients.**

   The Format Shape task pane opens with the Fill controls displayed.

6. **Select the Gradient Fill option.**

Lavender, Background 2, Darker 50%

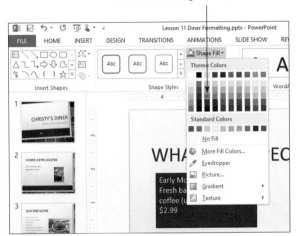

Figure 11-9

7. **Click the Preset Gradients button, and click the Light Gradient - Accent 1 preset.**

It's the first color in the top row. See Figure 11-10.

8. **On the Gradient Stops slider, click the Stop 2 of 4 marker.**

See Figure 11-11. Any color changes you make using the controls below the slider will apply to that particular stop point on the gradient line.

9. **Open the Color button's palette and click More Colors.**

The Colors dialog box opens.

10. **On the Custom tab, enter the following RGB values: Red 175, Green 103, Blue 219.**

11. **Click OK to close the Colors dialog box.**

12. **Click the third marker from the left on the Gradient Stops slider to select that stop.**

13. **Click the Remove Gradient Stop button.**

The Remove Gradient Stop button is the button with the red X on it to the right of the slider. The stop is removed, and the middle stop (which is the one you previously changed) is selected again.

14. **Click the up increment arrow on the Brightness box until it reads 30%.**

15. **Drag the middle slider to the center of the Gradient Stops slider.**

    Use the value in the Position text box below the slider to place the stop at the 50% mark.

16. **Close the task pane.**

17. **Save the presentation.**

Leave the presentation open for the next exercise.

Light Gradient - Accent 1

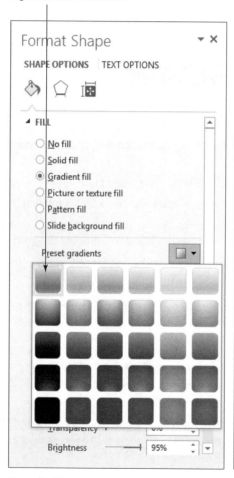

Figure 11-10

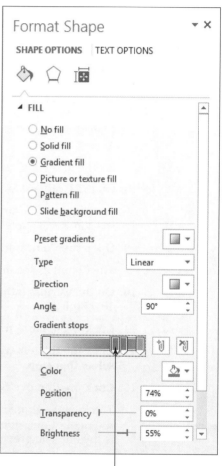

Stop 2 of 4 marker

Figure 11-11

Applying and removing borders

When you first create them, text boxes don't have borders, so they blend in with the slide background. You can add a border to any object, choosing a line style (solid, dashed, and so on), line color, and line weight (thickness). You can also remove the border from a text box at any time.

In this exercise, you remove the borders from two text boxes and apply different borders to two others.

Files needed: Lesson 11 Diner Formatting.pptx, *already open from the previous exercise*

1. **On slide 4, select the Quick Lunch text box.**

2. **On the Drawing Tools Format tab, click the Shape Outline button and then click No Outline.**

3. **Repeat Steps 1 and 2 for the Early Morning Eye Opener text box.**

4. **Select the Blue Plate Special text box.**

5. **On the Drawing Tools Format tab, click the Shape Outline button and then select the white square at the top of the palette (White, Background 1).**

   See Figure 11-12.

6. **Click the Shape Outline button, choose Weight, and choose the 6 point line.**

7. **Select the Dessert Special text box.**

8. **On the Drawing Tools Format tab, click the Shape Outline button and click Eyedropper.**

   The Eyedropper tool enables you to pick up a color from another object on the slide.

White, Background 1

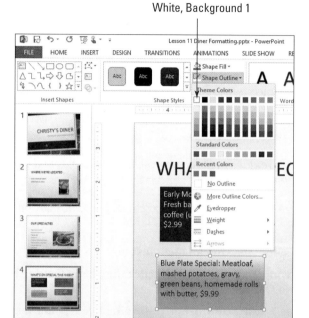

Figure 11-12

9. **Click the background of the Quick Lunch text box, picking up that color.**

   A border with that color is applied to the Dessert Special text box.

10. **Click the Shape Outline button, click Weight, and click 4 1/2 point.**

11. **Click the Shape Outline button, click Dashes, and click the Round Dot dotted line.**

   See Figure 11-13.

For more practice, try several other border colors, weights, and styles for the text boxes. For example, click the Shape Outline button and choose Weight⇨More Lines, click the Line Color tab, and try creating a gradient line.

12. **Save the presentation.**

Leave the presentation open for the next exercise.

Choose a dotted line.

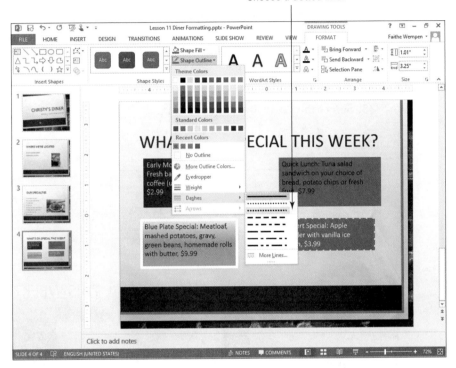

Figure 11-13

Applying shape effects

Shape effects are enhancements (such as shadow, reflection, glow, and bevel) that you can optionally apply to shapes and text boxes to dress them up. Some of the shape styles (covered earlier in the chapter) apply some of these effects, and you can also apply the effects separately.

In this exercise, you apply shape effects.

Files needed: `Lesson 11 Diner Formatting.pptx`, *already open from the previous exercise*

1. **On slide 4, select the Quick Lunch text box.**

2. **Click the Drawing Tools Format tab, click the Shape Effects button, and choose Bevel⇨Circle.**

   Circle is the first bevel effect under the Bevel heading. See Figure 11-14.

3. **Select the Blue Plate Special text box.**

4. **On the Drawing Tools Format tab, click the Shape Effects button and choose Shadow⇨Offset Diagonal Top Left (the last shadow in the Outer section).**

   See Figure 11-15.

5. **Select the Early Morning text box.**

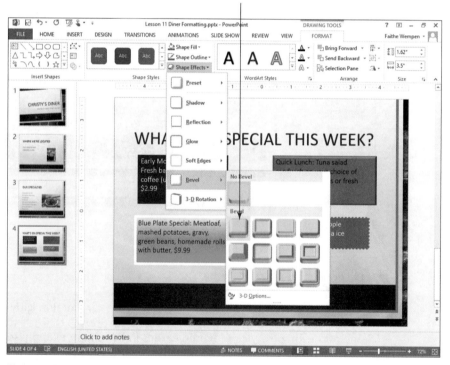

Circle bevel effect

Figure 11-14

Offset Diagonal Top Left

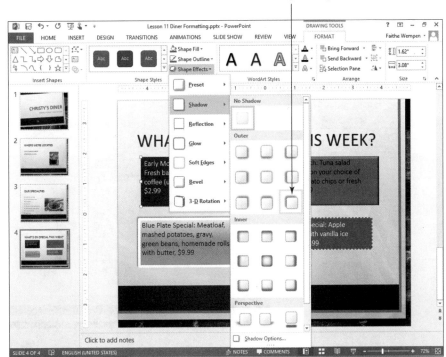

Figure 11-15

6. **On the Drawing Tools Format tab, click the Shape Effects button and choose Glow⇨Plum, 11 pt glow, Accent Color 1.**

It's the first option in the third row of the Glow Variations section. See Figure 11-16.

7. **Save the presentation.**

Leave the presentation open for the next exercise.

Plum, 11 pt glow, Accent Color 1

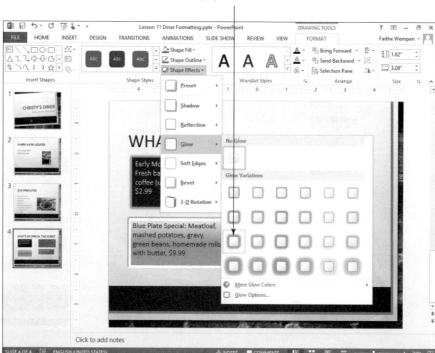

Figure 11-16

Turning text Autofit on or off

If you type more text than will fit in that text box (an especially common occurrence for a slide title), the text automatically shrinks as much as is needed to allow it to fit. This feature, called **Autofit**, is turned on by default in text placeholders. Autofit is very useful because it prevents text from being truncated.

In manually placed text boxes, a different Autofit behavior occurs by default: The text box itself gets larger as needed to accommodate the text.

Both of those behaviors can be very useful, but you may sometimes need to change the Autofit setting for one or more text boxes to achieve certain effects. For example, you may not want a manually placed text box to shrink if you delete some text from it, or it might be unacceptable to you for the font size used in the title of one slide to be different from that of another.

In this exercise, you change the Autofit setting for a text box.

Files needed: `Lesson 11 Diner Formatting.pptx`, *already open from the previous exercise*

1. **On slide 4, select the Blue Plate Special text box.**

2. **Try to enlarge the height of the text box by dragging its bottom selection handle downward.**

   It doesn't resize.

3. **Right-click the border of the text box and click Size and Position.**

   The Format Shape task pane opens.

4. **Expand the Text Box heading in the task pane to see its controls.**

   Text box options appear.

5. **Notice the current Autofit setting: Resize Shape to Fit Text.**

   This is the reason the text box shrinks and grows depending on the text in it.

6. **Select the Do Not Autofit option.**

   See Figure 11-17.

7. **Close the task pane.**

8. **Drag the bottom selection handle on the text box downward to increase its height by about ¼".**

   Use the vertical ruler to gauge the height. Notice that now the height is resizable.

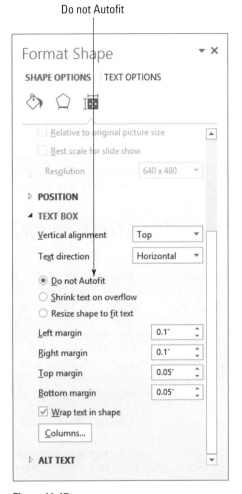

Figure 11-17

For more practice, try typing more text into one of the slides' title boxes than will fit and watch how it shrinks. Then change the text box's Autofit setting to Do Not Autofit and see how it changes how PowerPoint handles the text. Then change the setting to Resize Shape to Fit Text and see what happens.

9. **Save and close the presentation and exit PowerPoint.**

Inserting Graphics

You learned about inserting graphics in Word in Chapter 4, and inserting them in PowerPoint is very similar. The commands on the Insert tab in both applications include buttons for inserting a graphic from a file and also for inserting online images such as clip art.

However, PowerPoint has one big difference: placeholders. You have two ways of inserting graphics in PowerPoint: via the Insert tab (as in Word) and via the icons in a content placeholder. Depending on which method you choose, the graphic behaves differently.

The placeholder method offers several advantages. If you insert a graphic by using one of the content placeholders, the graphic integrates more seamlessly with the other content on the slide, and if you change to a layout that positions that placeholder differently or to a theme that arranges the placeholders differently, the graphic moves automatically to the new position. In contrast, if you insert a graphic by using the Insert tab's commands, it becomes a fixed, manually placed object on the slide, and it doesn't automatically shift when the layout shifts.

Inserting an online image from Office.com

In PowerPoint 2013, you access the Microsoft artwork collection via Office.com from within PowerPoint itself. This artwork collection includes both clip art illustrations (line drawings) and digital photographs. Use the following exercise to practice clip art insertion.

In this exercise, you insert an online image by using a placeholder and using the Insert tab.

Files needed: `Lesson 11 Greek.pptx`

1. **Open** `Lesson 11 Greek.pptx` **and save it as** `Lesson 11 Greek Restaurant.pptx`.

2. **On slide 2, click the Online Pictures icon in the empty content placeholder box.**

   The Insert Pictures dialog box opens, as shown in Figure 11-18.

3. **In the Office.com Clip Art search box, type** Greek **and press Enter.**

   Search results appear.

4. **Click an image that shows Greek columns, like the one in Figure 11-19, and then click the Insert button.**

   The image appears in the placeholder.

LINGO

Clip art images are line-based drawings that are compact in size and can be resized without losing quality. They aren't very realistic looking, though; it's obvious that they are drawn artwork.

Digital photographs are photos taken with a digital camera or scanned into a computer by using a scanner. They are very realistic, take up quite a bit of disk space, and can lose quality if you size them larger than their original size.

Type the word to search for here.

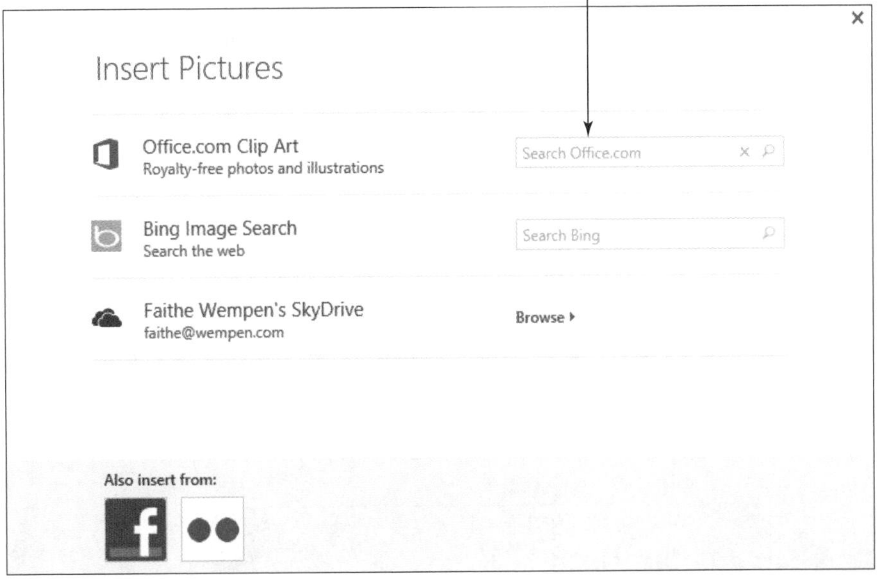

Insert Pictures

Office.com Clip Art
Royalty-free photos and illustrations

Search Office.com   ✕ ⌕

Bing Image Search
Search the web

Search Bing   ⌕

Faithe Wempen's SkyDrive
faithe@wempen.com

Browse ▸

Also insert from:

Figure 11-18

Use this image or one similar to it.

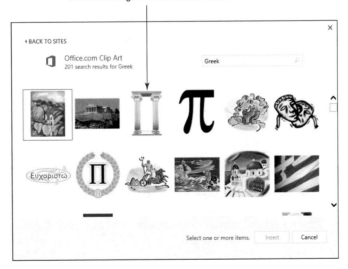

◂ BACK TO SITES

Office.com Clip Art
201 search results for Greek

Greek   ⌕

Select one or more items.   Insert   Cancel

Figure 11-19

5. **Click slide 5 to display it.**

This slide has no placeholder suitable for artwork.

6. **Click the Insert tab and click Online Pictures.**

The Insert Pictures dialog box opens. It's the same dialog box as shown earlier in Figure 11-18.

7. **In the Office.com Clip Art search box, type** phone **and press Enter.**

Images of phones appear.

8. **Click one of the clip art drawings (not a photograph) that shows a telephone and then click the Insert button.**

It appears in the center of the slide.

9. **Drag the picture to the upper-right corner of the slide, as shown in Figure 11-20.**

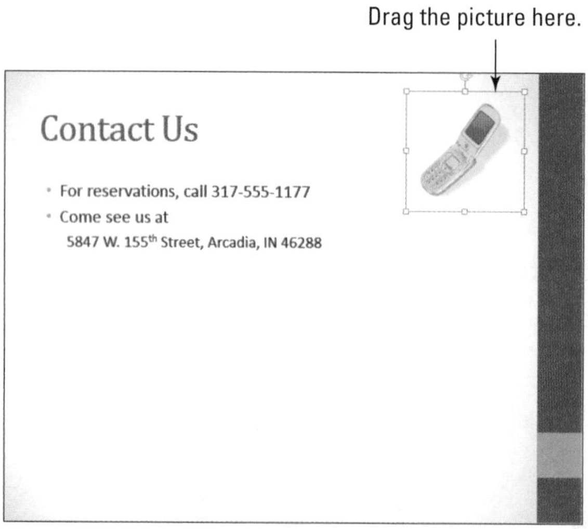

Drag the picture here.

Contact Us

 · For reservations, call 317-555-1177
 · Come see us at
   5847 W. 155ᵗʰ Street, Arcadia, IN 46288

Figure 11-20

For more practice, try changing to a different theme that positions the placeholders differently. Notice that the picture on slide 2 is repositioned automatically. However, the picture on slide 5 stays put regardless of the theme applied.

10. **Save the presentation.**

Keep the presentation open for the next exercise.

Inserting your own pictures

You can also insert pictures you've acquired yourself, either from someone else or from your digital camera or scanner. These pictures are stored as separate files on your hard drive or other media. PowerPoint supports many picture formats, including .tif, .jpg, .gif, .bmp, and .png.

Just like with online images, you can insert a picture either with the Insert tab's command or with the placeholder icon.

In this exercise, you insert pictures from files using a placeholder and using the Insert tab.

Files needed: Lesson 11 Greek Restaurant.pptx, *open from the previous exercise*

1. **On slide 3, in the content placeholder, click Pictures icon.**

   See Figure 11-21.

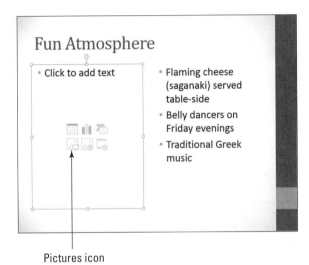

Pictures icon

Figure 11-21

2. **In the Insert Picture dialog box, navigate to the location containing the data files for this chapter. Select** flaming.jpg **and click the Insert button.**

   See Figure 11-22. The picture of the flaming cheese appears in the placeholder.

3. **Click slide 4 to display it.**

   This slide doesn't have a placeholder for a picture.

4. **On the Insert tab, click the Pictures button.**

The Insert Picture dialog box opens. It's the same dialog box as in Figure 11-22.

Select this picture.

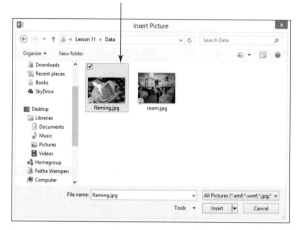

Figure 11-22

5. **Click room.jpg and click the Insert button.**

The picture appears in the center of the slide, overlapping the text.

6. **Drag the picture below the bulleted list.**

See Figure 11-23.

Large Parties are Welcome

- Upstairs meeting room accommodates 50
- No room reservation fees
- Meeting area has its own bar

Place the picture below the bulleted list.

Figure 11-23

7. **Save the presentation and close it.**

Leave PowerPoint open for the next exercise.

Creating SmartArt

SmartArt enables you to present text in a graphical way, bridging the gap between decorative images and ordinary text. With SmartArt, a plain bulleted list can become much more appealing to read. You can also use SmartArt to present information conceptually in ways that plain text alone can't achieve.

LINGO

SmartArt is a type of artwork you can create in PowerPoint or other Office programs. By using SmartArt, you can place text paragraphs in shapes and arrange the shapes to add visual meaning to the text. For example, an organization chart or a pyramid graphic conveys information about text by the text's position in the graphic.

Converting text to SmartArt

The easiest way to create SmartArt is to convert an existing bulleted list to SmartArt. That way you don't have to retype the text.

In this exercise, you convert a bulleted list to a SmartArt graphic.

Files needed: `Lesson 11 Manufacturing.pptx`

1. **Open** `Lesson 11 Manufacturing.pptx` **and save it as** `Lesson 11 Manufacturing SmartArt.pptx`.
2. **On slide 1, click in the bulleted list to move the insertion point there; then press Ctrl+A to select all the text.**
3. **On the Home tab, click the Convert to SmartArt Graphic button.**

   A menu of SmartArt styles opens. See Figure 11-24.

 You can point to a graphic type to see it previewed on the slide before you commit to a certain type by clicking it.

4. **Click the Basic Cycle graphic (the last graphic in the second row).**

   It's applied to the bulleted list.
5. **Save the presentation.**

Leave the presentation open for the next exercise.

Inserting a SmartArt graphic

If the text doesn't already exist in the presentation, you may find it easier to create a SmartArt graphic from scratch and then type the text in it as you go. You can choose from several graphic types, such as Process, List, Hierarchy, and Matrix. Each is well-suited for presenting a different type of information.

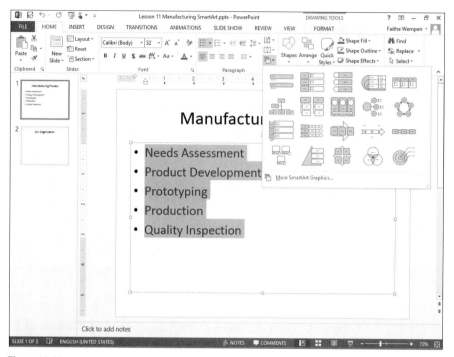

Figure 11-24

In this exercise, you create a new SmartArt graphic by using the Hierarchy graphic type.

Files needed: Lesson 11 Manufacturing SmartArt.pptx, *already open from the previous exercise*

1. **Display slide 2 and then, on the Insert tab, click the SmartArt button.**

   The Choose a SmartArt Graphic dialog box opens.

 If this slide had contained a content placeholder, you could have clicked the SmartArt icon in the placeholder to start this graphic. This slide didn't have a placeholder, so you're creating the graphic from the Insert tab.

2. **Click the Hierarchy category.**

3. **Click the Organization Chart sample.**

   It's the first sample in the first row. See Figure 11-25.

Choose this graphic type.

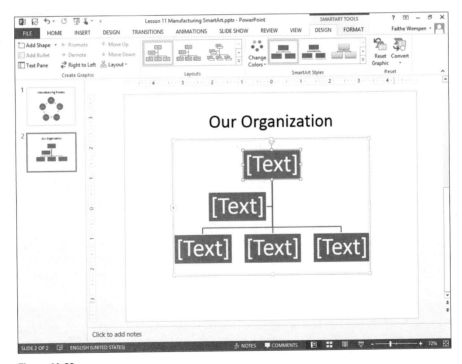

Figure 11-25

4. **Click OK.**

A blank organization chart appears, as shown in Figure 11-26.

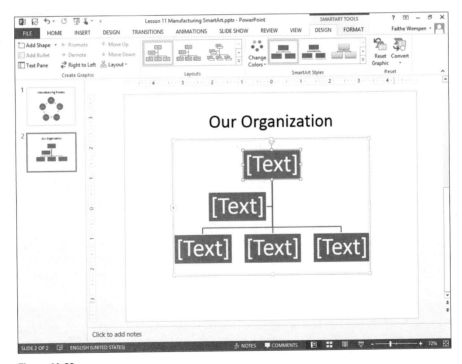

Figure 11-26

5. **Click in the topmost [Text] placeholder and type** Janet Green.

The text in the placeholder shrinks to accommodate the text, and the text placeholders in all the other boxes also change to that same size for consistency.

6. **Click the second [Text] place-holder and press Delete to remove it from the graphic.**

The graphic should now resemble Figure 11-27.

7. **Click in the leftmost of the three [Text] placeholders and type** Kim Fairfield. **Press Enter and then type** Director of Operations.

8. **Click in the middle [Text] placeholder and type** Brady Jackson. **Press Enter and then type** Director of Manufacturing.

9. **Click the rightmost [Text] placeholder and type** Eve Williams. **Press Enter and then type** Director of Personnel.

The graphic should resemble Figure 11-28 at this point.

10. **Click the Brady Jackson box to select it.**

11. **Click the SmartArt Tools Design tab and then click the Add Shape button.**

A box for a subordinate appears below Brady.

12. **In the new box, type** Ann Rayne. **Press Enter and type** Quality Assurance Manager.

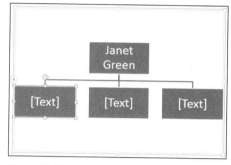

Figure 11-27

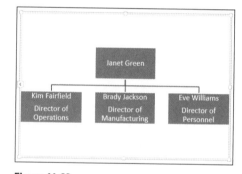

Figure 11-28

13. **With the new box still selected, click the down arrow to the right of the Add Shape button, opening a menu of new shape types.**

    See Figure 11-29

14. **Click Add Shape After.**

    A new box appears at the same level of hierarchy as the previous one.

15. **In the new box, type** Roger Park. **Press Enter and type** Equipment Manager. **Then click away from the graphic to deselect it.**

    The slide should look like Figure 11-30.

16. **Save the presentation.**

Leave the presentation open for the next exercise.

Choose Add Shape After.

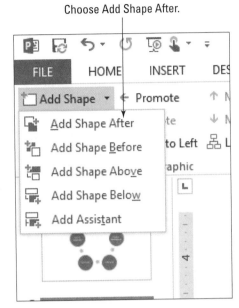

Figure 11-29

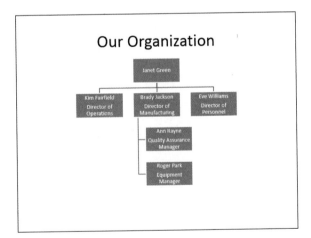

Figure 11-30

Modifying a SmartArt graphic

After creating a SmartArt graphic, you may want to modify it. Modifications can include changing the graphic type or layout, adding or removing shapes, and changing the order in which shapes appear.

In this exercise, you will modify a SmartArt graphic.

Files needed: `Lesson 11 Manufacturing SmartArt.pptx`*, already open from the previous exercise*

1. **On slide 1, click the frame of the SmartArt graphic to select the entire graphic.**
2. **Click the SmartArt Tools Design tab and then click the More button in the Layouts group.**
3. **Click the More Layouts button.**

   The Choose a SmartArt Graphic dialog box opens.
4. **Click the Process category.**
5. **Click the Continuous Block Process layout, as shown in Figure 11-31.**

   It's the first layout in the third row.

Continuous Block Process layout

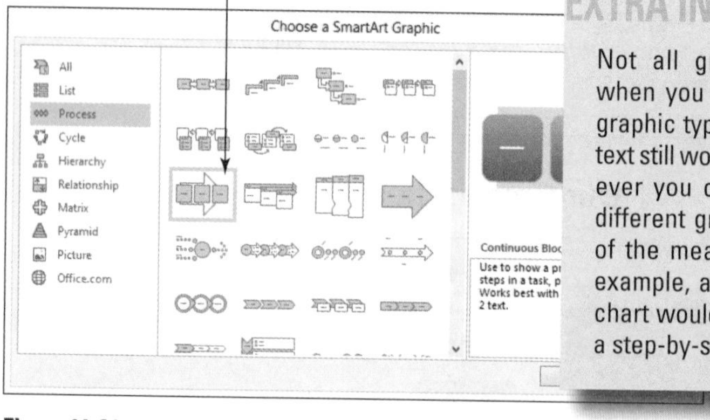

Figure 11-31

EXTRA INFO

Not all graphics make sense when you change to a different graphic type. In this example, the text still works logically, but whenever you convert SmartArt to a different graphic type, be aware of the meaning of the data. For example, a pyramid or hierarchy chart wouldn't work very well for a step-by-step process.

6. **Click OK.**

   The new graphic type is applied.
7. **On the SmartArt Tools Design tab, click the Right to Left button.**

   The graphic switches direction.
8. **Click the Right to Left button again.**

   It changes back to its original direction.
9. **Click the Text Pane button if the text pane does not already appear.**

   A text pane appears to the left of the graphic, as shown in Figure 11-32.

Text Pane button

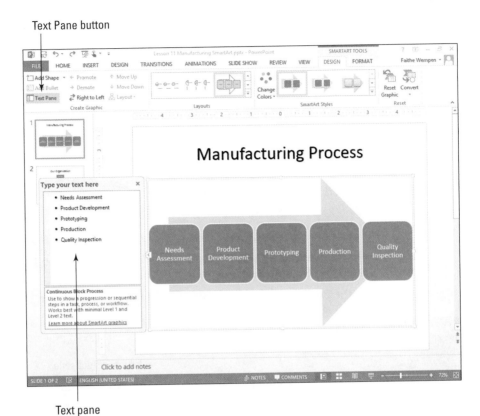

Text pane

Figure 11-32

10. In the text pane, change the word *Production* to *Manufacturing*.

11. Click the Close (X) button on the text pane to close it.

12. On the graphic, click the Quality Inspection shape and press the Delete key to remove it.

13. Save the presentation.

Leave the presentation open for the next exercise.

Formatting a SmartArt graphic

Various methods for formatting a SmartArt graphic are available. You can apply SmartArt Styles, for example, that format the entire graphic at once using a preset format that's tied in with the document's theme colors and effects. You can also change the colors of the graphic as a whole. Finally, you can apply formatting to specific shapes within a graphic, separately from the graphic as a whole.

In this exercise, you format two SmartArt graphics.

Files needed: `Lesson 11 Manufacturing SmartArt.pptx`, *already open from the previous exercise*

1. **Select the SmartArt graphic on slide 1.**

2. **On the SmartArt Tools Design tab, click the More button in the SmartArt Styles group, opening a gallery of choices.**

3. **In the Best Match for Document section, click the Intense Effect style.**

   See Figure 11-33.

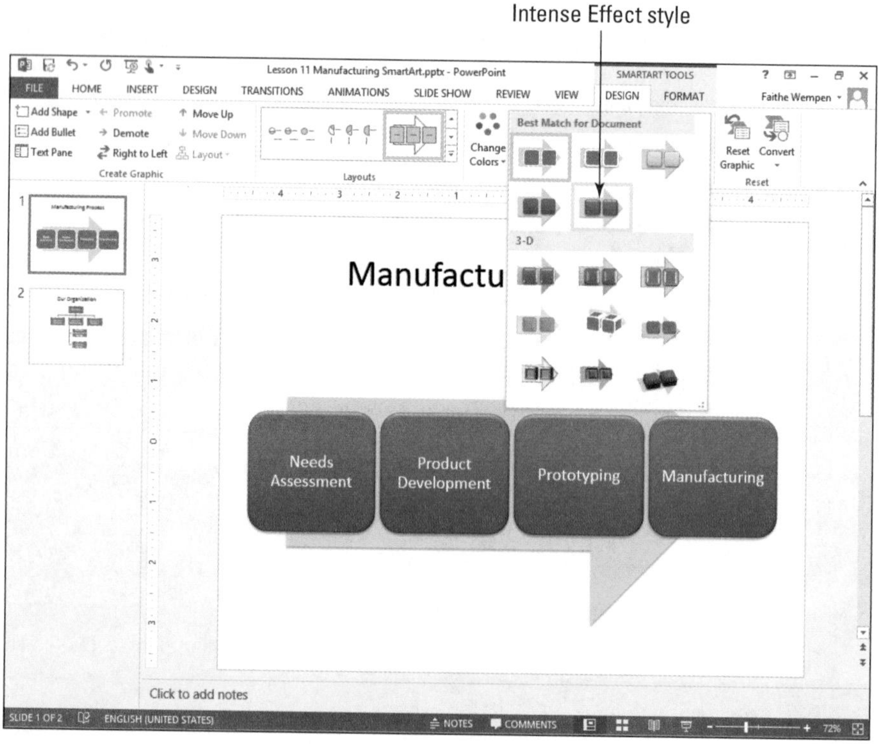

Figure 11-33

4. **Click the Change Colors button.**

   A gallery of color choices appears, as shown in Figure 11-34.

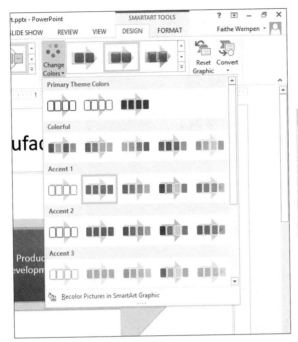

By default, a SmartArt graphic uses only one color. If you want a multicolored graphic, you must choose one of the color schemes from the Colorful section of the Change Colors button's menu.

Figure 11-34

5. **Click the Colorful – Accent Colors sample (the first one in the Colorful section).**

   The colors in the graphic change.

6. **Display slide 2 and select the SmartArt graphic.**

7. **On the SmartArt Tools Design tab, click the More button in the SmartArt Styles group, opening a gallery of choices.**

8. **Click Polished (the first sample in the 3-D section of the list).**

9. **Click the Change Colors button and select the Colorful – Accent Colors sample.**

   The graphic changes to show each level of the hierarchy as a different color, as shown in Figure 11-35.

10. **Click the Janet Green shape at the top of the graphic.**

11. **On the SmartArt Tools Format tab, click the Shape Fill button and click the black square in the top row of the Theme Colors section.**

    That shape becomes black, as shown in Figure 11-36.

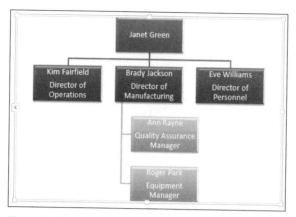

Figure 11-35

12. **Save the presentation and close it.**

13. **Close PowerPoint.**

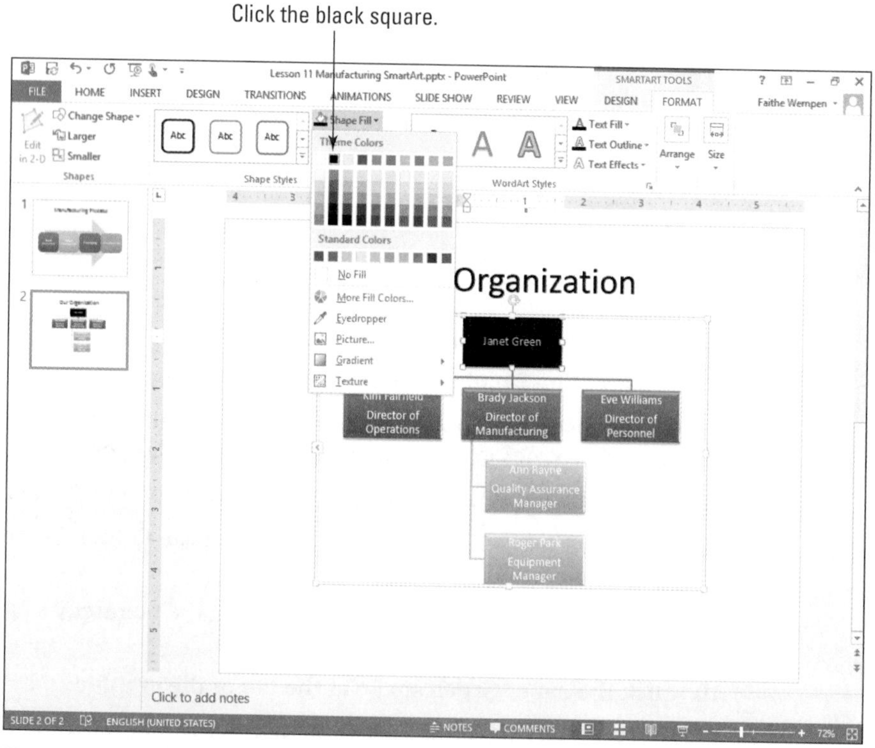

Click the black square.

Figure 11-36

Summing Up

Here are the key points you learned about in this chapter:

- ✔ A theme is a design set that you apply to a presentation to change several elements at once, including background, color scheme, fonts, and the positions of placeholders in the various layouts.

- ✔ To change the theme, click the Design tab, click the More button in the Themes group, and select a theme.

- ✔ To apply different colors, choose Design⇨Theme Colors. To apply different fonts, choose Design⇨Theme Fonts.

- ✔ You can apply shape styles to apply presets that include background fill, border, and effects all at once. Choose from the Shape Styles gallery on the Drawing Tools Format tab.

- ✔ To format a text box's fill, choose Drawing Tools Format⇨Shape Fill. To format a text box's border, choose Drawing Tools Format⇨Shape Outline.

- ✔ To apply effects such as shadow, glow, or bevel, choose Drawing Tools Format⇨Shape Effects.

- ✔ You can change a text box's Autofit setting to determine what happens when there's more text than will fit in the box at its current size. To do so, right-click the text box and choose Format Shape, click Text Box, and choose an Autofit setting in the dialog box.

- ✔ You can insert graphics via the placeholders on a slide's layout or via the Insert tab's buttons for inserting various types of content.

- ✔ To insert images from Office.com, click the Online Pictures placeholder icon or click Online Pictures on the Insert tab.

- ✔ To insert a picture from a file, click the Picture placeholder icon or click the Pictures icon on the Insert tab.

- ✔ You can convert existing text to SmartArt by clicking Home, Convert to SmartArt Graphic.

- ✔ To insert a new SmartArt graphic, click Insert, SmartArt or click the Insert SmartArt icon on a content placeholder.

- ✔ The SmartArt Tools Design tab provides options for changing the graphic type, style, and colors.

- ✔ You can format individual elements of a graphic from the SmartArt Tools Format tab.

Try-it-yourself labs

For more practice with the features covered in this chapter, try the following exercises on your own.

Exercise 1

1. **Open** `Lesson 11 Banking.pptx` **and save it as** `Lesson 11 Banking Formatting.pptx`.
2. **Apply the theme of your choice.**
3. **Change to a different set of theme colors.**
4. **Change to a different set of theme fonts.**
5. **On slide 7, format each of the text boxes in a different way.**
6. **Save the presentation and exit PowerPoint.**

Exercise 2

1. **Start a new, blank presentation.**
2. **Change the first slide's layout to Title and Content.**
3. **Use the Insert SmartArt Graphic icon in the content placeholder to start a new graphic.**
4. **Use a Horizontal Hierarchy graphic to create a tournament bracket graphic for a single-elimination sports tournament.**

   Figure 11-37 shows an example, but you can use your own sports teams.

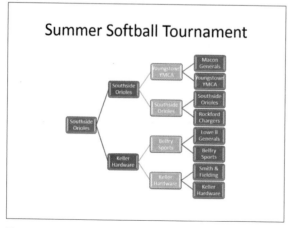

Figure 11-37

5. Apply the colors and SmartArt Style of your choice.

6. Save the presentation as `Lesson 11 Tournament.pptx` and exit PowerPoint.

Know this tech talk

Autofit: A setting that determines what happens when text overflows a text box. The box can enlarge or shrink to fit the text, or the text can change size, or nothing happens and the text is truncated.

border: A line around the outside of an object.

clip art: Line-based drawings that are compact in size and can be resized without losing quality.

color theme: A collection of color presets.

digital photograph: A photo taken with a digital camera or scanned into a computer using a scanner.

font theme: A collection of two font presets: one for headings and one for body text.

shape styles: Formatting presets that change an object's formatting in multiple ways at once, such as applying a border, a fill, and special effects.

SmartArt: A type of artwork you can create in Office programs, such as PowerPoint. You can use SmartArt to arrange text in ways that give it additional meaning.

theme: A design set that you apply to a presentation to change several elements at once, including the background, colors, fonts, and placeholder positions.

variant: A variation on a theme, often with different background colors and font colors.

Chapter 12

Adding Movement and Sound to a Presentation

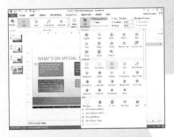

✔ Transitions *make the movement more interesting* from one slide to another.

✔ You can use animations to *call attention to specific objects* on a slide.

✔ Use entrance animations to *bring an object onto the slide separately* from the rest of the slide's content.

✔ With exit animations, you can *remove an object from a slide separately* from the rest of the slide's content.

✔ Animations called emphasis effects can *draw attention to an object* that is neither entering nor exiting.

✔ You can place a sound clip on a slide to *play back audio content* during the slide show.

✔ You can place a video clip on a slide so that the *video content is a part of the PowerPoint show.*

1. **What's the difference between a transition and an animation?**

Find out on page 411

2. **How do you speed up a transition effect?**

Find out on page 414

3. **Can you assign sounds to transitions?**

Find out on page 414

4. **How do you reorder the animation effects on a slide?**

Find out on page 417

5. **How do you apply an emphasis animation effect?**

Find out on page 419

6. **How can you copy the animation from one object to another?**

Find out on page 419

7. **Can you use a Flash video clip in PowerPoint?**

Find out on page 427

Have you ever heard the phrase "Death by PowerPoint"? It means being bored to death by a dull, long, lifeless presentation, usually with someone droning on about the slide's text-heavy content in too much detail.

To avoid causing this kind of agony for your audience, you can enliven your slides by adding movement and sound to them. You can set up different transition effects for moving from one slide to another, and you can animate the individual objects on a slide so that they enter or exit the slide or emphasize a certain point. (Don't go overboard in the other direction, though; too much bling can be worse than none at all.)

You can also add sound and video clips to a presentation. In earlier versions of PowerPoint, some types of video were difficult to integrate, but today's PowerPoint is greatly improved in this area, and you can integrate many sound and video types seamlessly into your show.

Adding Slide Transition Effects

You can apply transitions from the Transitions tab. Some of the transition effects have options that determine the direction of the action. For example, a Wipe transition might wipe from the left, right, top, or bottom, or from one of the corners. Other effects have no such options because they can happen only one way. If options are available, you can click the Transitions tab and choose them from the Effect Options button, which displays a menu when you click it.

LINGO

Transitions are movements from one slide to another. The default transition effect is None, which means the slide simply goes away and the next one appears. Some of the alternatives include Fade, Push, Wipe, Split, and Cut, to name only a few.

You can also set several other properties for a transition. You can assign a sound to it, for example, and you can control its duration (speed). You can choose when the transition should occur:

- ✔ On mouse click
- ✔ Automatically after a certain amount of time has passed

In the following exercises, you add transitions to slides and customize their options and properties.

Applying a transition to a slide

Each transition has default settings, so you can apply a basic transition effect with just a few clicks. You can then optionally fine-tune those settings later.

In this exercise, you apply several different transitions and then watch the presentation in Slide Show view to check them.

Files needed: `Lesson 12 Diner.pptx`

1. **Open** `Lesson 12 Diner.pptx` **and save it as** `Lesson 12 Diner Movement.pptx`**.**

2. **Select slide 1 and then, on the Transitions tab, select the Push effect:**

   - If you see the Push effect in the Transition to This Slide group, as shown in Figure 12-1, click it.

   - Otherwise, click the More button to open a gallery of transition effects and then click Push. See Figure 12-2.

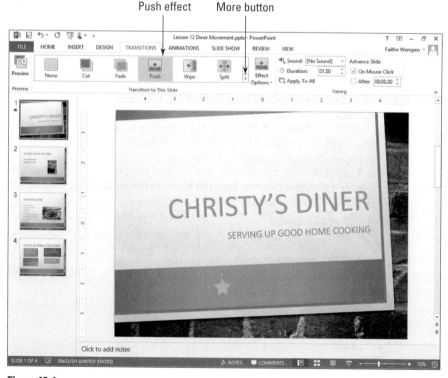

Push effect   More button

Figure 12-1

Push effect in gallery

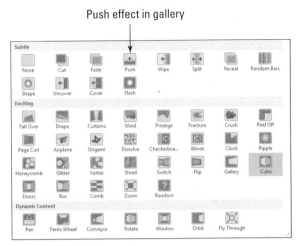

Figure 12-2

The Push effect is selected and is previewed on the slide. Notice that a star symbol appears below slide 1 now. This star indicates that a transition or an animation is associated with the slide.

3. **Select slide 2 and then select the Wipe effect:**

    • On the Transitions tab (shown in Figure 12-1), if you see the Wipe effect in the Transition to This Slide group, click it.

    • Otherwise, click the More button to open a gallery of transition effects and then click Wipe.

4. **Select slide 3, click More on the Transitions tab, and then click the Cube effect.**

5. **On the Slide Show tab, click the From Beginning button to watch the show and preview your transitions.**

6. **Click to move through the slides. When you reach the end of the slide show, click again to return to Normal view.**

7. **Click slide 3 to select it.**

8. **Click the Transitions tab and then the Apply to All button.**

    The transition effect from slide 3 (Cube) is now applied to all the slides in the presentation.

TIP

Using Apply to All is much faster and easier than applying the same transition effect manually to multiple slides. If you don't want it to affect certain slides, you can remove the transition from those slides later by choosing None as the transition effect for them.

9. **Repeat Steps 5 and 6 to view the presentation and check the transitions again.**

10. **Save the presentation.**

Leave the presentation open for the next exercise.

Changing a transition's options

Different transitions have different options available. Some of the transitions are directional in nature, so you have a choice of which way the transition moves. The direction could be toward a side of the screen, or it could be clockwise or counterclockwise.

All transitions have a Duration setting, which governs how quickly they occur. The longer the duration, the slower the transition. Most transitions take only a few seconds by default.

Finally, a transition can include a sound or not. PowerPoint has a short list of preset sounds it provides for your use; you can also specify a sound file that you have stored on your hard drive if you prefer.

In this exercise, you modify the settings for slide transitions and assign a sound effect.

Files needed: `Lesson 12 Diner Movement.pptx`, *already open from the previous exercise*

1. **Select slide 1 and then, on the Transitions tab, click the Effect Options button and choose From Top, as shown in Figure 12-3.**

   The transition is previewed on the slide.

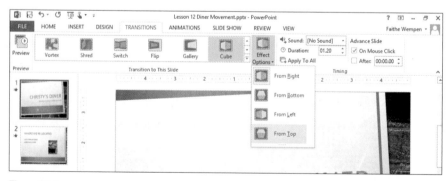

Figure 12-3

2. Click the down increment arrow on the Duration box once to change the duration to 1.00 seconds.

3. Open the Sound drop-down list and click Camera, as shown in Figure 12-4.

Figure 12-4

4. Click the Apply to All button.

5. Click the Slide Show tab and then the From Beginning button to watch the show and check your transitions.

6. Click to move through the slides. When you reach the end of the slide show, click again to return to Normal view.

7. Save the presentation.

Leave the presentation open for the next exercise.

Setting slides to advance manually or automatically

By default, slides advance on mouse click. That means that no matter how long you leave a slide onscreen, PowerPoint doesn't try to advance to the next slide until you give the signal. (That signal can be an actual mouse click or the press of a key, such as Enter, spacebar, or the right-arrow key.)

If you want some (or all) slides to advance automatically after a certain amount of time, you can specify this advancement on the Transitions tab. You can specify an automatic transition instead of or in addition to the default On Click behavior.

In this exercise, you set slides to advance automatically after a certain amount of time.

Files needed: Lesson 12 Diner Movement.pptx, *already open from the previous exercise*

1. **Select slide 1 and, on the Transitions tab, select the After check box.**

2. **Click the up increment arrow on the After text box until the value reads 00:05:00, as in Figure 12-5.**

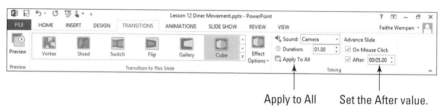

                     Apply to All   Set the After value.

Figure 12-5

3. **Click the Apply to All button.**

4. **Click the Slide Show tab and then the From Beginning button to watch the show and check your transitions.**

   Don't click; just wait for the five seconds to elapse so that the next slide will appear.

5. **When you reach the end of the slide show, click to return to Normal view.**

6. **Save the presentation.**

Leave the presentation open for the next exercise.

Animating Objects

You can create four types of animations in PowerPoint:

- ✔ An **entrance animation** governs how an object appears on the slide.

- ✔ An **exit animation** governs how an object leaves the slide.

- ✔ An **emphasis animation** makes the object do something to call attention to itself when it is neither entering nor exiting; this might include changing color, moving around, or making a sound.

- ✔ A **motion path animation** (not covered in this chapter) moves an object on the slide following a predefined path you specify. It's kind of like setting down model railroad tracks and letting the object be the train moving on the track.

LINGO

Animations are movements that are somewhat like transitions except they apply to individual objects on a slide rather than the entire slide. For example, you can animate a picture so that it appears after everything else on the slide has already appeared, or you can make the bullet points on a slide appear one by one rather than all at once.

Creating an entrance animation

Use an entrance animation whenever you want certain content on a slide to appear after the slide background has already appeared (and possibly other content on the slide, too). Any objects that you don't animate will appear at the same time the slide background does; any objects you animate will appear after that in a sequence you specify. After creating animations, you can modify and reorder them from the Animation Pane.

In this exercise, you create some entrance animation effects and order them by using the Animation Pane.

Files needed: Lesson 12 Diner Movement.pptx, *already open from the previous exercise*

1. **Select slide 1, and select the text box containing the slide's title,** *Christy's Diner.*

2. **Click the Animations tab and then the Add Animation button. In the Entrance section, select Fly In.**

   See Figure 12-6.

Fly In

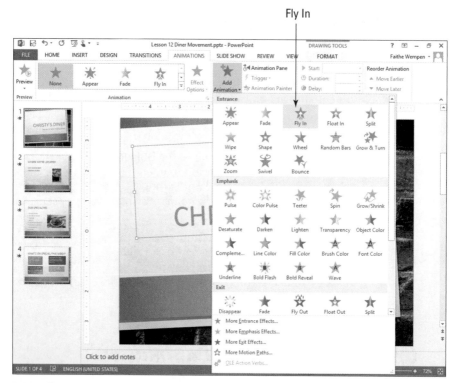

Figure 12-6

3. **Select the text box containing the slide's subtitle, *Serving Up Good Home Cooking*.**

4. **On the Animations tab, click the Add Animation button. In the Entrance section, select Grow & Turn.**

Notice that numbers appear next to the text boxes on slide 1, showing the order in which the animations will occur.

5. **On the Animations tab, click the Preview button to watch a preview of the animations on the slide.**

6. **Still on the Animations tab, click the Animation Pane button.**

A pane appears to the right of the slide, listing the animations on the slide.

7. **In the Animation Pane, click the first animation.**

8. **Click the down-pointing arrow button at the top of the Animation Pane.**

Figure 12-7

   The selected animation moves down to position 2, so the subtitle's animation is before the title's animation. See Figure 12-7.

9. **On the Animations tab, click the Preview button to watch a preview of the animations on the slide.**

10. **Save the presentation.**

Leave the presentation open for the next exercise.

Creating an emphasis animation

An emphasis animation calls attention to an object on a slide when it is neither entering nor exiting. PowerPoint offers many types of emphasis animations, including Grow/Shrink, Spin, and various color changes.

You can quickly copy animations from one object to another with the Animation Painter command. This command is handy when several objects on a slide should be animated identically.

In this exercise, you create some emphasis animations and copy an emphasis animation to multiple objects by using the Animation Painter.

Files needed: `Lesson 12 Diner Movement.pptx,` *already open from the previous exercise*

1. **Click slide 2 to select it and then click the photo on the slide.**

2. **Click the Animations tab and then the Add Animation button. In the Emphasis section, select Grow/Shrink.**

3. **Click slide 4 to select it.**

4. **On the slide, click the Early Morning Eye Opener text box.**

5. **On the Animations tab, click the Add Animation button. In the Emphasis section, select Teeter.**

   See Figure 12-8.

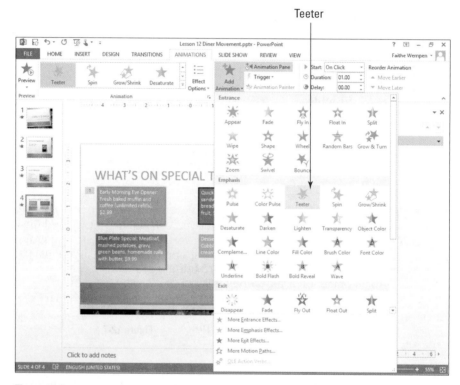

Figure 12-8

6. **On the Animations tab, double-click the Animation Painter button.**

   The feature turns on and stays on.

7. **Click each of the other text boxes on the slide (except the slide title) to copy the Teeter animation to them.**

   You can click them in any order you like.

If you had single-clicked Animation Painter in Step 6, it would have stayed on for only one usage and then turned off.

8. **Click the Animation Painter button to turn off the feature.**

9. **Click the Preview button to preview the slide's animation sequence.**

10. **Save the presentation.**

Leave the presentation open for the next exercise.

Creating an exit animation

An exit animation causes an object to leave the slide before the next slide appears. Without an exit animation applied, an object stays onscreen until the next slide appears. Exit animations are often used in combination with entrance animations to make an object enter, stay for a specified time, and then exit.

When you animate a text box that contains multiple paragraphs, each paragraph is animated separately, but you can collapse or expand the group of animations in the Animation Pane. You can format them as a group when collapsed, or you can expand the group to format an individual paragraph's animations separately.

In this exercise, you create an exit animation.

Files needed: Lesson 12 Diner Movement.pptx, *already open from the previous exercise*

1. **Select slide 3 and select the text box that contains the bulleted list.**

   Make sure you click the outside of the text box so that its border appears solid rather than dashed.

2. **Click the Animations tab and then the Add Animation button. In the Exit section, select Fly Out.**

   The bulleted list is animated. Numbers appear next to each item in the bulleted list on the slide, indicating their order in the animation. A single item appears in the Animation Pane, showing the entire animation sequence. See Figure 12-9.

Single item in Animation Pane for the entire series

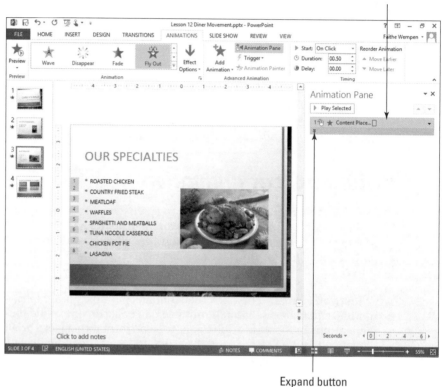

Expand button

Figure 12-9

3. **Click the Expand button below the animation in the Animation Pane to expand the list of animations in the group.**

   See Figure 12-10.

4. **On the Slide Show tab, click the From Current Slide button and click through the slide's content to see how the exit animation appears.**

5. **Press Esc to return to Normal view.**

6. **Save the presentation.**

Leave the presentation open for the next exercise.

Changing an animation's options

Animation options include the duration, the delay, and the sound effects assigned to an animation. You can set all these from the Animations tab. You can also set animation options via a dialog box interface.

In this exercise, you modify the options for animations.

Files needed: `Lesson 12 Diner Movement.pptx`, *already open from the previous exercise*

1. **Click slide 1 to select it and then click the Christy's Diner text box.**

2. **On the Animations tab, click the up increment arrow on the Duration text box until the Duration is set to 02.00.**

3. **Click the up increment arrow on the Delay text box until the Delay is set to 01.00.**

   See Figure 12-11.

4. **Click slide 2 to select it and then click the photo to select it.**

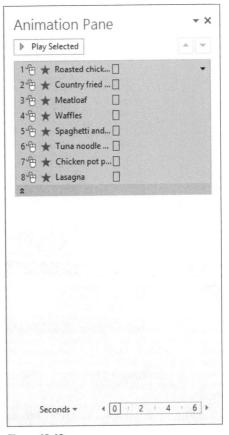

Figure 12-10

5. **On the Animations tab, click the Effect Options button. In the Amount section, select Huge.**

   The animation previews on the slide. The size is too large.

6. **In the Animation Pane, right-click the animation for the photo and choose Effect Options.**

   The Grow/Shrink dialog box opens.

Set the Duration. Set the Delay.

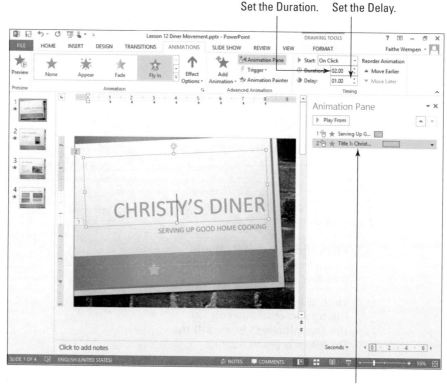

Figure 12-11

Selected animation

7. **On the Effect tab, open the Size drop-down list and, in the Custom text box, type** 175%.

See Figure 12-12.

8. **Open the Sound drop-down list and select Breeze.**

9. **Click OK.**

The animation previews on the slide, and the size of the growth is more appropriate.

10. **Save the presentation and close it.**

Leave PowerPoint open for the next exercise.

Set a custom value.

Figure 12-12

Inserting Sounds and Videos

Another way to make a presentation more interesting is to include multimedia content such as sounds and video clips. You can place clips directly on a slide and set them up to play either automatically or on click.

Inserting a sound clip on a slide

When you place a sound clip (sometimes called an audio clip) on a slide, a speaker icon appears to represent it. Playback controls appear beneath the icon, so you can control the clip during the show. You can set the clip to play on click or automatically.

> You can control whether or not the playback controls appear by selecting or deselecting the Show Media Controls check box on the Slide Show tab.

In this exercise, you place a sound clip on a slide and control its playback.

Files needed: `Lesson 12 Beethoven.pptx`

1. **Open** `Lesson 12 Beethoven.pptx` **and save it as** `Lesson 12 Beethoven Clip.pptx`.

2. **Click the Insert tab, click the Audio button, and select Audio on My PC.**

   The Insert Audio dialog box opens.

3. **Navigate to the folder containing the data files for this chapter.**

4. **Select** `Beethoven's Ninth.wma` **(see Figure 12-13) and click the Insert button.**

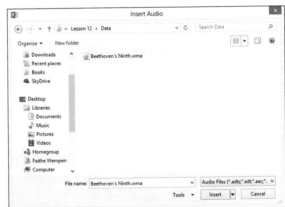

Figure 12-13

A speaker icon appears in the center of the slide, with playback controls beneath it. See Figure 12-14.

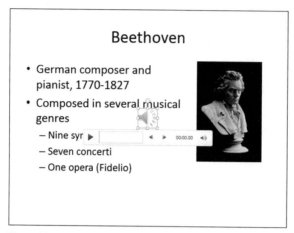

Figure 12-14

5. **Click the Slide Show tab and then the From Beginning button.**

   The slide appears in Slide Show view.

6. **Hover your mouse pointer over the speaker to see the playback controls and then click the Play button (triangle) in the playback controls.**

   The clip begins playing.

7. **Press Esc to return to Normal view.**

8. **Select the speaker icon.**

9. **Click the Audio Tools Playback tab, open the Start drop-down list, and select Automatically.**

   See Figure 12-15.

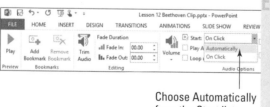

Choose Automatically
from the Start list.

Figure 12-15

EXTRA INFO

If this presentation contained multiple slides, this sound would stop playing when you advanced to the next slide. If you wanted the sound to continue across multiple slides, you would select the Play Across Slides check box.

10. **Select the speaker icon and, on the Audio Tools Playback tab, select the Hide During Show check box.**

    This step hides the speaker icon in Slide Show view.

11. **Click the Slide Show tab and then the From Beginning button.**

    The slide appears in Slide Show view, and the music starts playing automatically.

12. **Press Esc to return to Normal view.**

13. **Save the presentation and close it.**

Leave PowerPoint open for the next exercise.

Inserting a video clip on a slide

PowerPoint 2013 accepts video clips in a variety of formats, including Windows Media, Windows Video, QuickTime, MP4, and Flash. You can place a video clip on a slide either within a content placeholder or as a standalone item. You can also apply formatting to a video clip, such as a video style that governs the shape and appearance of the clip's frame.

Using a placeholder means that the clip will be resized or shifted as needed if you change layouts or themes; inserting a clip manually makes it stay as-is regardless of the layout or theme. To insert a video clip, click the Insert tab and then the Video button.

In this exercise, you place a video clip on a slide by using a content placeholder, and you apply a video style to it.

Files needed: Lesson 12 Run.pptx

1. **Open Lesson 12 Run.pptx and save it as Lesson 12 Run Video.pptx.**

2. **On the content placeholder, shown in Figure 12-16, click the Insert Video icon.**

    The Insert Video dialog box opens.

3. **Click the Browse hyperlink next to From a File.**

    The Insert Video dialog box opens. (This is a different dialog box from the one in the previous step, but they have the same name.)

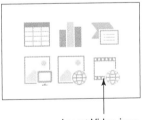

Insert Video icon

Figure 12-16

4. **Navigate to the folder containing the data files for this chapter and select** `AgilityRun.wmv`.

See Figure 12-17.

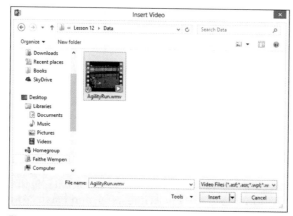

Figure 12-17

5. **Click the Insert button.**

The clip is inserted on the slide in the content placeholder.

6. **On the Video Tools Format tab, click the More button to open the Video Styles gallery.**

7. **In the Subtle section, click Center Shadow Rectangle (the second style).**

See Figure 12-18.

8. **On the Video Tools Format tab, click the Video Shape button and then click a rounded rectangle.**

The video clip's frame changes shape.

9. **On the Video Tools Playback tab, click Volume and then Low.**

This clip has a lot of background noise, and the sound is not integral to the meaning of the clip.

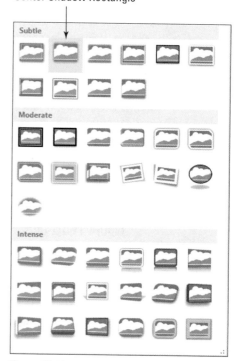

Figure 12-18

10. **Click the Slide Show tab and then the From Beginning button to open the slide in Slide Show view.**

11. **Click the Play button (the triangle) under the video clip to play it.**

    When you're done watching the video clip, press Esc to return to Normal view.

12. **Save and close the presentation and exit PowerPoint.**

 # *Summing Up*

Here are the key points you learned about in this chapter:

- ✔ Transitions are movements from one slide to another. You can set up transitions on the Transitions tab.

- ✔ To control the speed of a transition, set its duration. To automatically allow a transition to occur without a mouse click, set the After value to a number of seconds.

- ✔ By clicking Transitions and then Effect Options, you can specify a direction or other options for a transition effect.

- ✔ Animations make individual objects move. You can create entrance, emphasis, exit, and motion path animations.

- ✔ An entrance animation controls how and when an object enters the slide. If an object isn't animated, it enters at the same time as the slide's background.

- ✔ An emphasis animation calls attention to an object that is neither entering nor exiting. A motion path animation does the same thing, but it moves the object along a prescribed path.

- ✔ An exit animation controls how and when an object exits the slide. If an object has no exit animation, it exits when you transition to the next slide.

- ✔ Using the Animation Pane, you can sequence and fine-tune multiple animations on a slide.

- ✔ Using the Animation Painter, you can copy animation effects between objects.

- ✔ To insert a sound clip on a slide, choose Insert➪Audio.

- ✔ To insert a video clip, use the Insert Video content placeholder icon or choose Insert➪Video.

- ✔ After inserting a video clip, you can use the Video Tools Format tab's commands to control the appearance of the video clip frame. Use the Video Tools Playback tab's commands to control the clip's playback.

Try-it-yourself lab

For more practice with the features covered in this chapter, try the following exercise on your own:

1. **Open** Lesson 12 Greek.pptx **and save it as** Lesson 12 Greek Animation.pptx.

2. **Apply a different transition to each slide.**

3. **Apply animation effects to at least three objects on three different slides.**

Know this tech talk

animation: The movement of an individual object on a slide.

emphasis animation: An animation that occurs when an object is neither entering nor exiting the slide.

entrance animation: An animation that occurs as an object is entering the slide.

exit animation: An animation that occurs as an object is leaving the slide.

motion path animation: An animation that moves the object along a predefined path.

transition: A movement from one slide to another.

Chapter 13

Presenting a Slide Show

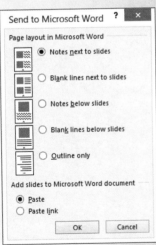

✔ Slide Show view enables you to *display a presentation full-screen* on a computer monitor or projector.

✔ Keyboard shortcuts make it easy to *move between slides* and temporarily black out (or white out) the screen.

✔ Right-clicking in Slide Show view opens a menu from which you can *jump to any slide*.

✔ The Pen tool enables you to *annotate slides with your own markup*.

✔ The Print command in PowerPoint enables you *print handouts in various arrangements*.

✔ Exporting handouts to Word provides *additional formatting flexibility*.

1. **How do you go back to the previous slide in Slide Show view?**

Find out on page 433

2. **How do you turn the screen white during a presentation?**

Find out on page 433

3. **How can you change the pen color when annotating a slide?**

Find out on page 437

4. **How do you customize the layout of a handout?**

Find out on page 439

5. **How do you export handouts to Word?**

Find out on page 441

*P*owerPoint 2013 gives you various methods for delivering your presentation: You can deliver a presentation live in a meeting room, broadcast it on the Internet, package it on a writeable CD, or send it out via e-mail, just to name a few.

This chapter focuses on the most popular delivery method: delivering a live show to an audience in person. You learn how to display a PowerPoint presentation onscreen, including how to move between slides and how to annotate slides with the Pen tools. You also learn how to print handouts, either in PowerPoint or in Microsoft Word.

For information about some of the other delivery methods, such as creating a CD or broadcasting and presentation, visit the Help system in PowerPoint or check out my book *PowerPoint 2013 Bible,* also published by John Wiley & Sons.

Displaying a Slide Show Onscreen

To give an onscreen show, use Slide Show view. It displays each slide full-screen, one at a time. For larger audiences, you may want to hook up a projector to your computer so the audience can see the slides more easily. (Pressing the Windows key and P connects a notebook PC to a projector or a second screen.)

In the following sections, you learn how to move around in a presentation, how to annotate slides, and how to save or discard the annotations afterward.

Moving between slides

To move from one slide to the next or to trigger the next on-click animation on a slide, click the left mouse button. That's all you need to know at the most basic level. You can also get much fancier than that about moving around. You can use shortcut keys to move to specific locations, and you can right-click and use the shortcut menu that appears to move around.

Right-click and choose Help in Slide Show view to get a list of the short-cut keys available.

You can also use the buttons in the lower-left corner of the screen in Slide Show view. They're very faint at first, but if you move the mouse pointer over one, it becomes solid. Click a button to open a menu or click the right- or left-arrow buttons there to move forward and back in the presentation.

In this exercise, you display a presentation onscreen and move around in it by using various methods.

Files needed: Lesson 13 Opa.pptx

1. **Open** Lesson 13 Opa.pptx **and save it as** Lesson 13 Santorinis. pptx.

2. **On the Slide Show tab, click the From Beginning button.**

   Slide 1 appears in Slide Show view.

3. **Click to move to slide 2.**

4. **Press the spacebar to move to slide 3.**

5. **Press the right-arrow key to move to slide 4.**

6. **Press the Enter key to move to slide 5.**

   You've just seen four different ways of advancing to the next slide.

7. **Press the Backspace key to move to slide 4.**

8. **Press the left-arrow key to move to slide 3.**

   Now you know two different ways of moving backward in a presentation.

9. **Right-click anywhere, choose See All Slides, and then click slide 1. (Opa!)**

   Figure 13-1 shows the thumbnail images that appear when you choose See All Slides.

Using this method, you can jump to any slide you want, at any time.

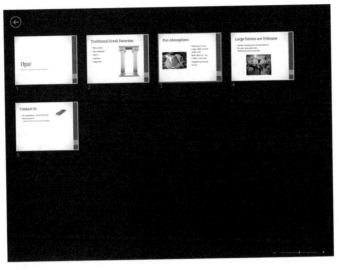

Figure 13-1

10. Move the mouse pointer to the lower-left corner of the screen and run the pointer over the icons there.

Figure 13-2 shows all of the icons. The first two are Previous and Next; you can use them to move between slides as an alternative to the keyboard and mouse methods you learned earlier.

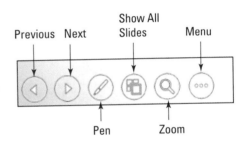

Figure 13-2

The Pen icon opens a menu from which you can choose a pen tool (Laser Pointer, Pen, Highlighter, or Eraser) and a pen color. These are covered in the next exercise.

The Show All Slides button provides an alternative to right-clicking and choosing Show All Slides, as you did in Step 9. It displays a gallery of slide thumbnails, as in Figure 13-2.

The Zoom button enables you to zoom in on a certain area of the currently displayed slide.

The Menu button displays a navigation menu from which you can jump to a custom show, set screen and arrow options, get help, and more.

Figure 13-3

11. **Click the Menu button.**

    A menu appears. See Figure 13-3.

12. **Choose the Last Viewed command from the menu.**

    Slide 3 reappears.

13. **Click the Menu button again, point to Screen, and choose Black Screen.**

    The screen turns black. You might use this to temporarily blank out the screen so you can have a discussion, for example.

14. **Right-click the slide and choose Screen⇨White Screen.**

    This step also blanks out the screen, except it turns white instead of black.

15. **Press Esc.**

    The presentation goes back to Slide Show view.

16. **Press B.**

    This is a keyboard shortcut for the Screen⇨Black Screen command. W is the keyboard shortcut for making the screen white.

17. **Press Esc.**

    Slide Show view closes, and you're returned to Normal view.

Leave the presentation open for the next exercise.

Annotating slides with the pen tools

Two pen types are available:

LINGO

As you're giving a presentation, you may want to make some notes on the slides, such as circling a word, underlining a phrase, or highlighting a key concept. The Pen tools enable you to do all those things. Making these changes is called **annotating**.

- ✔ **The Pen tool** draws a solid, thin line.

- ✔ **The Highlighter** draws wide, semi-transparent highlighting.

When you leave Slide Show view after using one of the pen tools, a dialog box pops up, asking whether you want to keep your ink annotations. If you choose to keep them, they appear on the slides as ink annotation objects, which are very much like line drawings that you might create by going to the Insert tab and clicking the Shapes button.

The Laser Pointer pen leaves no annotations on the slide. You can use it to point to areas of the slide as you're speaking.

In this exercise, you display a presentation onscreen and move around in it using various methods.

Files needed: Lesson 13 Santorinis.pptx, *already open from the previous exercise*

1. **On the Slide Show tab, click the From Beginning button to open slide 1 in Slide Show view.**

2. **In the lower-left corner of the screen, click the Pen icon, opening the Pen menu.**

3. **Choose Pen.**

   See Figure 13-4. The mouse pointer changes to a colored dot.

4. **Drag on the slide to underline the word *Opa!*.**

   It's underlined in red (the default pen color).

5. **Click the Pen icon and click Eraser.**

   The mouse pointer turns into an eraser.

Figure 13-4

6. **Click the line you just drew.**

   The entire line is erased. (You can't erase a portion of a line; it's all or nothing.)

7. **Click the Pen tool again and then click the Pen command on the menu.**

8. **Click the Pen tool again and then click the green square.**

   The pen color changes.

9. **Draw a green line under the word *Opa!*.**

10. **Press Esc to cancel the pen and return to the arrow pointer.**

11. **Click the left mouse button to advance to slide 2.**

12. **Right-click anywhere on the slide and choose Pointer Options⇨Highlighter.**

    This is an alternative way of accessing the Pen tools. See Figure 13-5.

13. **Drag the mouse pointer across the word *Saganaki*, highlighting it with the default highlighter color (yellow).**

14. **Press Esc to turn off the highlighter.**

15. **Click repeatedly until you get to the end of the presentation.**

    A box appears, asking whether you want to save annotations.

16. **Click the Keep button.**

    The presentation appears in Normal view with the ink annotations on the slides.

17. **On slide 1, click the green underline to select it, as in Figure 13-6. Then press Delete.**

18. **Switch to slide 2 and select the yellow highlight annotation there.**

19. **Drag the yellow highlight annotation up so that it's over the word *Baklava*.**

    See Figure 13-7.

Figure 13-5

Figure 13-6

20. **Save the presentation.**

Leave the presentation open for the next exercise.

Creating Handouts

When you print in PowerPoint, you have a choice of the type of printout you want. (Technically you can use any of these printout types as handouts, although the Handouts type is obviously custom-made for that purpose.) Here are the choices available:

- **Full Page Slides:** A full-page copy of one slide per sheet.

- **Notes Pages:** One slide per page, but with the slide occupying only the top half of the page. The bottom half is devoted to any speaker notes you typed into PowerPoint.

- **Outline View:** A text-only version of the presentation, structured as an outline, with the slide titles as the top-level outline items.

- **Handouts:** Multiple slides per page (two to nine, depending on your choice of settings), suitable for giving to the audience to take home.

- Moussaka
- Spanakopita
- Gyros
- Baklava
- Saganaki

Figure 13-7

LINGO

Handouts are paper copies of your presentation that you give to the audience. They give your audience something tangible to refer to and to take home. They can also write on the handouts to make their own notes. (Some handout layouts even include lines for writing.)

> **TIP** Different numbers of slides per page have different layouts. For example, if you choose three slides per page, the layout has lines next to each slide so the audience can take notes.

You can print the handouts directly from PowerPoint, or you can export them to Word for further formatting.

Printing handouts

When you print handouts from PowerPoint, the Handout Master's settings determine the details of how the handouts appear. You may want to customize the Handout Master before you print. The Handout Master settings apply only when you're printing the Handouts layouts, not when printing full-page slides, notes pages, or outline view.

In this exercise, you customize the Handout Master and then print handouts from PowerPoint.

Files needed: `Lesson 13 Santorinis.pptx`, *already open from the previous exercise*

1. **On the View tab, click the Handout Master button.**

   The Handout Master opens. It's a blank layout.

2. **On the Handout Master tab, click the Slides Per Page button and choose 3 Slides from the menu.**

   The layout changes to show placeholders for only three slides per page. See Figure 13-8.

3. **Deselect the Date check box on the Handout Master tab.**

   The placeholder for the date disappears from the layout.

4. **Still on the Handout Master tab, click the Handout Orientation button and choose Landscape.**

   The layout changes to show the three slides side by side. See Figure 13-9.

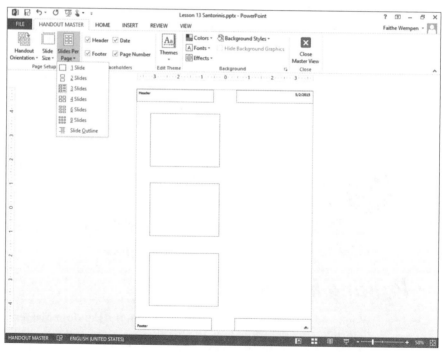

Figure 13-8

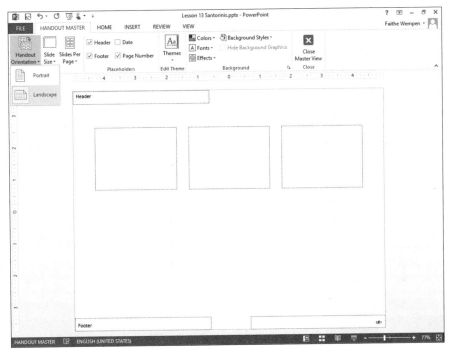

Figure 13-9

5. **Click the Close Master View button.**

6. **Choose File⇨Print.**

7. **Click the Full Page Slides button to display its menu and then choose 3 Slides.**

   The Print Preview shows the first handouts page with the layout you customized earlier. See Figure 13-10.

8. **Click the Print button.**

   The handouts print on your default printer.

Leave the presentation open for the next exercise.

Exporting handouts to Word

For more control over handouts, you can export them to Word. When they're in Word, you can make modifications that aren't possible in PowerPoint, such as changing the sizes of the slide graphics or adjusting the page margins.

In this exercise, you export handouts to Word and customize them there.

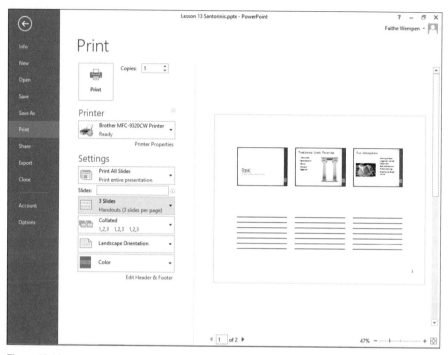

Figure 13-10

Files needed: `Lesson 13 Santorinis.pptx`, *already open from the previous exercise*

1. **Choose File⇨Export⇨Create Handouts⇨Create Handouts.**

   The Send to Microsoft Word dialog box opens. See Figure 13-11.

2. **Select the Blank Lines Next to Slides option.**

3. **Click OK.**

   The new Word document that opens contains the slides. The slides are placed in a three-column table:

   The first column contains the slide numbers, the second column displays the graphics, and the third column has lines for writing notes. See Figure 13-12.

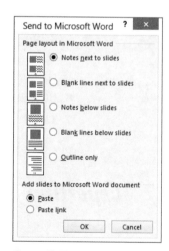

Figure 13-11

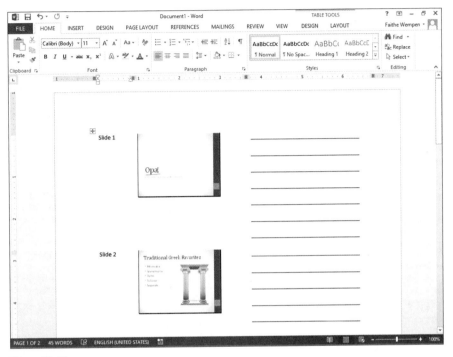

Figure 13-12

4. **Point the mouse pointer at the top of the rightmost column so that the pointer turns into a black arrow pointing downward. Click.**

   The entire column is selected. See Figure 13-13.

5. **On the Home tab, choose Line & Paragraph Spacing⇨1.15.**

   See Figure 13-14. The spacing of the blank lines in the rightmost column tightens up somewhat.

6. **In Word, choose File⇨Print.**

7. **Click the Print button to print one copy of the handouts with the default settings.**

8. **Save the document in Word as** `Lesson 13 Handouts.docx`.

9. **Exit Word.**

10. **Return to PowerPoint.**

11. **Save the presentation and exit PowerPoint.**

Mouse pointer

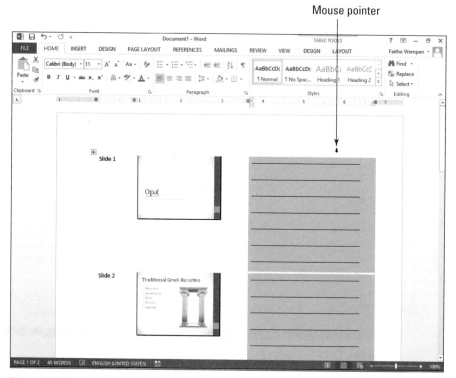

Figure 13-13

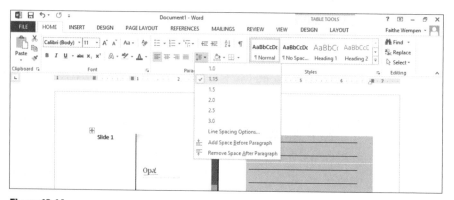

Figure 13-14

Summing Up

Here are the key points you learned about in this chapter:

- ✔ To enter Slide Show view, use the From Beginning or From Current Slide button on the Slide Show tab.

- ✔ To move to the next slide, you can press Enter, press the spacebar, press the right-arrow key, or click the Next Slide button in the lower-left corner of the slide.

- ✔ To move to the previous slide, you can press Backspace, press the left arrow key, or click the Previous Slide button in the lower-left corner of the slide.

- ✔ To jump to a certain slide, you can right-click, click See All Slides, and click the desired slide.

- ✔ To black out the screen, press B. To white out the screen, press W. To cancel either one, press Esc.

- ✔ To annotate a slide, right-click, click the Pen icon in the lower-left corner, choose Pen or Highlighter, and then drag on the slide.

- ✔ To print handouts, choose File⇨Print. Select a number of handouts per page and then click Print.

- ✔ To export handouts to Word for further editing, choose File⇨Export⇨ Create Handouts⇨Create Handouts.

Try-it-yourself lab

For more practice with the features covered in this chapter, try the following exercise on your own:

1. Open `Lesson 13 Airline.pptx` and save it as `Lesson 13 Airline Final.pptx`.

2. Watch the entire presentation in Slide Show view.

3. Export the handout to Word by using the Notes Next to Slides layout.

4. Make any changes you like in Word to make the handout more readable and attractive.

5. Print one copy of the Word document on the default printer.

6. Save the Word document as `Lesson 13 Airline Final.docx`.

7. Exit Word.

8. Return to PowerPoint, save the presentation, and exit PowerPoint.

Know this tech talk

annotate: To mark up a slide with the Pen or Highlighter tool in Slide Show view.

handouts: Hardcopy printouts designed for distribution to an audience.

Index

• A •

A4 paper size, 66
Absolute Position text box, 166
absolute referencing, 213–214, 233
access code, 4
Account Settings dialog box, 279–281
Account Type drop-down list, 278
accounts, e-mail, 275–283, 309
active cell, defined, 181, 201
Add Account dialog box, 276, 278
Add Animations button, 417–424
Add Shape button, 398
Add Subtitle box, 24
Add Title box, 24
adding
  borders to documents, 109–112
  contacts, 313–316
  e-mail accounts, 279–280
  shading to paragraphs, 112–114
  slide transition effects, 411–416
  text to slides, 23–25, 356–360
Address Book, 284. *See also* contacts
adjusting
  columns, 237–238, 240–241
  page settings, 62–66, 260–263
  rows, 237–239
advancing slides, 415–416
After line spacing setting, defined, 106
Align Left button, 16
Align Right button, 16
Align Text Left, 100–102
Align Text Right, 100–102
alignment, text, 100–102
all caps text attribute, 77
Animation Painter button, 420–421
Animation pane, 417–424
animations
  changing options, 423–424

  defined, 417, 430
  emphasis, 419–421
  entrance, 417–419
  exit, 421–422
annotating slides, 437–439, 446
AppData folder, 279
application, defined, 9, 54
Apply to All button, 413–414
applying
  background fill, 380–382
  backgrounds to worksheets, 242–244
  borders, 382–385
  horizontal alignment, 100–102
  shape styles and effects, 378–380, 385–388
  styles, 83–85, 121–124, 378–380
  text attributes, 77
  transitions to a slide, 412–414
Apps list, 11
argument, defined, 215, 233
aspect ratio, defined, 169, 172, 363, 367
Assign button, 130
Attach File button, 292
attachments
  contact information in e-mail, 324–325
  defined, 88, 94, 292, 308
  file attachments to e-mail, 292–295
  Send As Attachment button, 89
  viruses, 294
attributes
  defined, 77, 94
  text, 76–80
Audio button, 425
audio clip, defined, 425
Audio Tools Playback tab, 426
AutoFill, 192–193
Autofit text option, 388–389, 407
AutoRecover feature, 51–53
AutoSum button, 216
AVERAGE function, 221, 233

• *B* •

background
  filling in with color, 380–382
  for shading, 112–114
  worksheet, 242–244, 265
Backspace command, 69
Backstage view, 19, 41, 45, 54
Before line spacing setting, defined, 106
Bing (website), 157
Bing Image Search box, 160
blank document, creating, 13, 59–62
Blank Document command, 13
Blank Document icon, 60
blank presentation, creating new, 23,
  346–347
Blank Presentation template, 23, 346
Blank Workbook template, 180
blank worksheet in Excel, 20, 180
BMP file format, 26
Body Font drop-down list, 378
Bold button, 16
bold text attribute, 77
Border button, 110
borders
  adding to text, 109–112
  defined, 141, 153, 172, 382, 407
  presentation slides, 382–385
  table, 153–156
Borders and Shading command, 110
Borders and Shading dialog box, 155
Box button, 110
boxes
  Absolute Position text, 166
  Add Subtitle, 24
  Add Title, 24
  Bing Image Search, 160
  Cc, 284
  Clip Art text, 118
  Copies, 92
  Due Date, 327
  File Name, 43
  Name, 181
  Online Templates, 61
  Overview text, 361
  Search for Online Templates, 35
  Start Date, 327

Subject text, 285
To, 90
bulleted list
  changing bullet characters, 115–118
  creating, 114–121
  defined, 115, 141
Bullets button, 115, 117
Bullets tab, 129
business card option for contact, defined,
  324
buttons
  Add Animations, 417–424
  Add Shape, 398
  Align Left, 16
  Align Right, 16
  Animation Painter, 420–421
  Apply to All, 413–414
  Assign, 130
  Attach File, 292
  Audio, 425
  AutoSum, 216
  From Beginning, 413–414, 434
  Bold, 16
  Border, 110
  Box, 110
  Bullets, 115, 117
  Calendar, 272
  Center, 16, 100
  Change Colors, 403
  Change View, 328, 330
  Clear All Formatting, 84
  Clear Formatting, 80
  Close Master View, 441
  Collapse Dialog, 219
  Convert to SmartArt, 395
  Create, 22, 37, 62, 348
  From Current Slide, 345
  Custom Header, 263
  Custom Margins, 64
  Delete, 196, 303
  Dismiss, 333
  Draft, 36
  Editing, 19
  Effect Options, 423
  Email, 89
  Equation, 14
  Expand, 422

Expand dialog, 219
Expand the Folder Pane, 271
Fill, 194
Finish, 300
Font, 119
Font Color, 75, 131
Format, 126, 129, 254
Format Painter, 131–132
Full Page Slides, 441
Go, 218
Handout Master, 440
Handout Orientation, 440
Header, 15
Illustrations, 27
Increase Font Size, 75
Increase Indent, 103
Insert, 27–28, 195, 197, 242, 292
Junk, 306
Justify, 16, 101
Keep, 438
Landscape Orientation, 261
Letter, 261
Line and Paragraph Spacing, 106
Line Spacing, 106, 108
Manage Versions, 21
Margin, 63
Margins, 64
Maximize, 19
Menu, 435
More, 84, 122
More Layouts, 400
New Email, 292, 323
New Rule, 299
New Sheet, 199
New Style, 128
No Date, 331
No Scaling, 263
Normal, 344
Normal Margins, 263
Numbering, 115, 119
Open, 295
Orientation, 65
Outline View, 38
People, 273
Picture, 117
Pictures, 26–27, 394
Play, 426
Portrait Orientation, 261

Position, 166, 167
Preset Gradients, 381
Preview, 418
Preview File, 295
Print, 92, 257, 441
Print Active Sheets, 258–259
Print Selection, 259
Read Mode, 36
Reading Pane, 271, 288
Remove Gradient Stop, 381
Reply, 290
Reply All, 290
Restore Down, 17
Reverse Sort, 318
Right to Left, 400
Run Now, 301
Run Rules Now, 300
Save, 43
Save & Close, 314
Select All, 186
Send, 90, 286, 291, 292
Send As Attachment, 89
Send/Receive All Folders, 286, 293
Shadow, 110
Shape Effects, 386
Shape Fill, 380
Shape Outline, 382
Size, 65
Slide Show, 344
Slide Sorter, 38
Slides Per Page, 440
SmartArt, 396
Symbol, 117
Test Account Settings, 282–283
Text Box, 358
Text Effects and Typography, 78
Text Pane, 400
Theme Colors, 82
Theme Fonts, 81
Themes, 81
To, 323
Today, 68
To-Do Bar, 318
Undo, 17, 333
Video, 427
Video Shape, 428
Wrap Text, 164
Zoom, 181

• C •

calculating with formulas, 205–207
Calculator tab, 198
Calendar button, 272
Calibri Light-Constantia font theme, 82
Card view, 317
Cc box, 284
cell address, defined, 181, 201
cell cursor, 25, 54, 181, 182–183, 201
cells
   active, 181, 201
   AutoFill, 192–193
   copying data between, 190–191
   defined, 23, 179, 201
   deleting, 196–197
   editing, 188–195
   extracting with Flash Fill, 193–195
   formatting, 254
   formulas, referencing in, 207–209
   inserting, 196–197
   moving data between, 190–191
   named ranges, 222–226
   numbers in, 186–188
   printing selected, 257
   referencing on other sheets, 209–210
   typing in, 186–188
cells cursor, defined, 25
Center alignment setting, 100–102
Center button, 16, 100
Change Account dialog box, 281
Change Colors button, 403
Change View button, 328, 330
changing
   animation options, 423–424
   bullet character, 115–118
   column width, 240–241
   e-mail account settings, 277–279
   numbering style in list, 118–121
   presentation fonts, 376–378
   row height, 238–239
   saving locations, 45–49
   transition options, 414–415
   vertical spacing, 105–109
   views, 35–39
   worksheet structure, 195–197
character styles, defined, 124, 141
characters

   changing bullet, 115–118
   formatting text, 73, 94, 124, 141
Charts tab, 228
Clear All Formatting button, 84
Clear Formatting button, 80
clip art
   bullet characters, 118
   defined, 156, 172, 407
   inserting, 158–160
   presentation, inserting into, 390–391
   searching, 156–158
Clip Art text box, 118
Clipboard, 190, 212
close buttons, Excel's multiple, 12
Close Master View button, 441
cloud storage
   defined, 44, 54
   SkyDrive, 5, 41, 44–49
Collapse Dialog button, 219
color
   in Excel, 228, 255
   presentation slide, 372, 373–376, 407
   in Word, 73–76, 82, 95, 111
Color drop-down list, 111, 255
Color Model drop-down list, 375
Color Scale command, 228
Colors dialog box, 375
Colors list, 375
Column Width dialog box, 241
columns
   adjusting, 237–238, 240–241
   default widths, 237
   deleting, 195–196
   inserting, 195–196
   resizing, 150–153
   selecting, 149–150
   width, changing, 240–241
commands
   Backspace, 69
   Borders and Shading, 110
   Color Scale, 228
   Copy, 189
   Current Position, 134
   Cut, 189
   Define New Bullet, 117
   Define New Number Format, 119
   Define Send/Receive Groups, 287
   Delete, 69

Delete Sheet Rows, 196
Edit Document, 36
Format Page Numbers, 135
Ignore, 87
Insert Cells, 197
Insert Sheet Columns, 195
Last Viewed, 435
More Colors, 113
New Folder, 296
Online Pictures, 164
Open, 49–53
Outside Borders, 110
Page Down, 32
Page Margins, 134
Page Up, 32
Paste, 189
Pen, 438
Recent Workbooks, 20
Remove Page Numbers, 135
Save, 41–44
Save As, 40–44
Send, 90
Shift Cells Right, 197
Tab Color, 198
Top of Page, 134
Wrap Text, 162
Zoom, 33–39
Compatibility Checker dialog box, 44
contacts
    adding and editing, 313–316
    attaching to e-mail, 324–325
    defined, 313, 335
    deleting, 320–321
    filing, 319–320
    navigating the list, 316–319
    restoring, 320–322
    sending e-mail messages to, 322–323
    viewing, 273
contextual tab, defined, 14
contiguous cell range, defined, 183, 201
Convert Text to Table dialog box, 148
Convert to SmartArt Graphic button, 395
converting text to a table, 147–149
Copies box, 92
Copy command, 189
copying
    data between cells, 190–191
    formats with Format Painter, 130–132

formulas, 210–214
    slides in presentation, 353–354
COUNT function, 221, 233
COUNTA function, 221, 233
COUNTBLANK function, 221, 233
Create button, 22, 37, 62, 348
Create New Theme Colors dialog
    box, 376
creating
    custom table styles, 254–256
    document, 13, 59–62
    e-mail account, 276
    handouts, 439–444
    headers and footers, 245–247
    presentation, 346–349
    presentations with templates, 347–349
    rules to move messages, 299–302
    slides in presentation, 349–355
    SmartArt, 395–404
    styles in text document, 128–130
    task, 327–329
Creative Commons, 160
Current Position command, 134
cursor, cell, 25, 54, 181, 182–183, 201
Custom Header button, 263
Custom Margins button, 64
Customize Keyboard dialog box, 130
customizing
    Favorites list, 302–303
    footers, 137–139
    headers, 137–139, 263
    keyboard, 130
    page margins, 64
    Quick Access Toolbar, 17
    table styles, 254–256
    themes, 249–252
Cut command, 189

Damask theme, 81
data, copying and moving between
    cells, 190–191
data file, defined, 54
default file type, 41
default settings, 59

Define New Bullet command, 117
Define New Bullet dialog box, 117
Define New Number Format command, 119
Define New Number Format dialog box, 119
Define Send/Receive Groups command, 287
Delete button, 196, 303
Delete command, 69
Delete Sheet Rows command, 196
deleting
  cells, 196–197
  columns, 195–196
  contacts, 320–321
  e-mail messages, 303–304
  rows, 195–196
  slide objects, 365
  slides, 354–355
  tasks, 333
  text, 69
delimited data organization, defined,
    147, 172
Design tab, 81, 372
Detailed view, 328
dialog box launcher, 17
dialog boxes
  Account Settings, 279–281
  Add Account, 276, 278
  Borders and Shading, 155
  Change Account, 281
  Colors, 375
  Column Width, 241
  Compatibility Checker, 44
  Convert Text to Table, 148
  Create New Theme Colors, 376
  Customize Keyboard, 130
  Define New Bullet, 117
  Define New Number Format, 119
  Format as Table, 252
  Format Cells, 254
  Function Arguments, 219
  Header, 263
  Insert, 197
  Insert Picture, 26–27, 242, 393
  Internet E-Mail Settings, 282–283
  Junk E-Mail Options, 306
  Layout, 167
  Modify Style, 126–127
  Name Manager, 223

New Table Quick Style, 254, 256
  Open, 49–50
  Opening Mail Attachment, 295
  Options, 45
  Page Setup, 263
  Paragraph, 104
  Readability Statistics, 88
  Row Height, 238
  Rules and Alerts, 299–300
  Rules Wizard, 299–300
  Run Rules Now, 300
  Save As, 40–44, 44–49
  Save Current Theme, 250
  Search Text, 300
  Symbols, 117
  Zoom, 34, 181
dictionary file, 86
digital photograph, defined, 390, 407
Dismiss button, 333
DOC file format, 41
DOCM file format, 41
Document Formatting group, 84
documents. *See also* text
  creating, 13, 22–28, 59–62
  defined, 22, 54
  e-mailing, 88–90
  grammar checking, 85–88
  headers and footers, 132–139, 141
  inserting pictures, 156–161, 172
  lists, 114–121, 141
  opening, 49–53
  page settings, 62–66
  paragraph formatting. *See* paragraphs
  picture management, 162–170
  printing, 92–93
  saving, 40–49
  sharing, 88–91
  spell checking, 85–88
  styles, 83–85, 121–130
Documents folder, 44
Documents library, 44
DOCX file format, 40, 41
double underline text attribute, 77
Draft button, 36
Drawing Tools Format tab, 379–380,
    382–383
drop-down lists. *See* lists

Due Date box, 327
duplicating slides, 353–354. *See also* copying

 E

Edit Document command, 36
editing
  cells, 188–195
  contacts, 313–316
  text, 67–71
Editing button, 19
Editing group, 19, 194
Effect Options buttons, 423
Effect tab, 424
effects
  shape, 385–388
  text, 76–80, 95
  transition, 411–416
eLearning Center, 4
e-mail
  account setup, 275–283, 309
  composing message, 284–286
  contacts, attaching to, 324–325
  defined, 275, 308
  deleting, 303–304
  file attachments, 88–90, 94, 292–295, 308
  flagging, 305–306, 309
  interval setting for sending and receiving, 287–288
  managing incoming, 296–307
  manually sending and receiving, 286–287
  moving into folders, 297–302, 309
  reading, 288–290
  receiving, 286–290
  replying to, 290–291
  rules, sorting, 299–302, 309
  sending, 286–288, 322–323
Email button, 89
E-Mail tab, 280
emphasis animation, 417, 419–421, 430
encryption, defined, 277, 309
entrance animation, 417–419, 430
envelope template, 65
Equation button, 14
Equation Tools Design tab, 14
Essential SkyDrive Skills (website), 5

Excel. *See also* workbooks; worksheets
  AutoRecover feature, 51–53
  close buttons, 12
  defined, 9
  entering text, 23–25
  formulas, 205–214, 225–226, 233
  functions, 215–222
  interface introduction, 19–22, 177–186
  keyboard navigation, 32–33
  named cell ranges, 222–226
  Quick Analysis feature, 226–231
  themes, 247–256
exit animation, 417, 421–422, 430
Expand button, 422
Expand Dialog button, 219
Expand the Folder Pane button, 271
Expenses tab, 209–210
Export category, 21
exporting handouts to Word, 441–444
extensions, file, 26, 40–41, 54

 F

Favorites list, 271, 302–303, 309
File As, defined, 319, 335
file extensions, 26, 40–41, 54
file formats, 91
File menu, 19
File Name text box, 43
File tab, 19, 20
files
  attaching to e-mail messages, 88–90, 94, 292–295, 308
  dictionary, 86
  inserting pictures from, 161
  opening, 49–53
  saving, 40–49
fill, background, 380–382
Fill button, 194
fill handle, 192–193, 201, 212
Fill tab, 254
filters, Junk Mail, 306–307, 309
finding
  pictures on Web, 26, 158–160
  templates, 35, 61
  text, 300
Finish button, 300

first-line indent, defined, 102, 141
flagging e-mail messages, 305–306, 309
Flash Fill feature, 193–195, 201
Folder pane, 271
folders
  AppData, 279
  defined, 54
  e-mail, 286, 296–302
  subfolder, 48
Font button, 119
Font Color button, 75, 131
Font drop-down list, 74, 117
Font group, 16
Font Size drop-down list, 125
Font tab, 255
font theme, defined, 376, 407
fonts
  default, 59
  defined, 73, 95
  in presentation, 376–378, 407
  text, 73–76, 81–82
footer
  defined, 132, 141, 245, 265
  Header & Footer group, 15
  text document, 132–139
  worksheet, 245–247
Footer tab, 263
Format as Table dialog box, 252
Format button, 126, 129, 254
Format Cells dialog box, 254
Format Page Numbers command, 135
Format Painter, 130–132
Format Painter button, 131–132
formatting. See also themes
  cells in worksheet, 252–254
  lists, 119
  page numbers, 135
  paragraphs, 99–109, 130–132, 141
  picture, 26, 402–404
  table borders, 153–156
  text, 73–85, 130–132
  text boxes, 378–389
  worksheets, 241–247
Formula bar, 187, 189, 201, 206–207, 211–212
formulas. See also functions
  calculating with, 205–207
  cell references in, 207–209

copying, 210–214
defined, 205, 233
moving, 210–214
named ranges in, 225–226
order of precedence, 206
using, 205–210
From Beginning button, 413–414, 434
From Current Slide button, 345
Full Page Slides button, 441
Full Pages Slides, handout option, 439, 441
Full Screen Reading view, 36
Function Arguments dialog box, 219
functions
  AVERAGE, 221, 233
  basic, 221–222
  COUNT, 221, 233
  COUNTA, 221, 233
  COUNTBLANK, 221, 233
  defined, 215, 233
  inserting, 218–220
  MAX, 221, 233
  MIN, 221, 233
  NOW, 221, 233
  one-argument, 221
  SUM, 215–217, 221, 233
  TODAY, 221, 233

• G •

galleries
  Shape Styles, 379
  Theme, 371–378
  Variants, 374
  Video Styles, 428
GIF file format, 26
Go button, 218
grammar, checking, 85–88
graphics. See also clip art
  defined, 158, 172
  digital photograph, 390, 407
  file extensions, 26
  finding on Web, 26, 158–160
  inserting, 26–27, 117, 156–161, 242, 389–394
  moving, 165–168
  placement, 162–170
  raster, 157–158, 173
  resizing, 169–170

SmartArt, 395–404, 407
text wrap settings, 162–165
vector, 157–158, 173
Green Yellow color theme, 82
gridlines, defined, 153, 172
groups
  defined, 13
  Document Formatting, 84
  Editing, 19, 194
  Font, 16
  Header & Footer, 15
  Illustrations, 15–16
  Layout, 400
  Paragraph, 104
  Send/Receive Groups, 287
  Shape Styles, 379
  SmartArt Styles, 402
  Styles, 122
  Symbols, 13
  Themes, 372
  Variants, 374

• *H* •

Handout Master button, 440
Handout Master tab, 440
Handout Orientation button, 440
handouts
  creating, 439–444
  defined, 439–444, 446
  exporting to Word, 441–444
  printing, 439–441
hanging indent, defined, 102, 141
header
  creating, 245–247
  defined, 132, 141, 245, 265
  using, 132–139
Header button, 15
Header dialog box, 263
Header & Footer group, 15
Header & Footer Tools Design tab, 139
Header tab, 263
height, row, 237–239
Highlighter, defined, 437
Home tab, 19
horizontal alignment, 16, 100–102, 141
HTTP (HyperText Transfer Protocol),
  defined, 309

HTTP e-mail accounts, 275
hyperlinks in Page Setup, 263

• *I* •

icons
  Blank Document, 60
  book's icons explained, 3–4
  Line, 230
  Online Pictures, 390
  Pen, 437
  People, 313
  Pictures, 28
  Quick Analysis, 227
  Speaker, 426
  Stacked Column, 228
  Sum, 229
  Table, 230
  Video, 427
Ignore command, 87
illustration, defined, 158, 172. *See also*
    graphics
Illustrations button, 27
Illustrations group, 15–16
image, defined, 158, 172. *See also* graphics
IMAP (Internet Mail Access Protocol),
    defined, 275, 309
Inbox pane, 290, 294
Income tab, 210
Increase Font Size button, 75
Increase Indent button, 103
indentation, 102–105, 141
Info category, 20
inline image, defined, 159, 172
Insert button, 27–28, 195, 197, 242, 292
Insert Cells command, 197
Insert dialog box, 197
Insert Picture dialog box, 26–27, 242, 393
Insert Sheet Columns command, 195
Insert tab, 13, 358, 394
inserting
  cells, 196–197
  columns, 195–196
  functions, 218–220
  graphics, 389–394
  personal pictures, 393–394
  pictures, 26–27
  pictures from files, 161

inserting *(continued)*
  pictures from Web, 156–160
  ranges, 196–197
  rows, 195–196
  SmartArt graphic, 395–399
  sound clips into slides, 425–427
  video into slides, 427–429
insertion point, 27, 29, 54, 69, 95
Internet
  finding pictures on, 26, 158–160
  inserting graphics from, 156–160, 390–392
  templates on, 35, 61
Internet E-Mail Settings dialog box, 282–283
Internet Mail Access Protocol (IMAP),
    defined, 275, 309
ISP (Internet service provider), defined,
    275, 309
italic text attribute, 77

JPEG file format, 26
Junk button, 306
Junk E-Mail Options dialog box, 306
Junk Mail filters, 306–307, 309
justified alignment, defined, 141
Justify alignment setting, 100
Justify button, 16, 101

K

Keep button, 438
keyboard
  customizing, 130
  navigating with, 32–33
keyboard shortcuts
  cell cursor, moving, 182
  range selection, 184
  text attributes, 77

L

Landscape option, 65
Landscape Orientation button, 261
landscape page orientation, defined, 65, 95

Last Viewed command, 435
Layout dialog box, 167
layouts
  page, 62, 65
  print, 35–36
  slide, 356, 367, 400
  template, 62
Layouts group, 400
leading, defined, 106, 141
Left alignment setting, 100–102
legal brief template, 65
Letter button, 261
letter paper size (U.S.), 65
Line and Paragraph Spacing button, 106
Line icon, 230
line spacing, 105–109
Line Spacing button, 106, 108
Line Spacing drop-down list, 108
lists
  Account Type drop-down, 278
  Body Font drop-down, 378
  bulleted, 114–121, 141
  Color drop-down, 111, 255
  Color Model drop-down, 375
  Colors, 375
  contacts, 316–319
  Favorites, 271, 302–303
  Font drop-down, 74, 117
  Font Size drop-down, 125
  Line Spacing drop-down, 108
  numbered, 114–121, 141
  Printer drop-down, 92
  Priority drop-down, 327
  Save Changes In drop-down, 130
  Scope drop-down, 225
  Select a Function, 219
  Shading drop-down, 113
  Sound drop-down, 424
  Special drop-down, 104
  Start drop-down, 426
  Table Element, 254
  Tasks, 325–333, 335
  Time drop-down, 332
  To-Do, 325–333, 335
  Width drop-down, 111, 155
lost work, recovering, 51–53

• *M* •

macro-enabled file format, 41
macros, defined, 41
magnification, 33–39, 181
Mail interface in Outlook, 270–274. *See also*
   e-mail
Main Event theme, 372
Manage Versions button, 21
margins, page, 63–64, 134, 260–263
Margins button, 63, 64
MAX function, 221, 233
Maximize button, 19
memory, computer, 40, 49
Menu button, 435
Message tab, 292
messages, e-mail. *See* e-mail
Microsoft Office (website), 9, 156, 390–392.
   See also Office 2013
MIN function, 221, 233
Mini toolbar, 74
Mirrored margin option, 63
mixed reference, defined, 213, 233
Modify Style dialog box, 126–127
More button, 84, 122
More Colors command, 113
More Layouts button, 400
motion path animation, defined, 417, 430
mouse, 29–31, 190
moving. *See also* navigating
  cell cursor, 182–183
  data between cells, 190–191
  formulas, 210–214
  graphics, 165–168
  insertion point, 29
  messages into folders, 297–302
  slide objects, 360–362

• *N* •

Name box, defined, 181, 201
Name Manager dialog box, 223
named cell ranges, 222–226
Narrow margins option, 64
navigating
  in contacts list, 316–319
  with keyboard, 32–33, 182

  with mouse, 29–31
  in presentation, 340–342, 433–436
  Ribbon, 13–19, 349–350
New category, 21
New Folder command, 296
New Rule button, 299
New Sheet button, 199
New Style button, 128
New Table Quick Style dialog box,
   254, 256
No Date button, 331
No Scaling button, 263
noncontiguous cells, defined, 183
Normal button, 344
Normal Margins button, 263
Normal template, 59–60
Normal view, 33, 37, 367
Notes Pages, 342, 439
Notes pane, 37, 339, 342
NOW function, 221, 233
numbered lists, 114–121, 141
Numbering button, 115, 119
Numbering Library, 119
numbering pages, 133–135
numbers, typing into cells, 186–188

• *O* •

Office 97–2003 file formats, 41
Office 2013. *See also specific applications*
  eCourse introduction, 1–5
  entering text, 23–25
  exploring, 13–22
  inserting pictures, 26–27
  navigation, basic, 29–33
  opening an application, 9–13
  opening documents, 49–51
  recovering lost work, 51–53
  Ribbon, 13–19, 349–350
  saving documents, 40–49
  view, changing, 33–39
one-argument functions, 221
online course, 1–5
Online Pictures command, 164
Online Pictures icon, 390
Online Templates box, 61
Open button, 295

Open dialog box, 49–50
opening documents, 49–53
Opening Mail Attachment dialog box, 295
Options dialog box, 17, 45
orientation
　defined, 65, 95
　handout for presentation, 440
　page, 65–66, 260–263
Orientation button, 65
Outgoing Server tab, 282
Outline pane, 350–353
Outline view, 38, 367, 439
Outline View button, 38
Outlook. *See also* e-mail
　Address Book, 284
　contacts, 273, 313–325
　defined, 9
　interface introduction, 269–274
　tasks and To-Do lists, 325–333, 335
Outside Borders command, 110
Overall tab, 210
Overview text box, 361

P

Page Down command, 32
Page Layout tab, 62, 65
Page Margins command, 134
page settings
　adjusting, 62–66
　handouts from presentation, 439–441
　margins, 63–64, 134, 260–263
　numbering, 133–135
　orientation, 260–261
　paper size, 65–66
　size adjustment, 260–262
Page Setup dialog box, 263
Page Up command, 32
panes
　Animation, 417–424
　Folder, 271
　Inbox, 290, 294
　Notes, 37, 339, 342
　Outline, 350–353
　Reading, 271, 288, 295
　Slide, 339, 341
　Slides, 37, 339, 350–353
　Styles, 122, 125

paper size, 65–66
Paragraph dialog box, 104
Paragraph group, 104
paragraphs
　borders, 110–112
　break in, 99
　defined, 99
　formatting, 99–109, 130–132, 141
　shading, 112–114
　styles, 124, 142
password, e-mail account, 282
Paste command, 189
Pen command, 438
Pen icon, 437
pen tools, 437–439
People button, 273
People icon, 313
photograph, digital, 158, 173. *See also* graphics
Picture button, 117
picture from file, defined, 26. *See also* graphics
Pictures button, 26–27, 394
Pictures icon, 28
pixel, defined, 158, 173
placeholders
　slide, 356–358, 378–389
　text, 67–69
Play button, 426
PNG file format, 26
points, defined, 73, 95, 142
POP3 (Post Office Protocol 3), defined, 275, 309
Portrait Orientation button, 261
portrait page orientation, defined, 65, 95
Position button, 166, 167
Post Office Protocol 3 (POP3), defined, 275, 309
PowerPoint. *See also* presentations
　AutoRecover feature, 51–53
　defined, 9
　exporting handouts to Word, 441–444
　interface introduction, 339–346
　keyboard navigation, 32–33
　slide show, 433–439
　SmartArt, 395–404

templates, 23, 37, 347–349
themes, 371–378
views, 33–39, 342–346
PPT file format, 41
PPTM file format, 41
PPTX file format, 40, 41
presentations. *See also* slides
  animations, 417–424
  borders, 382–385
  creating, 22–23, 346–349
  defined, 22, 54, 339, 367
  graphics, 26–28, 389–394
  handouts, 439–444
  navigating in, 340–342
  sound clips, 425–427
  video, 427–429
Preset Gradients button, 381
Preview button, 418
Preview File button, 295
Print Active Sheets button, 258–259
Print button, 92, 257, 441
Print category, 21
Print Layout view, 35–36
Print Preview, 257
print range, 258–260, 265
Print Selection button, 259
Printer drop-down list, 92
printing
  document, 92–93
  handouts, 439–441
  layouts, 35–36
  page settings during, 260–263
  selected cells or ranges, 257
  slides, 439–444
  worksheets, 257–263
Priority drop-down list, 327
program, defined, 9
PST file format, 40
Push effect, 412

Quick Access Toolbar, 17, 43, 54
Quick Analysis feature, 226–231
Quick Analysis icon, 227

R

ranges of cells, 196–197
  defined, 183, 201
  formatting as table, 252–253
  naming, 223–226
  printing, 257–260
  selecting, 183–186, 257
raster graphic, defined,
    157–158, 173
Read Mode button, 36
Readability Statistics
    dialog box, 88
reading e-mail messages, 288–290
Reading pane, 271, 288, 295
Reading Pane button, 271, 288
Really Simple Syndication (RSS) feed,
    defined, 296
receiving e-mail, 286–290
Recent Workbooks command, 20
record, defined, 313, 335
references, cell, 207–214, 233
reminders, 331–333, 335
Remove Gradient Stop button, 381
Remove Page Numbers command, 135
removing borders from presentation,
    382–385
Reply All button, 290
Reply button, 290
replying to e-mail messages, 290–291
Report template, 62
resizing
  pictures, 169–170
  rows and columns, 150–153
  slide objects, 363–365
Restore Down button, 17
restoring
  contacts, 320–322
  lost work, 51–53
Reverse Sort button, 318
Review tab, 87
Ribbon, 13–19, 349–350
Right alignment setting, 100–102
Right to Left button, 400
Row Height dialog box, 238

rows
  adjusting, 237–239
  default height, 237–238
  deleting, 195–196
  height, changing, 238–239
  inserting, 195–196
  resizing, 150–153
  selecting, 149–150
RSS (Really Simple Syndication) feed,
    defined, 296
RTF (Rich Text Format), 91
rules, e-mail sorting, 299–302, 309
Rules and Alerts dialog box, 299–300
Rules Wizard dialog box, 299–300
Run Now button, 301
Run Rules Now button, 300
Run Rules Now dialog box, 300

● **S** ●

Save and Save As commands, 40–44
Save As dialog box, 40–49
Save button, 43
Save Changes In drop-down list, 130
Save & Close button, 314
Save Current Theme dialog box, 250
saving
  e-mail attachments, 294–295
  files, 40–49
Scope drop-down list, 225
ScreenTip, defined, 76
scroll arrow, defined, 29
scroll bar, defined, 29, 55
scroll box, 29–31, 55
Search for Online Templates text box, 35
Search Text dialog box, 300
searching
  pictures on Web, 26, 158–160
  templates, 35, 61
  text, 300
sections in presentation, defined, 348
Secure Password Authentication (SPA), 282
security
  password, e-mail account, 282
  viruses, 294
Select a Function list, 219

Select All button, 186
selecting
  cells in worksheet, 183–186, 257
  rows and columns, 149–150
  text, 71–73
selection handle, defined, 363, 367
Send As Attachment button, 89
Send button, 90, 286, 291, 292
Send command, 90
sending
  documents in different file formats, 90–91
  e-mail messages, 286–288
Send/Receive All Folders button, 286, 293
Send/Receive Groups button, 287
Send/Receive tab, 286, 287, 293
server address, 280
shade, defined, 76
Shading drop-down list, 113
shading paragraphs, 112–114
Shadow button, 110
shape effects, 378–380, 385–388, 407
Shape Effects button, 386
Shape Fill button, 380
Shape Outline button, 382
shape style, defined, 378, 407
Shape Styles gallery, 379
Shape Styles group, 379
Share category, 21
sharing documents, 88–91
sheet tabs, workbook, 178, 198, 201
Shift Cells Right command, 197
shortcuts, desktop, 9
Short-Term folder, 298
size. *See also* resizing
  page, 260–263
  paper, 65–66
  picture, 169–170
  text, 73–76, 125
Size button, 65
SkyDrive, 5, 41, 44–49
Slice theme, 248
Slide Master view, 361
Slide pane, 339, 341
slide show, 433–439
Slide Show button, 344
Slide Show tab, 344, 434

Slide Show view, 344
Slide Sorter button, 38
Slide Sorter view, 33, 38–39, 342
slides
  annotating, 437–439, 446
  creating, 349–355
  defined, 339, 367
  deleting, 354–355
  deleting objects within, 365
  duplicating, 353–354
  formatting, 376–389
  Full Page, 439
  graphics, 389–394
  layouts, 356, 367, 400
  moving between, 433–436
  moving objects, 360–362
  resizing objects, 363–365
  sound clips, 425–427
  text, adding, 23–25, 356–360
  transition effects, 411–416
  video, 427–429
Slides pane, 37, 339, 350–353
Slides Per Page button, 440
Slides tab, 372
small caps text attribute, 77
SmartArt
  converting text to, 395
  defined, 395, 407
  formatting, 402–404
  inserting, 395–399
  modifying, 399–401
SmartArt button, 396
SmartArt Styles group, 402
SmartArt Tools Design tab, 398, 400
SmartArt Tools Format tab, 403
sound clip, defined, 425
sound clips, inserting into slides, 425–427
Sound drop-down list, 424
SPA (Secure Password Authentication), 282
spacing, vertical, 105–109
sparklines, defined, 233
Sparklines tab, 230
speaker icon, 426
Special drop-down list, 104
spelling, checking, 85–88
Spelling and Grammar checker, 86

spreadsheet, defined, 178, 201. *See also*
  Excel
Stacked Column icon, 228
standard color, defined, 74, 95
standard paper size, 65
Standard tab, 114
Start charm, touchscreen, 10
Start Date box, 327
Start drop-down list, 426
style sets, 83–85, 95
styles
  creating new, 128–130
  defined, 121, 142
  document, 83–85, 121–124
  galleries for presentation, 379, 428
  modifying, 125–127
  numbered lists, 118–121
  shape, 378–380
  SmartArt Styles, 402
  Subtitle, 123, 125
  table, 254–256
  Title, 122
Styles gallery, defined, 121, 142
Styles group, 122
Styles pane, 122, 125
subfolder, defined, 48
Subject text box, 285
subscript text attribute, 77
subtitle placeholder, 68
Subtitle style, 123, 125
suite, defined, 9, 55
SUM function, 215–217, 221, 233
Sum icon, 229
superscript text attribute, 77
Symbol button, 117
Symbols dialog box, 117
Symbols group, 13
syntax, defined, 215, 233

Tab Color command, 198
Table Element list, 254
Table icon, 230
Table Tools Design tab, 253
Table Tools tab, 149

tables
  borders, 153–156
  converting text to, 147–149
  creating, 145–156
  custom styles, 254–256
  defined, 145, 173, 227, 233, 252, 265
  formatting from cell ranges, 252–253
  resizing columns and rows, 150–153
  selecting columns and rows, 149–150
Tables tab, 230
tabs
  Audio Tools Playback, 426
  Bullets, 129
  Calculator, 198
  Charts, 228
  contextual, defined, 14
  Design, 81, 372
  Drawing Tools Format, 379–380, 382–383
  Effect, 424
  E-Mail, 280
  Equation Tools Design, 14
  Expenses, 209–210
  File, 19, 20
  Fill, 254
  Font, 255
  Footer, 263
  Handout Master, 440
  Header, 263
  Header & Footer Tools Design, 139
  Home, 19
  Income, 210
  Insert, 13, 358, 394
  Message, 292
  Office Interface, 13–19
  Outgoing Server, 282
  Overall, 210
  Page Layout, 62, 65
  Review, 87
  Send/Receive, 286, 287, 293
  Slide Show, 344, 434
  Slides, 372
  SmartArt Tools Design, 398, 400
  SmartArt Tools Format, 403
  Sparklines, 230
  Standard, 114
  Table Tools, 149

Table Tools Design, 253
  Tables, 230
  Totals, 229
  Transitions, 412–416
  Video Tools Format, 428
  Video Tools Playback, 428
  View, 36, 38, 288
  worksheet, 178, 198, 201
tasks
  creating, 327–329
  defined, 325, 327, 335
  deleting, 333
  setting reminders, 331–333
  updating, 329–331
templates
  defined, 59, 95, 347, 367
  envelope, 65
  Excel, 180
  layouts, 62
  legal brief, 65
  online sources, 35, 61
  PowerPoint, 23, 37, 347–349
  Word, 41, 59–62
Test Account Settings button, 282–283
text. *See also* paragraphs
  alignment, 100–102
  attributes, 76–80
  Autofit, 388–389
  color, 73–76
  deleting, 69
  editing, 67–71
  effects, 76–80, 95
  formatting, 73–85, 130–132
  placeholder for, 67–69
  searching, 300
  selecting, 71–73
  size of, 73–76, 125
  SmartArt, converting to, 395
  table, converting to, 147–149
  typing, 23–25, 69–71, 186–188, 356–360
  wrapping around graphics, 162–165, 173
Text Box button, 358
text boxes, 35, 166, 284–285, 378–389
Text Effects and Typography button, 78
text message, defined, 324
Text Pane button, 400

Theme Colors button, 82
Theme Fonts button, 81
themes
    color in, 74, 82, 95, 372, 373–376, 407
    customizing, 249–252
    Damask, 81
    defined, 80, 95, 248, 265, 347, 367, 371, 407
    Excel, 247–256
    font, 376, 407
    formatting, 247–256
    Main Event, 372
    PowerPoint, 371–378
    Slice, 248
    Word, 80–82
    workbook, 248–249
Themes button, 81
Themes gallery, 371–378
Themes group, 372
TIF file format, 26
Time drop-down list, 332
tint, defined, 76
Title style, 122
To box, 90
To button, 323
Today button, 68
TODAY function, 221, 233
To-Do Bar button, 318
To-Do list, 325–333, 335
toolbars
    Formula, 187, 189, 201, 206–207, 211–212
    Mini, 74
    Quick Access, 17, 43, 54
Top of Page command, 134
Totals tab, 229
touchscreen, 10
transitions, slide, 411–414, 430
Transitions tab, 412–416
typeface, defined, 73, 95. *See also* fonts
typing
    numbers into a cell, 186–188
    in slide placeholder, 356–358
    text, 23–25, 69–71, 186–188, 356–360

underline text attribute, 77
underline words but not space text
    attribute, 77

Undo button, 17, 333
updating tasks, 329–331

variant in presentation, 373–376, 407
Variants gallery, 374
Variants group, 374
vCard, defined, 324, 335
vector graphic, defined, 157–158, 173
vertical line spacing, 105–109, 142
video, inserting into slides, 427–429
Video button, 427
Video icon, 427
Video Shape button, 428
Video Styles gallery, 428
Video Tools Format tab, 428
Video Tools Playback tab, 428
View tab, 36, 38, 288
views
    Backstage, 41, 45
    Card, 317
    changing, 35–39
    contacts, 273
    Detailed, 328
    e-mail attachments, 294–295
    Full Screen Reading, 36
    Normal, 33, 37
    Notes Page, 342
    Outline, 38, 367, 439
    PowerPoint, 342–346
    Print Layout, 35–36
    Slide Master, 361
    Slide Show, 344
    Slide Sorter, 33, 38–39, 342
viruses, computer, 294

Web. *See* Internet
websites
    access code, 4
    Bing, 157
    companion files, 5
    Essential SkyDrive Skills, 5
    extra information, 5
    Microsoft Office, 9, 156, 390–392

paper sizes explained, 65
Word tutorials, 93
width, column, 237, 240–241, 240–241
Width drop-down list, 111, 155
Windows 7, starting Office applications
in, 9, 12–13
Windows 8, opening Office applications,
9, 10–12
Windows Calculator, 205
Wipe effect, 413
Word. *See also* documents
AutoRecover feature, 51–53
borders and shading, 109–114
changing onscreen view, 33–39
defined, 9
importing handouts from PowerPoint,
441–444
keyboard navigation, 32–33
Ribbon, 13–19
styles, 83–85, 121–130
tables, 145–156, 173
tabs, 13–19
templates, 41, 59–62
themes, 80–82
tutorials for, 93
WordArt effects, defined, 77
workbooks
defined, 22, 55, 178, 201
scrolling in, 29–31
sheet tabs, 178, 198, 201
themes, 248–249
worksheets
background, 242–244, 265
blank, 20, 180

cells. *See* cells
changing structure, 195–197
columns. *See* columns
defined, 178, 201
footer, 245–247
formatting, 241–247
graphics in, 26–28
inserting sheets, 197–199
modifying, 197–199
previewing active, 257
printing, 257–263
rows. *See* rows
scrolling in, 29–31
Wrap Text button, 164
Wrap Text command, 162

• *X* •

XLS file format, 41
XLSM file format, 41
XLSX file format, 40, 41
XPS Viewer, 295

• *Z* •

Zoom button, 181
Zoom commands, 33–39
Zoom dialog box, 34, 181
zoom percentage, defined, 34
Zoom slider, 34
zooming, 33–39, 181

About the Author

Faithe Wempen, MA, is a Microsoft Office Master Instructor and the author of more than 100 books on computer hardware and software, including the *PowerPoint 2013 Bible* and *Excel 2013 eLearning Kit For Dummies*. She is an adjunct instructor of Computer Information Technology at Purdue University, and her corporate training courses online have reached more than one-quarter of a million students for clients such as Hewlett-Packard, Sony, and CNET.

Dedication

To Margaret

Author's Acknowledgments

Thanks to the wonderful editorial staff at John Wiley & Sons, Inc. for another job well done. You guys are top notch!

Publisher's Acknowledgments

Senior Acquisitions Editor: Katie Mohr

Senior Project Editor: Kim Darosett

Copy Editor: Virginia Sanders

Technical Editor: Mike Talley

Editorial Assistant: Annie Sullivan

Sr. Editorial Assistant: Cherie Case

Project Coordinator: Melissa Cossell

Cover Image: ©iStockphoto.com/GlobalStock

Math & Science

Algebra I For Dummies,
2nd Edition
978-0-470-55964-2

Anatomy and Physiology
For Dummies,
2nd Edition
978-0-470-92326-9

Astronomy For Dummies,
3rd Edition
978-1-118-37697-3

Biology For Dummies,
2nd Edition
978-0-470-59875-7

Chemistry For Dummies,
2nd Edition
978-1-1180-0730-3

Pre-Algebra Essentials
For Dummies
978-0-470-61838-7

Microsoft Office

Excel 2013 For Dummies
978-1-118-51012-4

Office 2013 All-in-One
For Dummies
978-1-118-51636-2

PowerPoint 2013
For Dummies
978-1-118-50253-2

Word 2013 For Dummies
978-1-118-49123-2

Music

Blues Harmonica
For Dummies
978-1-118-25269-7

Guitar For Dummies,
3rd Edition
978-1-118-11554-1

iPod & iTunes
For Dummies,
10th Edition
978-1-118-50864-0

Programming

Android Application
Development For
Dummies, 2nd Edition
978-1-118-38710-8

iOS 6 Application
Development For Dummies
978-1-118-50880-0

Java For Dummies,
5th Edition
978-0-470-37173-2

Religion & Inspiration

The Bible For Dummies
978-0-7645-5296-0

Buddhism For Dummies,
2nd Edition
978-1-118-02379-2

Catholicism For Dummies,
2nd Edition
978-1-118-07778-8

Self-Help & Relationships

Bipolar Disorder
For Dummies,
2nd Edition
978-1-118-33882-7

Meditation For Dummies,
3rd Edition
978-1-118-29144-3

Seniors

Computers For Seniors
For Dummies,
3rd Edition
978-1-118-11553-4

iPad For Seniors
For Dummies,
5th Edition
978-1-118-49708-1

Social Security
For Dummies
978-1-118-20573-0

Smartphones & Tablets

Android Phones
For Dummies
978-1-118-16952-0

Kindle Fire HD
For Dummies
978-1-118-42223-6

NOOK HD For Dummies,
Portable Edition
978-1-118-39498-4

Surface For Dummies
978-1-118-49634-3

Test Prep

ACT For Dummies,
5th Edition
978-1-118-01259-8

ASVAB For Dummies,
3rd Edition
978-0-470-63760-9

GRE For Dummies,
7th Edition
978-0-470-88921-3

Officer Candidate Tests,
For Dummies
978-0-470-59876-4

Physician's Assistant Exa
For Dummies
978-1-118-11556-5

Series 7 Exam
For Dummies
978-0-470-09932-2

Windows 8

Windows 8 For Dummies
978-1-118-13461-0

Windows 8 For Dummies,
Book + DVD Bundle
978-1-118-27167-4

Windows 8 All-in-One
For Dummies
978-1-118-11920-4

 **Available in print and e-book formats.**

 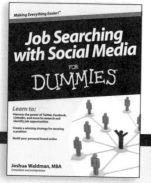